MUHLENBERG LI

S0-ADL-367

INNOVATIVE ORGANIZATION FOR POPULATION RESEARCH

The nature of the population problem is eloquently reviewed by traditionalists and futurists in the fields of demography, ecology, education, and philosophy. Biologists, physicists, social scientists, professional educators, industrialists, and a wide assortment of other disciplinarians have contributed to the investigation of how one might best attack one of the most enormous problems facing mankind.

The text also contains the observations of educators — from administration to faculty to students — who reflect exactly how the university might best serve to deal with this problem. It contrasts the considerations of leading administrators of universities, industrial and federal institutions regarding how each reviews his respective organization as best being able to address the population problem.

As a concentration of information and opinion, this text will help those who furnish the money for population work. It has application for those interested in institution building in any sector of the society. Any intelligent, informed layman will find it provocative for enhancing comprehension of the confusing issues facing everyone in this time of rapid change.

Few Americans are any longer unaware of, or naive about, the population and environmental crises confronting the world. The communications media have given continuing attention to these great threats to mankind. This book has a single intent . . . to examine the feasibility of organizing manmade institutions in a manner which will permit dealing more effectively with the population problem. It is designed to interest and help not only the researcher, scientist, and professional in the population field, but other groups as well, including those organizations and individuals who are oriented toward action in solving the problem, and for whom research is applicable in charting such action.

INNOVATIVE ORGANIZATION
FOR POPULATION RESEARCH

Innovative Organization for Population Research

Edited by

SYLVAN J. KAPLAN

Chief, Division of Plans and Objectives
National Park Service
Department of the Interior
Washington, D. C.

and

ROBERT K. McCORMICK

Congressional Correspondent
National Broadcasting Company

With a Foreword by

Philip A. Corfman, M.D.

Director, Center for Population Research
National Institute of Child Health and Human Development
National Institutes of Health
Bethesda, Maryland

CHARLES C THOMAS · PUBLISHER
Springfield · Illinois · U.S.A.

312
K17i

Published and Distributed Throughout the World by
CHARLES C THOMAS • PUBLISHER
Bannerstone House
301-327 East Lawrence Avenue, Springfield, Illinois, U.S.A.
Natchez Plantation House
735 North Atlantic Boulevard, Fort Lauderdale, Florida, U.S.A.

1971, by CHARLES C THOMAS • PUBLISHER
Library of Congress Catalog Card Number: 76-161168

With THOMAS BOOKS *careful attention is given to all details of manufacturing and design. It is the Publisher's desire to present books that are satisfactory as to their physical qualities and artistic possibilities and appropriate for their particular use.* THOMAS BOOKS *will be true to those laws of quality that assure a good name and good will.*

Printed in the United States of America
C-1

FOREWORD

THE world and our country are facing increasingly perilous and complex problems caused by growing numbers and concentrations of people. The problems created by such growth threaten levels of health and nutrition, retard economic progress, and contribute to social disorganization.

Unprecedented concern over population problems has resulted in an expanded Federal research effort, an effort which includes examining new ways to advance research progress. One initiative taken by the Center for Population Research staff has been our investigation of the feasibility of supporting population research centers at universities and other nonprofit institutions. Dr. Kaplan's activities for the Center for Population Research, which have culminated in this book, have given us a detailed perspective on the issues related to creation of these centers.

We are pleased that in July 1970 a population-research-centers program was established within the Center for Population Research. These centers will encourage scientists from a variety of disciplines to work together to investigate the complex and wideranging problems posed by population growth and concentration.

PHILIP A. CORFMAN

INTRODUCTION

IN THIS book we shall look at institutions which are or might become involved in studying "the population problem." It is a book made up of independently drawn conclusions of many brilliant scholars. The conclusions represent disparate, critical, and as often as not, partisan views. Some of the views expressed are irreverent; some may be considered down-right unpleasant. But their authors have one common characteristic. They want to help define the population problem, to consider ways to develop a critical mass of research resources with which to study it, and to suggest courses of action for implementing a program to resolve it.

Few Americans are any longer unaware of, or naive about, the population and environmental crises confronting the world. The communications media have given continuing attention to these great threats to mankind. There is an awesome element of drama in this threat which stimulates the imagination of the most beleaguered poor, the young dove, and the most war-preoccupied hawk.

In a sermon before his congregation in 1970, Robert Zoerheide[1] sharply summarized some of these critical issues in his opening remarks. They make an excellent introduction: "Facts to work the cradle by . . .

> World Health Organization: 3.7 births per second, 221 per minute, 13,260 this hour, 318,575 today, 2.2 million this week, 114 million this year. . . .
> Four fifths to nine tenths of the new babies who once died at birth now live. . . .
> One out of every 22 babies ever born (77 billion) is alive today.
> World population has passed 3 billion and will more than double, to 7 billion, in thirty years, at present rates. In six centuries man may expect an allocation of approximately one square foot of space upon which to stand. In 1,565 years, the weight of human beings will equal the weight of the world itself.
> U.S.A. . . . as the census clock ticks . . . a birth every seven and

one-half seconds . . . growth per year—three million . . . equivalent of a new city the size of Syracuse, Dayton, or Tulsa, about 250,000—each month. . . .

Happy Birthday, new American! You will use and pollute in a lifetime with:

> 56 million gallons of water
> 10,000 pounds of wheat
> 10,000 pounds of meat
> 28,000 pounds of milk
> > 1,800 pounds of garbage and trash (each garbage can costs $50 a year to empty. . . NYC)
> 70 million cars are on the road
> 4 million added last year

Each owner, in a lifetime uses

> 21,000 gallons of leaded gasoline . . .
> 72 million tons of carbon monoxide in the air
> 25 million tons of sulphur dioxide
> 12 million tons of uncaptured airborne particles.

Happy Birthday, new consumer, you have your whole life ahead of you. May you be physically strong, mentally awake, and morally straight . . . (and, may you be able to breathe)!"

The dramatics of this type of statistics are for openers only. This book has a single intent: to examine the feasibility of organizing man-made institutions in a manner which will permit dealing more effectively with the "population problem." It is designed to interest and help not only the researcher, the scientist, and the professional in the population field, but other groups as well, including those organizations and individuals, for example, who are oriented toward action in solving the problem, and for whom research is applicable in charting such action. As a concentration of information and opinion, it will help those who furnish the money for population work: members of Congress, Government policy-makers, the administrators of foundations and other funding organizations. Even beyond that, the book is aimed at the intelligent, informed and interested layman.

But before developing the ideas to be contained in the pages which follow, it might be stated that the welcome paid the newborn by Reverend Zoerheide might well be in the best Malthusian tradition. And since the spirit of Thomas Robert Malthus[2]

will be alluded to over and again in this document, either directly or by implication, perhaps a word about this forefather of
modern demography might be appropriate in the beginning.

Malthus was a pessimist of the first order, and he would have
endorsed the opening remarks of the sermon with solemn concurrence. He argued throughout his career that hope for happiness and a favorable quality of life is in vain, for population
will always outrun the availability of resources. Malthus envisioned that population would expand to the limit of subsistence
and there be held by pestilence, war, and famine.

The trends postulated by this position, the *Malthusian* position, although not entirely borne out by the facts of this present world of exponential rate of change and of explosive technology, nonetheless are sufficiently in consonance with the times
to lend support to Mr. Zoerheide's cynical greeting to the American neonate. The element of pessimism is there and cannot be
ignored.

On the other hand, this is not a book designed by pessimistic
reflection or based on defeatism or hopelessness. It is instead a
volume of hope—hope based on what might be done by population research centers. The contents of this document are the result of a year's study, visits to many American campuses, private
research institutions, and Federal agencies. They are also the
summary of ideas compiled from commentary provided me in
personal conversations with experts, at a conference on population sponsored by the Interdisciplinary Communications Program of the Smithsonian Institution at Belmont, Maryland, in
November 1969, at the American Association for the Advancement of Science meetings in Boston in December 1969, and at
a conference on the Management of Consolidated Research Institutions sponsored by the National Institute of Child Health
and Human Development at the Pan American Health Organization building in Washington in February 1970.

The ideas brought forward are positive thoughts by a selected
number of my many advisors. They were presented in this text
to ventilate the serious problems attendant to trying to develop
a program on the subject of population centers. The first prob-

lem I encountered as I began the year-long study was that of determining what precisely I could mean when I spoke of "centers." I quickly discovered that I had several terms with which
to contend. Two terms required delineation: "center" and "centers program." Ultimately, I concluded the "centers program"
perhaps might better be viewed as a "centers system." A "center," hereafter, will be used to classify a special interest group
of individuals who have coalesced their common objectives, usually under common sponsorship, and in reasonable proximity to
one another. The use of the word "center" is not essential, and
occurs more by practice than by necessity. Sometimes the special
interest groups being referred to are related by economic ties.
Sometimes they are not. Their funding may come from a variety of sources. They may be known also as departments, divisions, institutes, bureaus, and/or projects, as well as "centers."

The concept of a "centers program" is one that involves the
activities of clusters of special interest groups which may or
may not be in geographical proximity to each other. Lazarsfeld,[3]
in a paper referring to the intellectual issues with which institutes deal, remarks upon what may be the function of an individual center's program. He suggests that centers should have
the following four major functions: (1) do substantive research, (2) train younger research people, (3) relate the center's
work to general academic teaching in pertinent subject matters,
and (4) relate the work to the ongoing concerns of the outside
community in terms of service and advice.

Hence, the "centers program" might be envisioned as involving a knowledge creation component, an information distribution and feedback component, and an information application
and delivery component. As I begin this book and ask the input
of the contributors, I will be thinking of a centers program
which probably will be mission oriented. Initially, at least, I am
starting with the proposition that a centers operation will have
the collective function of seeking ways to influence population
growth, structure, and distribution in a manner that will improve health, raise standards of living, and preserve human dignity.

In the pages which follow, the questions posed will relate to whether the university can mount a centers program to deal with the "population problem." Effort will be made also to explore what contributions organizations other than universities might make in the search for answers to the questions raised by the "population problem." In all instances, the essays will be critical, objective, and not necessarily in support of a single viewpoint.

The term "population problem" is in quotes, because so many have said in guiding our thinking regarding centers development: "Know first what the problem is before you design the center to solve it!" This call for definition is given by Douglass Cater in the Section One of the book. The response has been magnificently provided by seven provocative papers in Section Two.

In this time of institutional change the question of the university's ability to deal with its obligations has come under attack from many fronts. For this reason answers have been sought from those in the universities who might be able to say whether, with all the prevailing stresses to meet the multiple roles the universities are expected to play, this institution can still perform the task of researching the population problem. Section Three of this book presents some thought-provoking facets of this issue.

The answers given in Section Three permit leading administrators from a variety of types of institutions to comment upon what their respective organizations can best do to contribute to the problem. Going a bit further, in Section Four, spokesmen from industry, national laboratories and nonprofit foundations join the presidents of two major universities in presenting their respective opinions.

A study of how existing population research centers function leads to an examination of the manner in which other types of research centers on campuses and in research institutions operate. We want to see whether an international center or a mental retardation center has a problem of function common to that of the population center, and whether these population centers tend to "cross pollenate" their findings and communicate with one another. If population problems are as all inclusive as they would seem to be, we want to determine if workers in special interest centers tend to cross disciplinary lines and to become intellectually or emotionally involved in the activities of their associates. Moreover, we must know if any mechanisms exist for work in the various types of centers to be collated, made relevant to the population problem, and packaged for different types of consumers. These matters are discussed in Section Five of this book.

Section Six contains evaluations of the foregoing commentary. Seventeen professionals, highly qualified to judge that which has preceded, were asked in a conference setting to review the symposium. Their thoughts help to draw conclusions on what needs to be done so that the population problem may be faced realistically.

From the wisdom of the experts, expressed in the first six sections, conclusions are derived in Section Seven from these proposed courses of action. This section is entitled "Insights and Afterthoughts," although one would be hard pressed to determine when in the chronology of these deliberations the "after" thoughts began; "evolution" of thoughts might better express the views developed in this section, thoughts intended to point directions toward which designers of institutional programs might move in formulating their plans for a mighty confrontation with the population problem.

If the ideas, the suggestions, and the recommendations in this book sometimes seem to point first in one direction then in another, it is due to the fact that the problem itself is complex and unique. Its intricacies are being explored with vigor and dedication, but it is still largely an unmapped area and we can give you only the directions considered most nearly reliable by those most familiar with the terrain.

Washington, D.C.   SYLVAN J. KAPLAN

CONTENTS

xiii

SECTION THREE

IS THE UNIVERSITY DEALING WITH THE POPULATION PROBLEM?

SECTION FOUR

WHAT CAN VARIOUS TYPES OF INSTITUTIONS CONTRIBUTE TO THE POPULATION PROBLEM?

SECTION FIVE

REACTIONS OF TENANTS AND LANDLORDS: CENTERS AND HOST MANAGEMENT

INNOVATIVE ORGANIZATION
FOR POPULATION RESEARCH

SECTION ONE

THE CHALLENGE

Douglass Cater sounds the keynote of this book by pleading that we not become so enshrouded with traditional academic behavior that we cannot recognize the time when change is required. Mr. Cater asks that we examine existing institutions, then show enough imagination to improve upon them.

Chapter One

THE CHALLENGE: INSTITUTION BUILDING

DOUGLASS CATER

IN HAWAII recently, I was told of the state senator who had difficulties with public speaking. A friend prescribed the Demosthenean exercise. He was to fill his mouth with marbles and each day throw one away. When he had finished the treatment, the friend told him, "Now that you have lost all your marbles, you should be able to give a good speech."

I feel in a somewhat similar predicament. Population is a subject about which I know next to nothing. I have had no experience in the administrative business of creating centers. My one excuse for writing this is that during my five years in the White House I developed a keen interest in that recondite subject known as institution building. As a backstage advisor on the President's health, education, and miscellaneous social programs, I had the rare opportunity to watch the spawning of a good many new institutions.

I grew interested not only in how they spawn, but how they grow, how they survive, and most particularly, how they become effective. Sometimes we forget that the last is the most important of all.

Two aspects of institution building strike me as pertinent: First, the Federal Government has increasingly had to be concerned about areas of public life with which it has never before been involved. It has met a need for institutions subsidized by government yet apart from government. In one area after another, we have been obliged to try for something that Lenin preached but never practiced—a withering away of the state. It remains one of the central problems of government today: how it can subsidize and strengthen activities which cannot and should not be subject to the inhibitions imposed by traditional governmental procedure and bureaucracies.

Second, our record of institution building in this quasi-gov-

5

ernmental area has not been an unqualified success. One comparative success story has been the National Science Foundation. So far the NSF has stayed free of political interference although it has been able to achieve impressive size over the years. The National Institutes of Health have been similarily successful, at least until the present. With the help of powerful friends in Congress, NIH obtained the funding for remarkable growth, and evolved successful cooperative relationships with the private sector of the research community. My former boss once expressed a degree of concern whether NIH was adequately concerned about bringing the results of its endeavors to the benefit of all citizens. Still, President Johnson concluded that NIH was a "billion dollar success story" and he declared himself a firm supporter.

There are other institutions whose success is not yet proven. The National Endowments of the Arts and Humanities were launched in response to a widely recognized need for federal support of these vital areas of the nation's life. So far, however, they have not proved whether they can grow at a pace nearly adequate to the need. Nor have they demonstrated whether they can remain successfully insulated from the political processes.

Similarly, The Corporation for Public Broadcasting was created to meet a pressing need in the field of educational television and radio. It was conceived as a foundation, separate from government, to stimulate a better quality of public broadcasting. The act was passed with the overwhelming support of Congress. A distinguished and independent board of directors was appointed. An outstanding man was made president of the Corporation. Yet its stouthearted efforts to claim enough revenues to make a measurable impact in this costly field were more heroic than effective. The possibility of long-term financing, insulated from the annual appropriation process, whether by a special tax or by a multi-year appropriation, became increasingly remote. There was resentment in Congress at the very notion that there should be this insulation.

Let me mention one more instance—this one an outright failure to respond to the needs of institution building. During the

Johnson presidency, there was public disclosure that the Central Intelligence Agency had been secretly subsidizing a number of private voluntary organizations, including the National Student Association. This created a prompt outcry in the press and after inquiry, this method of covert financing was cut off by Presidential order. A study made by Presidential committee reached the conclusion that there was urgent need for support of the international activities conducted by our many voluntary organizations. Without subsidy, these organizations would be incapable of playing a creative and peace-building role in world affairs. Yet only government could supply this subsidy. The second conclusion, equally familiar, was that the method of subsidy should be insulated from government. Our voluntary organizations should not be made an instrument of American foreign policy. The Presidential committee proposed a quasi-governmental institution, directed by distinguished leaders from private life. So far, however, there has not been any evidence that such an institution will be created or financed by the government.

One can examine the recent record of institution building and grow pessimistic. Yet the longer record shows that this country has been remarkably innovative when the need was clear: the liberal arts college, our great universities of science and technology, our institutes capable of both theoretical and applied research. It is time to be innovative again.

As we look at the population problem, I am doubtful that any of the earlier models will serve. The population explosion presents a unique challenge and will require a unique institutional arrangement. Examining the complexity of the problem and the time frame within which it must be met, one could conclude as engineers concluded about the bumblebee—that it cannot possibly fly. But the bumblebee, by prodigious flapping of its wings, does manage to fly. So it is in dealing with population —we must flap and fly.

It seems clear to me that we must establish three primary points about the building of this new institution: first, we need a clear definition of the problem. Second, we need the ablest people to work on it. Third, we must not be handicapped by traditional ways of doing things.

Defining the problem will require, I suggest, a great deal of imagination. What, for example, will motivate people to translate the population explosion into terms of individual family planning? Fear of future famine stimulated by advertisements in *The New York Times* will not do the job. Even if this message reached beyond the middle-income families which already practice family planning, it could have a reverse psychology. I am still depressed by my wife's visit to a family planning clinic in India where she discovered more women seeking advice on how to have babies than how not to have them. The fear of famine can produce the psychology that there is survival in numbers.

How do we set the deadlines which are so essential to decision making, particularly in nonregimented societies? We talk about the population bomb but we are vague about our timetable for defusing it. We need to set schedules for our efforts even if they are as arbitrary as President Kennedy's target date for reaching the moon.

How do we move rapidly to meet the population crisis without producing the political or social backlash which frequently results from trying to change mass social behavior? How do we avoid the developing suspicions that population restraints are somehow associated with racial prejudices and with genocide.

Finally, what does experience teach us are the best ways of reinforcing the appeal to man's reason in the matter of family planning? As we hopefully move into an era where social policy sets minimum family income, abolishes hunger and malnutrition, reduces infant mortality, cures killing diseases, and extends man's life span, how can we persuade man to adopt less cruel ways to avoid overpopulating the planet?

These rather random questions indicate my belief that defining the problem must go far beyond the province of population experts. Indeed, I would hope that giving wider definition to the problem may assist the technical experts in shaping their own priorities.

This leads to the second point—the recruitment of the ablest people. As my questions make clear, this search for talent should be widespread. We will need men and women whose primary expertise is in the rare art of institution building—from government, the universities, and private enterprise. We should call on constitutional lawyers to help chart a path through this perilous terrain that will hopefully bypass years of testing in the courts. We need economists, tax experts, psychologists, publicists, and finally, just plain politicians to contribute their perspectives. If ever there was compelling reason to break down the barriers between disciplines, the population crisis is it. Perhaps we can even set an example of working together that will carry over into other problem areas.

Finally, there is the third point—to avoid being handicapped by traditional ways of doing things. This does not mean total ignorance of those institutions which have been setting new traditions in problem solving. I would be interested, for example, in seeing a perceptive analysis of NASA's experience in charting man's journey to the moon, distilling its relevance—or irrelevance—to man's attempt to curb population growth. How much central direction, how much pluralism of effort should there be among the population centers? Should this ratio shift over time? More and more in our nuclear age, we recognize that it is necessary to achieve a critical mass if we are to achieve results and not fritter away our resources. What is the critical mass in dealing with the population crisis?

I hope that we will give free rein to our creative imagination. Our population endeavors must not follow the course of the evangelical religious faiths in my native Alabama whose moral exhortations create uneasy consciences on Sunday and backsliding during the rest of the week. Yet, we must take account of the opposite experience during the prohibition era when the strong arm of the law failed to make people change their habits. Population planning must find a middle way.

I have asked far more questions than I have suggested answers. My only hope is that I have not been guilty of the fault attributed to Henry James. "The trouble with Mr. James," said Mrs. Henry Adams, "is not that he bit off more than he can chew, but that he chewed more than he bit off."

WHAT IS THE POPULATION PROBLEM?

Robert Cook introduces this section, by providing historical perspective that no other person in this country could provide, since he is one of the real pioneers in the field.

Jerry Combs gives the demographer's analysis, without which there can be no realistic consideration of the population problem itself. Frank Fraser Darling gives an ecologist's viewpoint regarding the population problem and provides the reader insight into man's relationship to his environment.

Conrad Taeuber relates the population problem of the United States to the population problem facing the entire world. Herman Miller and Willis Harman reach far out into the future, as they envision it—Miller into the American future, Harman into the world future.

Arthur Campbell elaborates on the problem, emphasizing the research aspects.

Chapter Two

WHAT IS THE POPULATION CRISIS?

ROBERT C. COOK

THE population crisis is an accelerating multiplication of people. The population crisis is a disturbing and increasing imbalance between the resources of the earth and the human beings devoted to consuming those resources. The population crisis is an overbalanced dependency ratio which ends with nearly half of the people in a nation under the age of fifteen.

The population crisis is these things and many more. Most of the problems that the modern world is engulfed in are in one way or another related to the fact that the unprecedented multiplication of people is increasingly and alarmingly out of control.

The fable of the blind man and the elephant symbolizes the population crisis.

Each blind man feeling a portion of the elephantine anatomy has *his* picture of the population problem, and his own formula for a "solution."

And none of these formulae is likely to be very useful in bringing about an effective and humane balance in the number of births and deaths taking place in the world today.

Three propositions epitomize the major and essential elements of the population crisis:

1. The population crisis is a human artifact.*

2. In essence, the "population crisis" is easy to understand.

3. The population crisis is compounded by weird serendipities* trapped in ominous cultural lags.

Copyright 1970 by Robert C. Cook. All rights reserved.

* The author uses the words "serendipity" and "artifact" in a somewhat innovative fashion; he considers "serendipity" as including any sort of accidental or unexpected discovery, not just something good or helpful or beneficial. He regards "artifacts" as anything created by man, from the discovery of the vaccination process to the population problem itself.

TO BEGIN AT THE BEGINNING*

In one sense there has always been a population crisis. For a million years or more, the growth of man numbers was slow and precarious. The Four Horsemen and the Grim Reaper were rampant. The counterbalance between horrendous death rates and acute accent on fertility was the basis *sine qua non* for the survival of the family, the clan, the nation, the race.

Even with virtual prodigies of fertility, the effort to keep the human race in business was competing neck-and-neck with death. It has been estimated that during the million years before the "invention" of agriculture, the rate of population increase was so slow that fifty thousand years were required to double human numbers. Agriculture was one of the greatest of the cultural breakthroughs, which increased and somewhat stabilized the food supply, made village life and eventually city life possible, and set a pattern of existence where the development of the arts, the sciences, and simple technologies could make a beginning. Then population growth responded to growing stockpiles of increasingly powerful artifacts. The time required to double population was drastically reduced from five hundred centuries in the preagricultural Old Stone Age to sixteen centuries by the opening of the Christian era.

True, humankind had been concerned with population problems since "the beginning." When death occasionally took a partial holiday, births continued at the old rate, and a sudden eruption of population took place. The arithmetic of these microexplosions was understood by our ancestors of twenty-five hundred generations ago. Contraceptive formulae are found on Egyptian papyruses, and infanticide was widely practiced whenever death nodded. Eventually every one of these microexplosions of people was nullified, more or less, by the rampaging horsemen of war, famine, pestilence, and poverty.

The doubling time was slowly being shortened. A quarter billion man-creatures living on the earth at the time of Christ

---

* For confirmation of historical and demographic material stated in the following pages, the reader's attention is directed to References 4-17.

grew to a half billion about the time the colonization of North America got under way in the early fifteenth century. This moderate acceleration has steadily and relentlessly increased since that time. Until two centuries ago, the number of births in the world each year exceeded the number of deaths—*on the average,* with great short-term variability—by only a small fraction of 1 percent a year. But the balance which had continued for a million years was slowly shifting.

Man has moved from the cave to the skyscraper on a burgeoning mountain of artifacts. The earliest artifact may have been the sharpened end of a stick to be used to impale food and to protect against aggressive neighbors—humans and other mammals. The use of fire is an artifact. The wheel, the alphabet, agriculture, the development of villages and cities—these are all human artifacts; some of them very simple, some of them extremely complex.

By its ability to invent and improvise, the human breed has reached a pinnacle never even approached by any other form of life.

MAN: THE MAGICIAN'S APPRENTICE

Smart as he has proved to be, man has never quite managed an effective control of the complex interplay of the forces he has enthusiastically undertaken to manipulate. The road from A to B seems clear and straight enough, but often it is not. Fire kept a cave warm in winter. It kept wolf packs at bay. But it could also burn the hard-working householder out of his newly created hogan.

The "invention" of agriculture—the idea of organizing food production, both animal and vegetable—took aeons to develop. Ten thousand years ago, this initially simple artifact had reached a point of complexity where human existence entered a new phase: stable communities became possible, then villages and cities and the maintenance of larger populations. Even so, when crops failed, starvation took over. Famine was tempered but not eliminated. The seven fat years and the seven lean years predicted by Joseph in Egypt came to pass—and this sine-like curve of the fat and the lean years was to continue for nineteen hundred years after the birth of Christ. Man, the magician's apprentice at the center of all these ramifications, did not know what he had set in motion. Nor did he give a thought to where it was taking him, or what the consequences—good *and* bad—might be.

Those who were architects of the great irrigated agricultures of five thousand years ago, operating with the assurance of the ignorant, did not anticipate that the end result of their inspired efforts would be to make a desert of what was for so long a garden spot: most of Asia Minor and much of the eastern Mediterranean area.

As we are discovering today, man has not changed very much. He is still throwing switches and turning valves with the happy abandon of the village idiot. He now finds himself trying to control a massive array of self-perpetuating, self-activating juggernauts, which, uncontrolled, portend catastrophe.

The beginning of the nineteenth century will be circled in red in the history of the future. That date marked the invention of the superartifact that set the population rocketing skyward. It marked the opening of a new area of technology. It was the discovery of vaccination by James Jenner[4] in 1796. The era of the microbe hunters and the virus hunters began. What Ralph Linton[5] labeled "the age of faith and epidemics" suddenly began to fall apart. The neck-and-neck race between the stork and the Grim Reaper came to a sudden end.

But innovators have rarely led happy lives. They have branded themselves as heretics and dangerous radicals, fortunate if they escaped with their lives.

James Jenner neither drank the hemlock nor was burned at the stake. But the opposition to this great discovery was violent to the point of hysteria. The priests considered this trifling with God's prerogative of giving and taking life according to His whims, to be blasphemous. The physicians considered Jenner an upstart and a charlatan. The lawyers hoped that a vaccinated child would die so that Jenner could be tried for murder. But Jenner had one outstanding sales pitch in his favor. What the priests, the doctors, and the lawyers had to say did not stop mothers from bringing their children to be given the lifesaving

175916

scratch on the arm; and the opposition collapsed. Within two years, the number of deaths from smallpox in the city of London declined from over two thousand to little more than six hundred yearly.

This was only the beginning. Within scarcely more than a century, most of the major epidemics and infectious diseases were under control. The brutal death rates which were the heritage from the remote past suddenly ended.

For a million years and more, human numbers were held to a very slow rate of increase because of the horrendously close bal- ance between the number of births and the number of deaths. Jenner *et al.* changed all that, and very suddenly. Nobody—not the physician nor the priest nor the lawyer nor the statesman— had any intimation of what was happening. Human arithmetic was not considered a subject worthy of study in the early 1800's. Nor does it appear on many curricula even today. The ultimate significance of this most portentous event in human history was unanimously ignored.

If the champions of the old order who saw vaccination as a defiance of the divine plan had stood their ground to the last ditch, things might have turned out differently. But as it actually happened, the Lord was "relieved" very quickly of His responsi- bilities in the "taking away" department. The new offensive against death was transferred as rapidly as possible to the De- partment of Health.

The failure to recognize the potentially devastating conse- quences of a profound imbalance in births and deaths is the es- sential element in the population crisis. The "population prob- lem" is not due to some extraneous force—some whim of provi- dence. It is not due to an increase in the number of sunspots. It is not due to any sudden escalation in the reproductive powers of the human species. It is due to a series of artifacts invented by man. Unless compensating artifacts can very quickly be de- veloped to restore by humane means the balance between mod- ern low death rates and the number of births in the world, that great human innovation, death control, will end by being not a blessing but a disaster.

THE FATAL IMBALANCE

Before Jenner, a compelling concern with high fertility was an essential element of every human culture. This concern colored the traditions, the mores, and the emotional imperatives of the entire human race. Cultural anthropology has accumulated an impressive documentation of sex mythology, sex totemism, sex ritual. Fertility rites designed to increase the productivity of crops, herds, and humans were universal.

The very sudden emergence of highly effective death control encountered no concerted opposition. But the deeply felt concern with fecundity, an essential to survival over aeons of time, inhibited any effective pressure to bring births into balance with declining deaths. The emotional drive to increase and multiply had the most august auspices. It was heavily reinforced by that biologically implanted urge which Malthus labeled "the attraction between the sexes" and by an emotion which has been termed "polyphiloprogenitiveness"—a sense of well-being and happiness amidst a swarm of children.

What happened in those parts of the world where death control first began to be effective is a remarkable demonstration of the fundamental good sense of the human race when it is given time to be exercised.

For a century after Jenner, death control grew gradually in effectiveness as death rates slowly declined in northern and western Europe. In response to no overt stimulation birth rates began a downward trend about two generations later. In less than two centuries, this "demographic transition" had extended across the industrial countries of Europe and North America. A new pattern of balance became established with fewer deaths and fewer births. This spontaneous adjustment to new conditions made it possible for human cultures to survive—even advance—in spite of death control. Under the cultural, social, religious, and economic conditions existing in this area—Europe and North America—the ancient parity of births and deaths is well on the way to being restored, though by means not even yet clearly understood.

Throughout the remainder of the world, death control technology did not become massively effective until toward the end of World War II; Ceylon is an example: In just two years the death rate declined from twenty-one to fourteen per thousand, and only a few years later, to eight per thousand. Since 1944, the birth rate has declined by 10 percent; the death by more than 60 percent. A generation after the break in the death rate, there are now in Ceylon four births to every death, and the population is doubling in twenty-nine years. For the world as a whole, the annual score of births and deaths stands now at about 125 million births and 55 million deaths—an excess of some 70 million births.

The essential arithmetic of this situation was not understood 175 years ago. Even today—with the crisis now upon us—it is not receiving the attention it must have. The actions to be taken and the artifacts to be evolved to check this devastating mushrooming of people are already overdue and the clock ticks on.

ACTS OF GOD AND ACTS OF MAN

Man has long shown a remarkable ambivalence regarding the benevolence of the Creator. There is an enormous literature testifying eloquently to God's ardent concern for His chosen species here on earth—created in His own image and charged with "dominion over all creatures."

A different picture is revealed in the popular concept formalized as a legal principle that "Acts of God" are devastatingly unpleasant. Such acts are conceived to be inevitable accidents; such as extraordinary interruptions of the usual course of events—lightning, tempests, etc.

Many "Acts of God" are modest enough: a house struck by lightning, a boat overturned by a tempest and all on board lost. More ambitious divine interruptions of the "usual course of events" devastate cities, even nations. On November 1, 1755, an earthquake destroyed the city of Lisbon, killing sixty thousand. On May 8, 1902, Mount Pelée, on the island of Martinique, blew up, killing thirty thousand. In June 1970, an earthquake in Peru destroyed many towns and cities, and killed some thirty thousand people. Encyclopedias and almanacs list scores of disasters. The total death and destruction due to such "Acts of God" is almost incalculable.

One of the most remarkable features of such extraordinary interruptions is the speed with which human initiative can, on occasion, make good the devastation. The dead were buried, and Lisbon was rebuilt. Martinique soon became a tropical paradise again. There are exceptions, of course. Pompeii was so deeply covered with volcanic ash that it waited nearly two thousand years to be disinterred by archeologists. When the "dead" volcano Thera (or Santorin) blew up in the Aegean Sea about 1450 B.C., the Minoan civilization of Crete was crippled and the entire balance of power in that area was changed. This "Act of God" probably affected man's destiny more than any single event since the last glaciers began to retreat north twenty thousand years ago.

The United Nations has been concerned about population almost since its inception. Only recently has a commission on "Disasters" been established. One can predict that this will develop into an effective arm of the United Nations quite rapidly —and will be effective long before the increasing concern in the U.N. with population has a comparable impact.

A different category of disasters has plagued humankind over the centuries. Perhaps because they have never been recognized for what they are and how they are caused, they have been far more difficult to rectify. These are the "Acts of Man." Five thousand years ago, man the artificer had reached the point where he had the technology at hand to create great urban civilization. Without exception, these impressive acts of man proved to have within them the seeds of their own destruction. Mohenjo-Daro, Hammurabi's Babylon, and other early civilizations in the great river valleys of Asia and Africa vanished because "Acts of Man" had devastated the environment beyond the power of man to repair.

By modern standards, the technologies of these ancient civilizations were puny. But given time, the power available turned many fertile lands into desert. The shining exception is in Egypt, where a force of nature has for five millennia and more protected the valley of the Nile from the ravages of man. Now it appears that even there the more powerful modern technologies may be moving toward the destruction of the Nile Valley. The Aswan High Dam threatens to do what two hundred centuries and more of less sophisticated artificers left undamaged. This huge structure appears to be releasing the same kinds of forces which destroyed the irrigation cultures of the ancient world.

Man's ability to cope with "Acts of God" is impressive. His ability to recognize the consequences of his own more devastating mistakes is a story with few chapters but with even fewer happy endings. To say that "Acts of Man" are beyond the power of man to deal with, might be overly pessimistic. But for effective correction to be possible, such acts must be recognized for what they are; and the arts of "Master Magicians," rather than the bunglings of apprentices, must be brought to bear with consummate new skills to make the essential corrections.

Until very recently in the time scale of history, man has been able to evade the ultimate payment for ecological overgrazing, so to speak, by moving to new pastures. Today there is nowhere else to go.

Now at long last, "Acts of Man"—consequences of unbridled and irresponsible application of some of his newer artifacts—are reaching the point of global devastation. It is a fair question whether trips to the moon and the rising pressures to explore the rest of the solar system with not too deliberate speed, may be in part symbolic, and are perhaps the final stage in this long flight from reality. Unfortunately—or fortunately—there is no prospect that science fiction will provide the means to beg the question of the ages.

THE SUPER ARTIFACT

Let us leave *Homo apprenticus* for a bit, and return to the blind man examining the elephant.

Unfortunately for the future welfare of the human species, these blind men are the authorities who are charged with doing something about the "population crisis." They are telling each other and the world about the elephant as he is revealed to them. And they are formulating—or fomenting—plans and policies they tout as "solutions for the population problem."

And how are they doing?

Not well at all!

Essentially, the problem is crystal clear, and kindergarten simple: For a million years, natural forces maintained a slowly deteriorating balance between births and deaths. Then the *big* artifact came along—Jenner and death control.

It is astonishing that none of the wise men of the race had any inkling of the plunge toward disaster and devastation that death control could bring. In 1927, just at the time the population of the planet was mushrooming up to the *second* billion mark, the first World Population Conference was held in Geneva. The preponderant conviction of the 123 solons there assembled was that the big problem of the early future was underpopulation *not* overpopulation! The population of Europe was expected to decline first, and the other continents would follow.

These blind men had no doubt that they knew their elephant!

There is another fable that illuminates this grotesquely ominous situation. As reported by Aesop, the mice recognized a grave problem: the cat. A high-level conference was convened. After much talk, one mouse genius came up with the solution "bell the cat!" After thunderous applause, a committee was appointed to do the job and the conference adjourned, without designating which heroic mouse should do the job.

In the solution of the population crisis, the "cat" has been identified: a devastating cultural lag, a tradition-bound obsession with a level of fertility which was a positive and essential good as recently as only a century ago, but which today is a catastrophe.

How to bell the population cat remains an utter and frightening nightmare. The balance between births and deaths each year must be restored. A very substantial proportion of these excess births must be prevented, otherwise all the talk—all the policy formulations—remain massive exercises in futility.

But how? If the number of births in the world cannot be brought into approximate balance—and very quickly—with the number of deaths, growth will inevitably and ultimately be checked by the Napoleonic formula: problems ignored eventually solve themselves. The population crisis will ultimately and inevitably solve itself by a rise in the death rate. This is not the way we would like it; but in the end that's the way it will be unless man can create a better method.

If the problem is to be solved in a context of human decency, the birth rate worldwide will have to be brought into balance with the modern death rate. This allows no alternative to a reduction of the number of births by from 50 to 70 million each year. Obviously, none of the proposals now being considered, and none of the operational plans now in being, offer any prospect whatever that such a reduction in fertility will occur quickly enough to avert the "Napoleonic solution." That "Nature and Nature's God" may be building toward the *other* solution is suggested by the emergence in Asia of a virulent strain of cholera which is spreading alarmingly in Asia and Africa.

The increasing concern about the population crisis is encouraging. But remedies so far attempted or proposed are far too little and too late. They are unimaginative, poorly planned, and pathetically inadequate to deal with the crisis. They notably lack any tincture of that essential ingredient of the successful artificer: the inventive faculty. This faculty has been applied with brilliant success in the mechanical, chemical, electrical, and other arts. An invention has been defined by the courts as the successful solution of a problem by "means that are *not obvious* to a person skilled in the art." Obvious means to solve problems are called "combinations." They do not constitute inventions and they cannot be patented. None of the fertility control expedients now being applied or advocated could possibly be considered by the Court of Customs and Patent Appeals as being more than low grade "combinations."

It is increasingly popular to talk about "social invention." In a mouse convocation, those who used such a phrase might be forgiven, for mice have never invented a mantrap—or even a cattrap. For human beings to evoke "social invention" when they appear to have no concept of what invention is—or involves—puts them on the same intellectual level with the mice.

Yet historical record leaves no doubt that human cultures can and sometimes have gained effective control of fertility. Such control was well under way in France before the end of the eighteenth century. Such control was becoming effective in Ireland before the potato famine of 1848-50. When the potato was introduced into Ireland about 1690, the population stood at about a million. This cheap and easy way to grow food ignited a population explosion which reached eight million a century and half later. Then the potato blight provided a Napoleonic solution. The crop failed for three years; a million Irish starved and more than a million emigrated. This was, however, only the capstone on the Irish version of fertility control; adopted with remarkable unanimity by the people in defiance of the church, the patriots, and the government, it was already on the way to success before the potato famine. The control was based on a spontaneous growth of public opinion that demanded that a couple wait for a "place" to be made for them by the death of their parents before they could marry. Many never married and late marriages produced few children. With low fertility and continuing emigration the population is now about three million.

In Italy, where the obsession with "the more bambinos the better" was traditional, the people countered Mussolini's ukase to start turning out the cannon fodder needed for the new Imperial Rome by cutting sharply back on the birth rate.

Between 1947 and 1957, the Japanese people[13]—not the government—cut the birth rate in half by resorting to massive induced abortion. This is the most dramatic reduction in a birth rate of which there is record. Such examples as these prove that human fertility can be controlled. By comparison, expedients which today are being undertaken in the developing countries are simplistic and unimaginative to the point of naivete.

It has been the position of this writer for the last several years that the solution of the population crisis would be found neither in the drug store, in the laboratories of biophysiology, nor in the birth-control clinic. Without this essential ingredient —the development of the *will* and the *determination*—the ultimate ideal contraceptive will fail. It appears to be established as a matter of historical record that if the will be strong enough, the pill and the IUD are not necessary. The Irish turned the trick with very little contraception of any kind. The people of the United States reduced the birth rate to the lowest point in its history in 1933-35 without benefit of pills, IUDs, or any of the other more modern gadgets. Solution of the problem appears to be in the area of the inventive stimulation of motivation based on an effective understanding of the basic elements of human arithmetic. Like attaching the bell to the cat, this seems easy enough at the verbal level, but it is not easy in practice. A truly effective changing of men's and women's minds about so primeval and fundamental a matter as procreation is a major undertaking.

The total attack on fertility gets back to that fundamental property of the human species—the application of the human mind to the development of artifacts. In order to counter some of the more potent artifacts which have gone beyond the control of the magician's apprentice, powerful retro-artifacts are critically needed. The first must be a sure-fire means to put the threat of atomic holocaust permanently under wraps; the second, an effective, quick-acting means to restore that ancient and necessary balance between births and deaths.

Of these two artifacts, the latter will prove to be by far the most complicated. Wide-ranging social, economic, ecologic, political, religious, anthropological, and other interactions are involved. The relatively simple corrections which intervened in the industrial West in the unhurried tempo of a vanishing culture can hardly be expected to be effective in today's frenetic world.

A brief exploration of one area of this enormous complex will illustrate the point. This comprises the matter of *hidden motivations* which without question are powerful determinants of the reaction of human beings to fertility control.

As a point of departure, it may be pointed out that Norman Himes'[14] concept of the "Vital Revolution" meant that in effectively tinkering with death and birth, man had in fact begun to play God in a way not possible prior to that time. This set in motion a train of partly overt, partly hidden reactions which even yet are not fully recognized, let alone understood.

To play God is a frightening undertaking, and it is not surprising that the responsibilities it entails are evaded or denied. Death control has universal approbation. It is conceived as an absolute good, with hardly any thought to the consequences of upsetting the age-old balance between births and deaths.

On the other hand, birth control, necessary to maintain a safe balance as death rates decline, has tended to arouse deep opposition and profound emotional turmoil. To avoid looking straight at the realities of this situation, miracles are hoped for: food from the sea, space travel, pie in the sky for everybody—so much pie that all of God's children will become so fat they will stop breeding.

The truth is that these and other blindfold attempts to escape looking at the realities confronting us today are heading our planet and its human passengers toward catastrophe. The world eagerly accepts the rapid and widespread control of mortality, but is content to evoke no more than wishful thinking to deal with the ensuing imbalance between births and deaths.

There are hundreds of causes of death. There is only one cause of birth, and that is centered right in the tangled nexus of emotional tensions, taboos, and associated perplexities and complexities, which constitute perhaps the major stock-in-trade of the psychiatrist. If by some biological miracle mankind could be redone along the lines of the aphid and could reproduce satisfactorily by a process reminiscent of the Immaculate Conception, the psychiatrists' couches and consultation rooms would be far less crowded than they are today.

Some aspects of the population industry have very little erotic octane. A tabulation of vital statistics or a chart of population densities around the world is hardly calculated to set the libido spinning, even though it may carry a portentous message. My experience over more than two decades of writing and talking about the population question in most varied contexts convinces me that the obsessions and the evasions and the fleeing from reality which one constantly encounters in discussion of this surpassingly important matter have a powerful sexual component. This goes back into the centrally sex-obsessed nature of the Judeo-Christian culture of the West. The complex of reactions will certainly not be the same in some other cultures, even in other Western subcultures. Hence no unitary formula will suffice.

The United States, that land which Dr. Albert Ellis[15] once described as "addled, straddled, and spraddled in its attitudes toward sex," has perhaps more than its fair share of irrational taboos, which afford all around us impressive examples of how crypto-sex complicates the population question. It may even be responsible, at least in part, for the ingenious theory that man's future is in outer space: that we can dump our surplus population on the moon or on Mars, or on some other handy planet.

Admittedly, the chain of action-reaction culminating in such intellectual non sequiturs is long and well concealed, but it is there for the searching. I have no doubt that if these strong illusions are tracked down, they will be found to be based ultimately and fundamentally on sex and on early conditioning which usually persists for life.

This hidden sexual component which creates such formidable blockages to facing the population crisis squarely has not received the attention it deserves. That it is so enthusiastically neglected is a matter of very considerable importance. Nearly a quarter of a century ago, a distinguished British psychologist, Dr. J. C. Flugel,[16] set forth in detail the nature and the mechanisms involved in some of the sexually based compulsions in opposition to fertility control and even to discussing the matter. What Dr. Flugel has to say, although it has largely been ignored, is as valid today as it was in the mid 1940's. His thoughts are best stated in his own words:

> Sexual restraints and taboos, we have implied, may be looked upon as an aspect or manifestation at the human level of the general biological antagonism between individuation and genesis. . . . What we are, however, undoubtedly justified in asserting, and what is of much greater immediate importance to us here, is that this general sex taboo (which in one form or another is a feature of human society and which is certainly not least developed in our Western culture), together with the psychological conflicts around sex

which it engenders, plays a big part in the somewhat strange and ambivalent attitudes that humanity . . . has adopted toward Malthus's principle. . . .

A taboo, however, as Wundt, Freud, Frazer, and other eminent students of the subject have pointed out, implies a double attitude —an attitude of disgust or prohibition overlying one of attraction and desire. For men do not trouble to prohibit actions that nobody is tempted to perform. . . . Now an interesting fact about Malthusianism is that the resistance to it appears to spring from two sources: from the sexual taboo itself and from the underlying sexual urge—both in their different ways providing motives for the rejection or neglect of the principle in question. A strong taboo, therefore, implies a strong desire (even though this may sometimes be an unconscious one).

Dr. Flugel emphasized the varied aspects of the sexual conflict and attitudes regarding control of fertility. Discussing the castration complex, Flugel makes this observation:

Civilized man's attitude to his sexual impulses and organs is curiously ambivalent. On the one hand—as in a traditional Christian morality and in the general—they are looked upon as a source of impurity and sin, treated with contempt and subjected to the sternest measures of control. On the other hand, they are also a source of pride and pleasure, something intimately connected with our sense of power, dignity, and self-esteem, something the loss of which would wound us very deeply. . . .

Such deep-seated conflicts obviously lead to highly emotional, amply confused, and most varied reactions. One example is the widespread confusion regarding fertility and virility. This bit of folk wisdom implies that an individual, a group, or a nation which has low fertility has low virility. This mushrooms out into the cannon-fodder complex not unknown around the world today. There is no close relationship between mere numbers of human beings and effective military power, else Mainland China would be far and away the greatest and most powerful nation on earth. China's technological achievements in recent years have been impressive, but she will become a great power only if she is able to achieve a technological and industrial breakthrough. Progress in this area is actually impaired by the low living level of her people and her high rate of population increase. Yet we find ourselves repeatedly exhorted to attempt the impossible task of outbreeding the Chinese. This, the argument runs, would demonstrate our virility! In actual fact, it would seriously endanger the orderly development of our complex industrial economy.

Narrowing down this thought—there are the contradictory emotions which on many occasions center around the arrival of a new child. There is much joy in this event, but there can also be serious concern as to how this bundle from heaven will affect the family exchequer, the prospects for education, and other mundane worries of the older children. Dr. Flugel points out that in a significant number of cases, this produces a curious Freudian lapse:

> Finally, as regards death wishes towards children in civilized societies, the present writer is aware of two cases in which the father, writing to have notices of the birth of a child inserted in a newspaper, asked for the notice to be placed among the list of "deaths" and the editor of one well-known paper subsequently stated that such a slip was not so very uncommon.

Dr. Flugel's observations are limited to a small sector of the human race—the Judeo-Christian culture of the Western world. This is an area where great progress has been made in reestablishing the ancient birth-death balance. Yet even in this relatively favorable situation, much remains to be done. In other cultures, the same fundamental, human mechanisms are operative. The analysis of the motivating "pressure points" which move the psyche to make up its mind is an enormously important and very complex area.

To sketch in a few pages even a crude outline of the population crisis is impossible. If this impressionistic view of its enormous range and complexity creates a picture which carries a sense of concern and urgency the effort is justified.

Pretty-pretty simplistic prescriptions for a cure or a solution are bound to fail. The elephant that the blind men are attempting to explore is so large and so complicated that those with 20/20 relational vision find it hard to comprehend.

Rudyard Kipling once said that "the Gods of the Copybook Maxims are the last of the Gods to die." In a sense not intended by Kipling, these copybook gods might have an especial relevance to stimulating the production of human "copies"—to giving aid and comfort to the stork. To the extent that they delay the dawn of reproductive sanity they imperil the future.

Perhaps the time has come when the last survivors of these most fundamental of the "copybook gods" will be forced to join their colleagues who have had to take sanctuary over the centuries in the Edens and the Valhallas, free to range the earth only between midnight and dawn on midsummer's night.

In a sense it can be said that the past is dead and the future is not yet born. There is only the present.

While the past is beyond our powers to touch or to change, the future is malleable. And such is the power of the mind of man to contrive new artifacts that it becomes possible at least to dare to think of such a portentous and mind-stirring challenge—a challenge terrifying in a way, but which can no longer be eroded.

Nothing less than a new morality may be the necessary undergirding of this superartifact so essential to make the future safe. The distinguished physiologist, the late Anton Carlson,[17] drafted the specifications for the kind of human competent to be the architect of such a future:

> As I see it, the person who has developed some control of his greed, his vanity, and his fears; who has developed to the limit of his brain the accumulated understanding of man and the universe, and who thinks in terms of his fellowman—that is, the human race—not for the day, for tomorrow, or even the next hundred years, but for the future at least as long as our human past; and who at the same time uses all his influence, without violence or coercion, to prevail on his fellowman to follow his example, that individual is entitled to the connotation "wise."

Man's destiny is not beyond the moon somewhere in outer space. With a potential future as long as his past, man has the power to create either a desert or to add to the glory of the incredibly beautiful planet which is our home. How this great adventure turns out depends on whether the human species has the wisdom, the compassion—and the guts—to do the job.

Chapter Three

A DEMOGRAPHER VIEWS THE
POPULATION PROBLEM

JERRY W. COMBS, JR.

THERE are two sets of issues regarding population we shall discuss here. The first of these relates to how the population "problem" is to be defined. What criteria shall we use? What shall be our measure of too little or too much? The second set of issues relates to the means of population control. When it has been decided that we have enough population or too much, how shall its growth be curtailed? Neither issue can be discussed solely as an exercise in rationality, since in the final analysis, even the definition of the problem has to cope with basic issues of human and social values. The second is more loaded with such questions, however. For since "control" always involves the manipulation or the "modification" of human behavior, we must cope with questions of freedom, of "legitimacy," of religious beliefs, the proper sphere of political or governmental action, and changes in the social structure. These issues must be resolved at all levels of our society.

The arguments to be advanced can be briefly stated. Many criteria are proposed to measure the nature of the population problem. Each will give somewhat different answers. Thoughtful men will disagree on the importance to be attached to the different criteria. Nevertheless, this generation is challenged to sift through the research and the discussion of the various issues and reach some sort of subjective judgment regarding the ultimate, desirable level of population size. If we do not, the impersonal forces of the universe will ultimately set such a limit, quite inconsonant with our current values of the good life, and with no regard at all for the fate of modern civilization.

The greater challenge will be to achieve population control within acceptable limits. Population growth does not lend itself very well to decision making at the top. The millions of parents-

31

to-be who make these decisions are influenced by their personal predilections, their social training and conditioning, their reference groups and the friends whose good opinions they value, their religious beliefs, their anticipated income, their aspirations for themselves and their children, and their optimism or pessimism with regard to their chances of obtaining a proper mixture of children and other worthwhile ingredients of what is for them the good life. The meaningful pressures which may be applied by society occur through bringing about appropriate states of mind among the individual men and women on the "baby production line." Political constraints—whether operating directly through laws or indirectly through education, economic controls, or other means—can be exercised only when they implement a consensus within the body politic already arrived at, and when that consensus not only approves the goals professed out also tolerates the sanctions by which the rules, regulations, and laws are implemented. When you cry, "Action Now!" on this front, you must look deeply within your own souls.

In brief, what I am saying is that no government, by itself, certainly not a democratic government, is going to solve the population problem. Neither is the population problem going to be solved by scientists—chemists, biologists, or behavioralists—nor are the solutions going to be forged in the laboratories of the nation's drug companies, nor will they be manipulated by systems analysts feeding masses of data into hungry computers. The solution to the problem of population is going to be forged and fashioned in the hearts and minds of human beings who wish to occupy this planet with as much comfort, dignity, and grace as their intelligence, ingenuity, and humanity can afford. Moreover, the specification of the problem and its solution will probably question some of the old verities, challenge the conventional wisdom, contradict some cherished shibboleths, and undermine some very profound and previously unquestioned virtues. For when growth is no longer valued, when the mighty and prolific threaten our existence, the foundations of our social order are shaken. Land values cease to increase, Chambers of Commerce can no longer advertise a "growing community," men may no longer gamble on the increase in land values in the ghetto, and we may find ourselves making do, at slower speeds, on yesterday's roadways rather than new and bigger superhighways. Taxes may well rise, too. Without a growing population, floating bond issues to be amortized by the next and more numerous generation may appear finally for what it is, an evasion of this generation's responsibility. New modes of coping with problems will have to be designed.

But we may conceptualize in the process a new and more profound sense of individual and community responsibility, a new sense of rights, and a new notion of man's relation to himself and his environment, his past, and his future.

DEFINITION OF THE PROBLEM

Now to the issues. How do we define the problem?

World Population Growth

The most startling way to pose the population dilemma is to talk about what is happening on a world basis. A large part of the audience is probably already very familiar with it. I shall be brief. At the beginning of the Christian era—which is, after all, very recent—the world's population was probably in the range of a mere 250 to 350 million persons. Admittedly, this figure is based on a great deal of conjecture, but is plausible enough to have gained widespread acceptance. Had it been twice that figure or only half, the generalization that mankind's growth up to that time had been extremely slow would obviously be true.

It continued to be relatively slow until the dawn of the modern period. In 1650 there were, again very roughly, about 545 million persons in the world. A century later, in 1750, the population of the world is estimated to have increased to about 728 million, only four million of whom lived in North America, and only eleven million of whom lived in Latin America. Hardly more than two centuries later, sometime after the year 1960, based on researches carried out under the auspices of the United Nations, the population of the world had reached three billion persons, or more than four times the number estimated for 1750, and is racing toward four billion. If fertility rates remain at the level observed around 1960, and the level of mortality continues to decline at rates consistent with its recent declines (I am abridging the assumptions somewhat here), the population of the world will reach 7.4 billion by the year 2000, and would increase to 22.3 billion in the year 2040 if growth rates projected for the year 2000 continued. This would mean an average density of the world (excluding Antarctica) of 428 persons per square mile, whereas the average density in 1960 was only fifty-seven per square mile.

Now these are extreme projections, illustrating potential growth. If fertility drops, or if mortality rises or ceases to decline, the realized populations in the years 2000 and 2040 will be less. U.N. estimates made a few years ago set the range, on various assumptions of fertility decline, between 5.3 billion and 6.8 billion for the year 2000, and between 8.5 and 14.8 billion in 2040. Even the lower estimates are sobering when it is remembered that the highest rates of growth are in those regions of the world with very low levels of living, where economies are already strained. In recent years their growth rates have been rising. In the period 1940-50, the growth rate of world population was less than 1 percent per year, but has been rising toward 2 percent. In the developing countries, because of the decline in mortality and the high fertility, growth rates are between 2 and 3 percent per year, as high as 3.5 percent in several.

In the United States, European countries, the U.S.S.R., Japan, and Oceania, growth rates are substantially lower than in the underdeveloped, or "developing" countries. Their great surge in population growth, during which mortality was declining faster than fertility rates, and during which their rates of growth were almost double that of the rest of the world, came in the several centuries before 1900, and never, except in countries being rapidly developed, like the United States, where migration also was important, attained the rates of growth presently observed in the developing countries. Fertility is much lower in this block of countries. European growth rates have recently been below 1 percent per year, and the United States is growing at the present time at only about 1 percent per year. In the post World War II period, of course, there were somewhat higher levels of fertility throughout the West. In the United States the rate of growth in the 1950's was about 1.6 percent. Since 1957 the birth rate in the United States has been going down again, but the downward trend is not expected to continue. In the last year there are signs that the birth rate is stabilizing, and unless fertility per woman in the childbearing period declines, the birth rate will rise in the next decade because of the increase in the proportion of women in the childbearing ages as a result of the post World War II baby boom. Consequently, some increase in population is certain, even though fertility declines, and an increase in population to about 300 million in the year 2000—about 50 percent above the current population—is a reasonable expectation. The problem in the United States and Europe, and a few other countries, such as Japan—whether considered numerically or in terms of growth rates—is of a different order from that in the underdeveloped countries; but almost everywhere, population is increasing.

To put the problem of population in terms of growth is one way to set the problem and to define it, and it frightens some people almost to death, but not enough of them to solve the problem.

Food Supply

We need to look more closely at the implications of food supply. The first of the derivative issues is simple—can we feed these many people? Malthus raised the same issue almost two hundred years ago, and the pundits and scientists and the industrialists and the farmers of the world have gone about refuting him ever since. We think we eat well today, at least some of us, and there's little doubt that there will be food enough in the United States for at least 100 million more mouths. As for the world as a whole, the nutritionists tell us that if we simply set ourselves to the task, make sufficient investment, change our methods of tillage, cultivate the ocean shelves, stack people up more densely in the cities so there is still land untrod, and change our eating habits and our tastes sufficiently, we can feed the anticipated increment of the world's population for at least the next thirty years.

There are, of course, some sleepers in this argument which tend to displease a person like me who is accustomed to a diet of hamburgers and other choicer cuts of beef, and whose stomach is inconvenienced by grains and grasses not predigested. But food, they tell us, is not really the measure of the problem. We can grow and still eat enough to grow. Eventually, food may be a limiting factor, but not at seven billion persons. I accept the appraisal that mankind can meet this challenge! But it only means to me that we are not in danger of starving, which I believe is all the nutritionists are saying. They are also implying, I think, that we can continue to eat better, and with less effort, if we grow more slowly, which is also a matter we should consider.

Economic Growth and Population Growth

Man needs more than food. He needs clothing, some heat to keep him warm, some activity, houses, hammocks, chairs, beds, radios, refrigerators, automobiles or scooters, bicycles, all sorts of fashionable regalia, etc., and this leads us to consider another criterion by which population growth is judged—the economic dimension.

Economists are in the enviable position of being able to work both sides of the street on the matter of population. In the 1930's when population growth in most western European countries was grinding to a halt, the decline was felt to be an imminent reality in just thirty years or so, even in the United States, the economic hue and cry was that no population growth was a terrible disaster. Their arguments carried a certain credibility. The world's economy, particularly that dominated by the Western world, was in a state of stagnation, coincident with the declining rates of population growth. Not only that, but population growth, by increasing the demand for land and for all manner of other consumer items, provides one of the basic stimuli for savings and investment, since growth in itself will generate a rewarding return. Our economy is geared to expanding markets. Without question, the cessation of population growth altogether will require some profound adjustment of the economic institutions as we know them if we are to continue to have the kind of prosperity to which we have become accustomed.

Most economists are agreed, however, that the rapid rates of population growth in the developing and underdeveloped countries set limits not only upon the increase in per capita income in those countries but upon the growth of the economies themselves. So much of current income must go directly into food and clothing, that savings for capital investment—whether voluntary or imposed by the system—are severely limited. Slower rates of growth would not only enable the population to live better now but would permit increased savings and investment to provide a more rapid growth of capital. Less need be spent for education if there were fewer children, and the overall quality of training could be improved. Slower growth, or no growth at all, is seen as an essential condition for a more rapid improvement in the level of existence for peoples in these countries.

Demographic Structure

A similar distinction must be made between developing and developed countries when we look at the next criterion by which population growth can be evaluated: that of demographic structure. In the absence of charts or other visual aids, and for the benefit of those who may not be familiar with questions of age structure, I shall simply state that what I am referring to is the relationship between age groups in a society. Populations having high fertility characteristically have a large proportion of children in relation to the adult population. Lower fertility rates reduce this proportion of children, so that there are proportionally larger numbers of adults and therefore a larger number of effective workers. In essentially agricultural societies the difference may not be of great significance, since children may become economically productive at relatively early ages; but in complex societies requiring extensive education prior to becoming economically active, the difference is significant from several standpoints. In societies with lower fertility, there is less investment of money and manpower to educate the next generation of workers and a greater proportion of the population can be effectively employed, leading to greater production of both goods and services.

The transition from high to low fertility rates, however, complicates this general picture, because of the short run fluctuations in age structure. From the standpoint of economic efficiency, the immediate effect is salutary. The burden of dependency is reduced, that portion of the population born in the preceding period when birth rates were high, as they grow older, enter the economically productive age groups, and for several decades we have an exceedingly productive population. We had such a population in 1930 and 1940. As these workers continue to grow older, however, and reach retirement age, the burden of dependency shifts in character, and we have a larger proportion of people in the older age groups, and relatively smaller proportions to take their place in the economically active ages. This has more than economic implications. It has social implications because the institutional mechanisms for caring for the aged are different from those for caring for children, and there are political implications growing out of the fact that older people are thought to be more conservative and less innovative than the young, and they may preempt positions of power and prestige, and slow down the processes of change, and so forth. Universities may cease to grow, the average age of professors gets older, their radicalism grows barnacles, employment opportunities for younger would-be professors are diminished. So, if you have a bias against age, you can paint a very ugly picture of the ossification that takes place, not only in education, but in society generally.

It is certainly an issue relevant to an assessment of population growth. The demographic significance is less, of course, if the birth rate, though declining, does not fall to the replacement level, and so generates some continued growth. It is greater if it falls and stays at the replacement level. The effects we are talking about, however, are more important for short-run considerations than for the long-run, for when fertility stabilizes at any level, the population structure will eventually become normalized, the people born in the period of high fertility will finally die, and subsequent generations of youth may not find the situation so diabolical.

Thus, those who advocate drastic declines in fertility levels may expect considerable intellectual opposition from the standpoint of both the economic and demographic implications of such a development. These implications clearly support a reduction in the rate of population growth in the developing countries, but it can be argued that they do not so clearly support reduction of fertility to the replacement level in the already developed, highly industrialized countries.

Political Power

I shall mention the criterion of political power only briefly and in passing. Population growth, as an instrument of political power, has had advocates in the past, most recently and notoriously in the case of Nazi Germany and Fascist Italy. It is not among current arguments openly advanced by nations today; it is, however, an aspect of population which enters people's consciousness at various levels and has to be taken account of. Last summer in India I was reminded by any number of people, always confidentially, that Hindus feared if they restricted their fertility they would soon be outnumbered by Muslims and Christians, who did not restrict theirs. In the United States there is a reflection of an emphasis on numbers as a source of political power in the charges of genocide directed toward the delivery of family planning services to the poor, and notably to minority groups. It has to be taken account of as an unstated aspect of opposition to programs of fertility limitation, and cannot be blindly passed over as a consideration of national power.

Resources and the Environment

The more telling arguments for reduction of rates of population growth in all countries to the point of stability emerge from considerations of resource utilization and environmental debasement. The resource argument stems from the basic premise that we dwell in a finite world. In the final analysis the Malthusian argument was based on the same premise. The second premise on which arguments over the continued availability of resources rests is that modern technology is a vast consumer of nonrenewable mineral and fossil resources, so that the conditions under which the present and probable future population of the world can continue to maintain and advance its levels of living are tenuous indeed. Man has a long history of depletion of natural resources. One flight from New Delhi, India, to Cairo, to Rome is sufficient to convince a traveler that ancient civilizations, with far smaller populations, completely deforested the regions in which these ancient civilizations flourished, for there is hardly a tree or a green patch to be seen. It is red, rocky, barren. Greenery persists in the more temperate climes, where civilization is more recent, but in the United States the red clay hills of the South and the dust bowls of the Midwest also attest to man's propensity to devastate his environment. Man's ingenuity in seeking new resources to exploit, and the ethnocentric tendency to view present success as evidence of special virtue, tends to becloud the lessons of history. Western civilization is still young and impetuous. It still has iron, coal, and the fossilized remains of the earth's prehistoric period; it still has the enormous resources of scientific rationality and specialization, and the flexibility to move from one exhausted resource to another more plentiful and to fabricate substitutes in our laboratories and manufacturing plants, the cost of which may be absorbed in the general prosperity. It is thus an optimistic and rather conceited approach we take to our environment which tends to make us feel that when one thing is gone we will be able, through our ingenuity, to find something better. Though the earth is finite, it does contain enormous resources still. And for almost every foreseeable shortage, there are foreseeable innovations to forestall the consequences of their loss.

Now, I cannot find incontrovertible evidence that in thirty years, or sixty, or a hundred, those resources on which our civilization is utterly dependent will be exhausted, and bring about its collapse. Like land, and space, and food supplies, we can visualize enough to keep going—in the short-run, or in the foreseeable future—particularly if we maintain a parochial view of the problem, and assume that the resources elsewhere, in Canada, or Africa, or wherever, will be ours to exploit. Thus, it is relatively easy to dismiss the occasional, even though increasingly vocal, prophets of doom as either misinformed, narrowly specialized, carried away by excessive zeal, or logically inconsistent. Certainly 100 million more people in the United States, bringing us to a density of approximately ninety to one hundred per square mile, is not likely to devastate us.

It is only when we break out of the strictures of short-run forecasts or free ourselves from the parochial or provincial view, and contemplate the extraordinary task of bringing the rest of the world up to the kind of living standard which we enjoy, that our complacency is shaken. Harrison Brown,[18] for example, has pointed out that with no population increment at all, it would require all the factories in the world at the present time, working around the clock, one hundred years to create merely the capital equipment necessary to bring the level of living of the rest of the world up to that enjoyed in the United States. At current rates of growth of population, the time required would be four hundred years. What, we may ask, are the implications of these figures for our reserves of raw materials?

Perhaps more relevant to our own situation, it is when we begin to raise questions about the hidden costs incident to our technological processes, and focus not upon the depletion of specific resources so much as upon the consequences of the system which feeds upon them, that we begin to wonder whether the pursuit of growth, economic or demographic, carries with it any real long-range benefits. We can go offshore and further for our oil, as we are doing; we can invent methods of desalinization of water, as we are doing; we can build our cities larger and build greater superhighways, as we are doing, and we can invent methods for disposing of wastes and curbing pollutants. But are we not, in fact, long before we reach the point of the utter exhaustion of our resources, losing our way in technological prowess? Is not the very quality of life deteriorating?

The issue is, I believe, as much philosophic as scientific. It is an issue in which there are useful scientific and factual inputs, but its resolution involves to a far greater extent questions of values which are not essentially mensurable by scientific instruments. We cannot use cost-price analysis to set a value on the additional hour of commuting time, by car or subway, or justify the rationality of giving up single-family houses for apartment living closer to one's work. These are values which individual psyches must adjudicate. Controlling pollution is a cost which society, and individuals in it, must bear; and the added cost of such control which is attributable to the increase in population must be spread among all those alive. Furthermore, we are beginning to appreciate the effect upon our living conditions of the heat generated by the continued conversion of fossilized fuel. We have been discussing recently the establishment of new cities to absorb some of the impact of our increasing population in order to protect already existing cities. But the requirement for water to disperse the heat generated by industry is likely to further concentrate urban development along our coastlines. Many observers of the modern scene already believe our cities are unmanageable and ungovernable, simply because of the complexity of their problems. And many people who live in them are growing increasingly disenchanted with the inconvenience, the stresses, the filth, the crime, and all their other problems. But in a sense, we are stuck with our cities, and the technology which spawns them, and to give them up is to invite disaster—lower levels of living, rising death rates, etc. We are precariously balanced on a treadmill; we dare not get off.

Some critics find the ecological argument weakened by a loose specification of the population-pollution equation. Clearly *pollution does not arise from population*. The pollution arises from our technological process, from the pressures of modern living, and from the complexity of life organized around these processes, including our concentration in cities. The pollution of our public lands, the refuse that litters our beaches, are not so much a reflection of the density of population in this country, as of the affluence deriving from our technological accomplishments that enables vast numbers of us to utilize these outposts of nature. *Population is thus not the culprit, but one of the multipliers.* We can control pollution by constraints on our technology, and I believe we must. We can solve many of our other problems by altering our institutions more responsively to some of the maladjustments incident to the conditions of the twentieth-technological century. I believe we must. But having said this, whatever the level of technological development and its resultant pollution capacity, population does operate as a multiplier. It is one factor subject to control. What needs to be examined in far more detailed terms than has so far been done, is the proposition that the better you live, the fewer people you need, and that at some point the choice is explicitly and overwhelmingly between fewer people and more progress, or between more people and a declining average welfare. I do not think we can answer this question in precise, scientific terms, with the information we have. I suspect that the answers we arrive at eventually, as those we arrive at now, are going to be heavily loaded with subjective judgments and tastes and varying admixtures of information. We ultimately come back to the basic premise that mankind does live in a finite world, that he has, through his technological prowess, unleashed an amount of population growth in the world that already prevents much of the world from living well and that some day population growth will stop, either through man's foresight and self-control or through forces quite beyond his control. The problem of judgment comes in balancing the advantages—if any—of uncontrolled population against the advantages of population stabilization and technological progress. No one wants to live less well.

As a man who grew up in the relatively uncrowded milieu of a small southern town, whose zeal for the fleshpots of the city could be amply satisfied by the opportunities in nearby Atlanta, whose population then was something of the order of 125,000 or so, who postponed marriage to about age thirty, and who found the desire for parenthood richly satisfied by two daughters, I am not distressed by the appeals of the environmentalists. While I am not convinced that they can document their more exaggerated predictions of disaster in the near future, the logical argument that unless fertility is reduced, population must ultimately be controlled by an increase in the death rate, coming about from a variety of reasons, cannot be refuted. Moreover, it is difficult to demonstrate, except in terms of short-run interests of particular groups, the advantages to be derived from continued population growth anywhere. I like people, but my interests are easily satisfied by those available, and their multiplication does not promise any increase in either my opportunities or capacity for friendship. I certainly see no possible justification for opting for more people at the expense of whatever level of living is possible. As one well past that magical age, I find nothing appalling in a population whose average age is forty, and I can assure those here whose age is half that, that their next twenty years are going to speed past much faster than their last twenty. Furthermore, I believe it is within the ingenuity of man to cope institutionally with the economic adjustments required by a cessation of population growth. Some generation is going to have to face this reality. And it would seem to me that this one is as adequately equipped to face it as any that is likely to come after.

I therefore think it legitimate, in fact, responsible, to ask: "If eventually, why not now?" And since what I shall say, in what follows, will document the impossibility of doing it now, or tomorrow, it is certainly responsible to ask: "Why not begin now?"

ISSUES: THE REGULATION OF MAN'S NUMBERS

We turn now to the issues of population control. How can it be done? Shall we leave it to nature, or forestall it by our own initiative, courage, and ingenuity? I opt for the latter, and so will ignore with only a passing mention the view that the problem may solve itself eventually. When the population of the world reaches the ultimate carrying capacity of the earth or the ultimate level of tolerance for men themselves, then famine, starvation, disease, war, misery, or atomic catastrophe will take care of the problem, restore a workable balance between men and their environments. Those that survive may be able to adjust to it. Such a view is both morally and intellectually untenable. The issues I shall discuss are those relating to the control of fertility which, hopefully, may forestall the more horrifying or "natural" controls.

The Demographic Transition Theory

A good many years ago it was generally accepted doctrine within the demographic community that the conditions of life in a highly developed, industrialized and urbanized society would lead almost automatically to a reduction of fertility. As man forsook the rural environment, where the family was the unit of labor and children were viewed as economic assets, and took up residence in the city, with its rationalization of human relationships, secularization of values, and rising aspiration levels, the value of children changed from economic assets to liabilities, and fertility decline followed as a matter of course. This change had taken place in all of the Western world, where technological progress, resulting in the decline in the death rate, was followed by those conditions speeding the decline in fertility. It was assumed that the same chain of events would follow in the developing countries, that a decline in the death rate was a precondition of modernization, since it facilitated the growth of a trained and competent labor force, but that the ensuing urbanization would result, as it had in the West, in declining fertility. To a point, this theory is still partially valid. Fertility did indeed decline in the Western world, so far, in fact, that there emerged fears that Western civilization was in danger of extinction because the time was coming when the countries affected would no longer reproduce themselves. In country after country in the early 1930's fertility was barely above the replacement level. Today, as we have already noted, fertility in the Western world is low, generating growth rates of 1 percent per year or less.

Two things happened, however, to undermine confidence in the theory of the demographic transition as a dependable safeguard against too much growth. With improved economic conditions following the depression of the 1930's, fertility rates rose again, and the postwar prosperity following World War II was accompanied by an unprecedented "baby boom" lasting until late in the 1950's. It thus became apparent that fertility was affected, not solely by the urban conditions of an industrial society, but by other processes as well, so that fertility close to the replacement level could not under all circumstances be assumed even in the highly industrialized countries of the West. Secondly, it also became apparent that drastic reduction in mortality was possible in less developed countries without accompanying social changes presaging eventual fertility declines. Because life everywhere is so highly prized, people readily adopt the very adequate techniques, such as sanitation, immunization, and the use of insecticides, that will soon reduce the death rate. Social changes which involve the reconceptualization of the value of children come more slowly, as a result of economic and other changes, which cannot be imported so easily, and it became clear that the tremendous population growth following the reduction in mortality had come so rapidly that it was impeding the other anticipated changes.

Voluntary Family Planning

In this context, soon after World War II, a major effort was launched to introduce into the developing countries mechanisms for promoting the adoption of family planning. There has been some tendency to exaggerate the possibility of achieving substantial results through the introduction of voluntary family planning, but in the defense of this effort it is fair to say that it was the only politically feasible approach that could be made at the time. The voluntaristic aspect made the export of devices tolerable to countries smarting under centuries of imperialistic domination, and it could be incorporated to some extent within the context of health services. Unfortunately, though perhaps predictably, the successes have not been as great as hoped for. Success has been limited largely by an overdependence upon gadgetry and a lack of emphasis upon, or the absence of techniques to bring about, motivations to adopt any form of birth control. Limited success has been achieved, of course, in the introduction of sterilization, IUDs, and to some extent, the pill, where these methods were culturally acceptable. Too frequently, however, they have been adopted by people only after they already had a large number of children, and the effort has been handicapped by the lack of trained personnel to distribute the information, prescribe and fit the devices, or perform the necessary operations. The greatest failure has resulted from lack of knowledge relating to the cultures and the social organization supporting high fertility and the inability to bring about changes in the society that would facilitate the practice of family planning. Where such changes have occurred, as in Japan, which had already industrialized prior to World War II, and in Taiwan, fertility decline has been rapid. There the decline may have been facilitated by, but was certainly not initiated by, the availability of family-planning services. On the other hand, despite its lack of short-term success, this effort has introduced into many countries the concept of family limitation, which may eventually be implemented as the required social changes occur; and it has undoubtedly stimulated the development of techniques in the field of contraception (such as the IUD and the pill) designed to overcome cultural objections to the more traditional methods.

In the United States and western Europe, the practice of family planning or contraception was adopted long before there were organized efforts to advocate it or provide services. Family planning as an organized endeavor was largely instrumental, not in promoting the practice of contraception, but in leading an attack upon restrictive legislation which made the practice difficult. Following the impetus given the organization by success in these efforts, it then moved into education and has promoted the practice of family planning and family limitation in rural areas and among the poor, and has provided services and various contraceptives to those who could not afford to buy them through commercial channels. Voluntary family planning, here and abroad, however, is improperly labeled "population control," though it may be somewhat instrumental in that direction. By its very nature, it addresses itself everywhere to individual welfare and the right of individuals to control their own fertility according to their own desires. It is almost a fatal confusion in the United States to equate governmental programs of delivering family planning services to the poor as population policy. To do so obscures the manifest benefits that derive from delivering family-planning services to that portion of the population which does not have access to the commercial sources of supply and medical services available to the more affluent, and it easily leads to the notion that they are campaigns directed "against" the poor.

A second weakness in the concept of voluntary family planning as policy is the implicit assumption that a sufficient desire for family limitation already exists if only a satisfactory technique, some "ideal" contraceptive, can be provided. It is true, of course, that there are cultural and personal preferences for methods. Coitus interruptus seems to have been quite acceptable to Europeans long before the condom, the douche, or the diaphram came into vogue. Males in some societies reject it. Female sterilization caught on in Puerto Rico, male vasectomies seem to have a vogue in India, the IUD is popular and acceptable in some, a traumatic experience in others, and abortion is popular in Japan and many eastern European countries. But everywhere it is not the appeal of the contraceptive, but the socially reinforced determination to prevent a birth that is the key to successful contraception. Where the family size desired is high, or avoidance of a birth not salient, it is not practiced carefully.

Boys who know they are going to experience severe difficulties if they father an illegitimate child do not depend on Saran Wrap or cola douches, but neither do they need the pill.

Transformation of the Social Structure

Reduction of fertility from relatively high to lower levels requires changes in the social structure which bring about a change in the meaning of children. In the developing countries the changes have to be radical and involve the shift from predominantly agricultural to a predominantly industrial-urban society. We do not know whether intermediate transformation, such as the change in the organization of agricultural production, can effect such changes, though this is possible.

In the Western world, as we have already noted, the radical transformation has already occurred. What further changes are required to assure continued reduction or the maintenance of fertility at or near the replacement level are not nearly so drastic. Where in the developing countries, fertility must be reduced by more than half, in the United States fertility could be reduced to the replacement level by a reduction of only an average of one child per family, or from something over three to slightly more than two. A number of such changes that would facilitate such a reduction have been proposed.

De-emphasis of the Family

When we talk about changes in the social structure, we are actually talking about changes in the system of attitudes and behaviors by which people relate to one another and the system of beliefs and sanctions, rewards and punishment, by which these behaviors are taught and reinforced. The "surplus," if you wish to call it that, of approximately one child in each family in the United States grows out of the fact that our composite system of values has led in the recent past, at any rate, to relatively early marriage, eventual marriage of a very high proportion of the population, few childless marriages, and an ideal family size that stresses three and four children. There also seems to be some upward bias to size of completed family because of the desire for at least one son.

The key to virtually all proposals to reduce fertility is to suggest a cultural de-emphasis of the family as primarily a childbearing institution. Such de-emphasis involves changes in social behavior facilitating the postponement of marriage and childbearing to later ages, stress upon roles for women involving activities other than childbearing, and liberalization of sexual norms which permit the satisfaction of the sex drive independently of marriage. Our cultural emphasis, with legal reinforcement, is essentially pro-natalist, it is argued, since our socialization process emphasized marriage as the "normal" adult condition, stresses children as the "ultimate" satisfaction in marriage, and idealizes the role of mother for women. Paralleling this emphasis, then, are social pressures upon individuals to marry, and as early as possible, tendencies to penalize those individuals who choose to live outside the family framework, punitive sanctions against homosexuality, tax laws which penalize the unmarried, and the like. Social changes which would facilitate and encourage the postponement of marriage, provide socially acceptable roles for the unmarried, allow more tolerance toward sexual deviance, and provide rewarding opportunities for women, whether married or not, outside the home, would, it is argued, bring about a considerable reduction of fertility, at least in the Western world, without the imposition of any more rigid controls.

The problems here are simply that one does not speak them into being. Social structures are complex, their various parts interdependent, they serve multiple purposes for individuals and for society, and require a high degree of integration. Since the family serves multiple purposes, not only as the primary institution for child nurture, however it may be reinforced by outside agencies, but also for the psychological needs of men and women as well as children, tampering with it is delicate. Unless the status of women is radically transformed, and they give up childbearing within a family framework altogether, the institution requires legal safeguards to protect the interest of women who continue to bear children within that framework.

These legal safeguards, in turn, automatically define the status of women as different from men, and this definition may subtly or not so subtly interfere with equal rights of women and thus interfere with their opportunities to pursue careers on a basis of equality. Furthermore, parents and teachers have difficulty in training girls for dual roles in society, with resultant personal conflicts for mature women. The woman who chooses both a family and a career is definitely handicapped in the latter.

If, on the other hand, society encourages women to work and pursue careers, it must perforce do so not only in the interest of population control but on the premise that both society and the woman derive other benefits as well. Then we read the proposal that to afford women and society these benefits, we should make available child-care centers, nursery schools, and lengthened school days, which will allow women to combine motherhood and careers. And so, the population purposes may be lost sight of.

The change in sexual norms may not always have predictable consequences. Modern American society has over the last several decades gone quite far in tolerating sexual experimentation out-

side of marriage. But this permissiveness has probably not contributed at all to the reduction of fertility—rather, perhaps to
its increase. Within the urban society which combines permissiveness with considerable freedom for the young, there has
been an increase in premarital pregnancy, an increase in illegitimacy, an increase in early, often forced marriages, and a greater
incidence of divorce. Early marriages, by increasing the exposure of married couples at the more fecund periods of life, facilitate larger families. Manifestly, the greater availability of
abortions would reduce the illegitimacy and forced early marriages, but it would raise problems of its own. Similarly, it seems
to me that societies have some difficulty maintaining tolerant attitudes toward deviant sexual practices. Tolerance within a context of general but not punitive disapproval is one thing; tolerance carried to the point of approval, in the sense of "normative," almost implies that the behavior will be taught with im-
punity, a perhaps not desirable consequence, so that tolerance
tends to be unstable until societies work out functional ways to
control its effects.

This is not to say that changed attitudes toward the family as
a childbearing institution are undesirable—simply to say that
controlling the direction of change is difficult. People make
their institutions. They use them as they can for their private
purposes. It takes societies time to work out an equilibrium between individual and group needs. And purposes shift.

Other Institutional Changes

Some reduction of values relating to childbearing could come
from changes in educational emphasis. Examination of the curricula of the average public school exposes an almost complete
void in content directed toward family-life education. There
are smatterings here and there of courses or units in personal
hygiene, some sex education (frequently under attack), home
economics courses, and basic studies of human biology. In colleges we have "how to do it" courses in marriage. In the middle
schools which my daughters attended, there was an innovative
unit in human ecology introduced a few years ago. But hardly
anywhere are there courses or units dealing with the costs of
rearing children, or such alternative consequences of marrying

early or late in terms of career, personal fulfillments, or the benefits to be derived from postponing the first birth. By and large, families do not educate their children in these matters. To suggest that your child has created problems for the marriage, or interfered with Daddy's career or thwarted Mother's pursuit of her personal aspirations, would be to suggest to the child it was not wanted, and damage its psyche. So we are silent, and we fail to communicate vital information. The school should not be silent.

The school, however, as a public institution, will not be responsive to this need until it is forced into it by the enlightenment of its officials or by public demand. To bring it about is the task of all who have a stake in the educational process.

Another institution possessing the capability of altering family values is the church. Many churches in this country have long since adopted secular views with respect to the practice of contraception and family size, but some fundamentalist Protestant groups, and especially the Roman Catholic Church, maintain decisively pro-natalist doctrines. If these religious groups, through their ministries and priesthood, could see their way clear to distinguish between the morality of sex and the wisdom, perhaps also the morality, of childbearing—to view the morality of sex within the context of responsibility, love, and sensitivity to and appreciation of the human personality and to view the morality of childbearing purely within the context of the welfare and development of both the child and parents—the practice of contraception would suddenly be transformed from an evil to be avoided or expiated to a form of "higher" morality. Such transformations of emphasis do occur within religious traditions. Moral obligations are reinterpreted in the light of new conditions of life. God has, according to the Scriptures, revealed himself in new ways with fresh messages, and religious institutions have been responsive. Perhaps we are not too far away from this one, but it must come from within the groups themselves.

Governmental Policy

We could go further in the discussion of societal influences which might in one way or another affect the fertility performance of members of our society and elaborate them far more fully than has been done. We ought now, however, to turn to the issue of governmental policy.

I know it is popular among some groups to attribute the government's inaction in the area of population policy to a failure of leadership. I do not entirely subscribe to this view. The charge may be more apt in connection with a wide range of regulatory activities concerning food, drugs, environmental pollution, and degradation, where one or another institution of society may be shown to have been unresponsive to the public welfare; but population policy involves the potential regulation of behavior in the most fundamental of all institutions, the family, to which all of us are associated in one way or another. Authoritarian regimes, controlled by a small clique maintaining its power by force, has much greater flexibility in manipulating the pressures brought to bear on individuals through a variety of institutions and policies. A democratic society, responsive though it may be to a variety of power groups in one aspect or another of the life of that society, is very largely constrained in its manipulation of values and behaviors within the family, particularly when those constraints are obvious, by the consensus within that society as to both the goals to be achieved and the sanctions which can be applied. Anyone taking a broad view of attitudes and sentiment in this country at the present time must recognize that there is a wide diversity of opinion with respect to the need for population control and a very great reluctance to accept controls which imply the loss of individual freedom. The lack of agreement on goals circumscribes the ability to impose indirect controls which still leave the sense of individual freedom. It is noteworthy, I believe, that a more liberal attitude toward abortion, while supported and given impetus by groups very concerned with population limitation, nevertheless is given legal expression as a "right" of a woman "not to bear a child she does not want." Governmental programs providing family planning services are proffered in the same terms. This is not to say that attitudes toward population are not undergoing change, or that sentiment for more positive action is not growing and may eventually bring that action about. It is to say that the consensus regarding these matters is a necessary condition, and that the justifications for whatever public policy is adopted must be prepared in advance so that they appear not merely rational or logical but acceptable innovations as well. Preparing this essential groundwork will require a great deal of philosophical, humanitarian, and legal thought to bring our various value systems into a framework consistent with the achievement of lower levels of population growth, at the same time our institutions adjust to the consequences of such slower growth.

Repeal of Restrictive Laws

When there is such a consensus, Government can, of course, act in a variety of ways to influence individual behavior. One of these is the legislative repeal, or court nullification, of laws which interfere with fertility control. State legislatures, together with state courts, are now in the process of repealing or modifying laws against abortion. From the standpoint of fertility, these modifications of the law will undoubtedly have a salutary effect, although their modification has been couched primarily in terms of the welfare and "rights" of individuals. They illustrate vividly, however, that such legislation does depend upon a very broad base of public opinion, mobilized to its support by a variety of motives. Considerations of population have not been dominant.

Public Welfare

Since our Government is committed to the provision of many kinds of services, both of the sort that are out of reach of all individual citizens and those that are out of reach of groups in special need, it has the capacity within current frameworks of influencing population through the provision of services. Family-planning services for the poor fall in this category. As noted earlier, it is unfortunate that family-planning services, which are most defensible and supportable as the extension to the poor of services already available commercially to the more affluent, have been labeled by the overenthusiastic as "population control" measures. As in the case of the modification of the abortion laws, I believe the broadest support of these measures has been motivated by welfare considerations.

Direct Incentives and Disincentives

A more direct approach to influencing population growth is the establishment of various incentives or disincentives. An example of the former is the payment for a vasectomy, as is done in India, or the provision of extra retirement benefits for those people limiting their fertility throughout their lives, as has been implemented in Mauritius. Some claim is made that income tax deductions for children are also incentives, although I fail to see how anyone supports a child on the tax saving he gets from a $625 exemption. Tax provisions relating to single persons are perhaps more punitive, but again, hardly offset the cost of supporting a nonworking wife. Even small incentives, however, if combined with other forces within society tending in the same direction, may tip the scales significantly in the desired direction. Again, they depend upon some sort of consensus regarding social values and legitimacy.

Indirect Incentives

Governments also have the capability of applying indirect incentives. It has frequently been pointed out that the Government housing policy following World War II, by making available cheap loans for veterans and others to purchase housing, probably contributed to the increase in fertility in the late 1940's and early 1950's—an unanticipated consequence of a program designed with other purposes in mind. Shifts in housing policy have been advocated to speed integration. Since, as is well known, fertility seems to be responsive to economic conditions, it may be possible, if the public would permit it, to have economic policies determined for their intended effect upon population growth. But how many, it may be asked, would opt for an economic slowdown and high unemployment rates, in order to increase the economic pressure on individuals to restrict their fertility? Population distribution can also be determined in a limited way by decisions to locate installations or activities in one or another locality. While such approaches have great potential, what Government can do in these respects is manifestly limited by the fact that until population control becomes an overriding public consideration, a variety of other factors will carry more weight.

Direct Restraints

The final issue in the control of population is that of the application of direct, legal restraints. A few people have so far timidly advanced such propositions, the usual responses to which are cries of outrage at the mere comtemplation of such a radical departure from traditional values. Even those who might otherwise espouse restriction of fertility in the interests of both individual and societal welfare, bridle at the kinds of sanctions which are implied by the realistic enforcement of a legal maximum number of children. If the freedom to bear a child is taken away, what freedom is left? Who will make the decisions, or enforce the law, and on what basis? How will such laws be enforced: by mandatory sterilization, or severe penalties falling perhaps heaviest on the "illegally born," or how? You could contemplate a century or more of test cases in the courts, legal and political jockeying. The problems raised by this issue are formidable, and perhaps the better part of wisdom would be to dismiss it entirely.

But we are talking about issues, and eventually this particular issue may be raised more seriously than it is now. If indeed, at some future date, there should develop a widespread consensus that a slower rate of population growth is in the interest of all, and that other indirect restraints within the social, economic, and political framework were not achieving the desired result, what would be left? Granting, then, that this possibility will depend upon a much greater consensus about the necessity for population control than currently exists, we can at least venture some comments.

First of all, should the time come when there is an overwhelming consensus within the body politic (or the society) that no more growth is beneficial, then the action of deviants—that is, those who refuse to abide by the consensus—will be perceived as threatening the welfare of the rest. Do recalcitrants, under these conditions and assumptions, have a right to assert individual rights inimical to the best interests of all the rest?

Secondly, all the indirect restraints, acting through the value systems of individuals, actually are effective with respect to those who are most vulnerable: the highly motivated, the rational, those whose religious values tolerate the restraint, etc. As one of my friends and colleagues, William Peterson, has written in one of his papers: "As a democrat, I am for freedom; but as a sociologist, I recognize that no man is free."

Third, if we can contemplate transformations in the social structure, the reconceptualization of religious values and teachings, may we not also contemplate that societies, in their wisdom, wrestling with a brand-new problem in a universe redefined and viewed from a different perspective, may reinterpret in the interests of all the definitions of human freedom and of human responsibility consistent with the new dimensions of life? Granted, that it will be a tedious exercise. Granted, that the consequences of the new definitions will have to be carefully assessed. But we do, ultimately, define rights of individuals in terms of their responsibilities as citizens within the broad context of needs of social systems and the flexibilities possible within them. And I daresay, this is one of the issues that will involve a great many thoughtful people as this country and the world move toward their rendezvous with what may be mankind's greatest challenge: limitation upon his own numbers in the interest of his own long-range welfare.

A few thoughts may be added, however, about the effectiveness of setting some legal maximum, and the groups most likely to be affected by such maxima. Using data from the 1960 Growth of American Families, it is noted that already, in that year, 65 percent of American families expressed a desire to have three or fewer children, leaving approximately 35 percent of families desirous of four or more. Only 15 percent were determined on more than four. If four children were the legal maximum, the average size of family would have been reduced from 3.1 children to 2.8 children, a reduction of about 10 percent, but not enough to have guaranteed population stability. Restriction to a maximum of three children would have reduced the average number to 2.5, another 10 percent, which would have left room still for a slight population growth. Thus, in the United States such a restriction would have just about curtailed population growth in the long run, but, perhaps surprisingly to you, the 20 percent reduction would have been achieved by restraints placed upon 35 percent of the families. Most of these families, of course, since they tend to be in the lower income groups, may have been benefited in terms of their economic welfare, but, unless they were appreciative of the favor, would represent an extremely large pressure group against the invocation of realistic sanctions imposed by a democratically elected Government. Furthermore, these larger families who would feel the restrictions most, are disproportionately represented among blacks and among Catholics. Another 10 percent reduction could be achieved by making the maximum two children, but then a whopping majority, 64 percent would be subject to the legal prohibition.

Thus, when the educational process, the institutional transformations, the shift in values, which would make direct legislative restraints practicable, had been brought about, the chances are that such legislation would be needed only to sanctify consensus already achieved, or to reinforce legislative restrictions of a more indirect nature. After all, laws which embody sentiments of the body politic may be useful even though they never have to be enforced.

These are the issues—perhaps not all, but a reasonable sample. They set the context and dimensions of the decisions that will someday have to be made if man is to control his destiny. The complexities of the problem are not its terrifying aspect. *It is the fact that the decisions require the agreement of so many with respect to so many aspects of their private and public lives.* Perhaps we can simplify it. Perhaps it all boils down to the simple decision not to have so many children, to the simple recognition that in the end the interests of the individual and of his society and of those who come after are all one and the same. I wish you all well as you reach your own decisions—in the public interest.

Chapter Four

RISING POPULATION AND ECOLOGY

FRANK FRASER DARLING

MY KNOWLEDGE of human population phenomena does not match my general interest. I know nothing of the mathematical side of demography nor, as an ecologist, have I ever been able to master the mathematical aspects of animal populations. I have been more interested in observational studies of social behavior and the ecological results.

Man's skill in buffering himself from the sheer physical environment is at once a blessing and a serious hazard, because he not only buffers his body but his mind as well. He forgets that though his head is in the clouds, his feet are in the muck, or makes himself believe the distance between ankle and knee represents a time span which allows him to assure himself that science will find a way. Too much of technology goes to more buffering and too little to prevention or radical cure of deleterious factors.

As I see it, human population pressure can be studied profitably from three angles, but in overlapping fashion: (1) social influences and consequences, (2) ecological consequences on the whole habitat, and (3) localized and global pollution.

Human beings in close, massed proximity tend to react very much like many other mammals, of which there are published studies, notably J. Calhoun's[19a, 19b] on rats in planned situations, and Paul Errington's[20] on muskrats in the wild. There arise antisocial behavior, footloose tendencies, withdrawal, and so on. We can see these phenomena quite plainly in human aggregations such as crowds and in overcrowded living conditions, especially when the areas of such similar conditions are large. The human being, however, has greater potential for adaptive response to these conditions. The Chinese in the past have tended to exist in closely packed conditions and have managed quite well. The city of Hangchow during the Southern Sung and Mongol peri-

59

ods could not expand spatially because of water, so, like New York, it built upward and by 1275 A.D. had passed the million mark. The poorer districts held a population of 324 persons per acre. A very fair measure of law and order seems to have been maintained by consent of the people, not by stern repression. The present-day city of Hong Kong also seethes and is full of wickedness, yet it is safer for a pedestrian to walk its streets at night than it is in Washington, D. C. Wickedness is not necessarily raw aggression; in fact, its most successful expression is in refined and sophisticated pursuits, and aggressive behavior is deplored. In short, the Chinese of the past have developed exceedingly polite manners, a phenomenon which is also found among very warlike tribes. One such warrior once said to me, "Had we not observed good manners none of us would have survived."

Now what we might call the Western nations have recently developed behaviorally on a line where good manners are not so essential to survival. Rudeness seems to be accepted as one of the rights of democracy. Some students in their common room in a New Zealand University recently asserted this supposed right by remaining seated with their feet on the table when visited by Queen Elizabeth II. One might say that *her* good manners saved the situation. She did not raise any of them by the ear, which some of us might have been inclined to do. From lack of good manners it is an easy step to definite aggressive behavior as a means of getting or doing what you want. It is an interesting reflection on modern behavior in Western overcrowded conditions that law proves inadequate and, paradoxically, liberal public opinion comes to a position of exceptional tolerance and benignity toward antisocial aggressive behavior. As one such liberal put it to me about the crime of child murder, "The victim is incidental, not the basis on which you deal with the murderer."

Places of extremely high density in Western situations are also, in general, areas of great mobility of population. There are many footloose individuals in Errington's usage, with consequent lack of social responsibility. The more tolerant the regime and the more uncertain becomes public opinion on genuine ethical grounds, the more social irresponsibility becomes accepted behavior. Crime and antisocial behavior in old-established rural situations is much less in proportional occurrence because folk have fairly settled and established places in the society, and being so well known, each individual prefers to maintain a relatively respected position. The immense increase in shoplifting and petty thieving in urban Britain instigated a survey from which it was recently reported that only a small percentage of those caught recognized any moral responsibility. It was a way of life. Court probation was no deterrent, because no moral responsibility was accepted.

Our deeper questioning of ethical behavior toward our less fortunate brethren is, of course, entirely right and the way we should hope to progress, but the consequences for the innocent in a time of uncontrolled population increase are deplorable. Security-guarding of banks, shops, warehouses, and so on is now taking up a considerable fraction of manpower for no productive purpose and represents a definite tax, raising the cost of living.

I am making no pronouncements. I am merely observing that increasing population pressures are producing antisocial behavior which is being met by public opinion of advancing humaneness. The hiatus may be our Achilles' heel. A population policy designed to lessen population pressure seems an obvious necessity. In general, our humane attitudes in public administration favor population increase in so many ways, such as antenatal and postnatal care, child allowances, eradication of tuberculosis, inoculation, and so on. These are measures to which we are rightly committed and they should not be brought forward as factors in population increase to be questioned, but as a concomitant there must be widespread and insistent education and propaganda on the subject of personal responsibility in human reproduction. This needs a crash program using all the new mass media at our disposal.

Repressive action in this field is, in general, undesirable; but I do think that enforced sterilization should be accepted for the more reproductive of the socially irresponsible, and voluntary sterilization should be encouraged as a social benefit. To this end, there should be definite research in surgical techniques leading to success in reversing sterilization. Success in this is now rather above 50 percent, which is not good enough. Easier abortion procedures may be unpleasant and are no final remedial measure, but they should be tolerated in our present urgent need until they are found unnecessary.

The ecological consequences on the planet have, in general, been ignored. The human flat foot itself can have quite surprising depressive influences on vegetation and soil structure, but when we add the ancillary means of movement, animals, railways, motor cars, and what not, large acreages of land are used up in potentially productive areas. I remember going around a village in India which had not existed three years before. The baked earth roads, the density of huts and peripheral degradation of vegetation gave one the false impression the village had been there since prehistory. All this flat-footedness in three years!

A more sophisticated society with growing leisure is depressive and abrasive on habitat to an increasing extent. Seacoast is an early sufferer. Sand dunes and salt marshes are damaged quickly by increasing density of leisure seekers. The U.S. National Park Service has to exercise a good deal of cunning and expertise in dealing with the abrasive hardware and flat feet of leisure seekers and culture vultures. This Service should be consulted for its revealing information on human impact on habitat even when there is obviously no desire on anyone's part to injure anything. The visitors to national parks are even supposed to be learning how to preserve their heritage.

The phenomenon of gaseous exchange in photosynthesis by plants is one of the first items in any biological education. We take it for granted and most people forget about it altogether. The plant absorbs carbon dioxide and exudes oxygen. Splendid. We tend to forget also that many human activities tend to depress photosynthesis in general, and certain aspects of it in particular. Also, our civilization of combustion based on fossil fuels is using up oxygen and pumping out carbon dioxide, as well as adding vast quantities of particulate carbon to the atmosphere.

Throughout history and prehistory, forests have been felled

and there has even been some sense of righteous satisfaction in felling forest, making room for more human beings. The role of the forest as a kind of natural sewage farm, converting wastes, purifying atmosphere and water, and maintaining levels of habitability has scarcely been recognized. The ecologist can explain all this at length, but one small point is worthy of emphasis: Photosynthesis in forests locks up carbon for long periods, whereas grass and food plants recirculate it rapidly. The forests and oceans are the great lockers-up of carbon dioxide. The forests are still being depleted at a prodigal rate. The Matto Grosso in Brazil is being burnt out, pushed out, or destroyed in any feasible way to create indifferent grazing for scrub cattle. The carbon dioxide of the atmosphere has risen 10 percent in this century, and there have been ominous signs of glacial recession and oceanic warming, which latter means carbon dioxide is being released. The so-called "greenhouse effect" of rising carbon dioxide would normally be checked by greater refulgence of growth of forest, but as the forest is losing out and so much carbon is being released from fossil fuel by the internal-combustion engine and generation of electricity, the natural balancing influences of forest and ocean are being impaired.

I have given the above as one example of ecological consequences of uncontrolled increase of human populations. There could be many others.

The third field of consequence of human population increase of interest to the ecologist is that of the pervasiveness of pollution of air, water, and soil. Pollution at present is a function of population, though I would strongly contend that it need not be so. Since man began smelting metals, living in aggregations, and developing industrial processes he has got rid of as many wastes as possible as cheaply as possible, by using the force of gravity in the flow of rivers. Some wastes, like sulphur dioxide, have just been blown off into the air.

As yet, there have been no good inventories of pollution nor far-reaching tabulation of effects. So-called economics have ruled that all industrial processes must get rid of their wastes, toxic or merely visually unpleasant, as cheaply as possible. This did not matter so much in earlier times with a human population of the planet in only an initially emergent phase, but the industrial revolution of the last two hundred years has brought pollution to a crucial pitch. Industrial processes are but half the trouble; the remainder is the direct result of the necessary aggregations of people depositing raw sewage into watercourses. Tertiary sewage treatment is still a very small proportion of the whole in several industrial countries; the United States is markedly deficient in this respect.

Pollution of watercourses and water sources is now so prevalent that not only is it a hazard to health but it is leading to shortage of usable water at a time when industry is calling for much more water.

Pollution of water leads on to the food question, because many lakes have died or are dying through eutrophication, the deoxidation of the lower layers and their filling up with nitrogenous and phosphatic compounds inimical to life. Lake Erie is the prime example but the phenomenon is widespread. Further, organic pollution going downstream to the estuaries has not only killed the fish en route but has cut out vast areas of shellfish beds. There has been a direct diminution of protein food, of which the world population is short. Starch is quite easily produced, but at a cost to direct protein-producing areas such as marshes.

But we are dealing here with the pollution aspects and it should be emphasized how food production by modern methods (so necessary because of the numbers of mouths) is adding to the pollution. Organic fertilizers such as farmyard manure helped soil structure and sponge quality to hold plant nutrients in the soil. Newly broken prairie soils had a large store of humus accumulated through time, and as this has been used up and mineral fertilizers substituted, pollution of watercourses by runoff has increased. Very heavy dressings of mineral fertilizers are now used, although a large proportion of the nutrient salts will be lost in the drainage water, subsequently to endanger life in the rivers and lakes.

The growing human population has further developed what, seen philosophically, are almost panic measures in protein production, such as broiler chickens, intensive veal, and feed-lot cattle. The disposal of the organic manure from such operations has become a problem and the watercourses have too often been used once more as open sewers. What is even more fantastic is that the cheap protein of broiler chickens for U.S. consumers is made possible by the scooping up of Peruvian anchovies from the Pacific to form fish meal for the broilers. Peru's human population is chronically short of protein.

I would suggest that the world has not yet attempted very seriously to make a global reorientation of population, food needs and production methods, pollution effects, and the general ecological picture. Such U.N. organizations as Food and Agricultural Organization, U.S. agencies such as Agency for International Development and so on, are too much concerned with belly filling regardless of consequences or side effects. Robert McNamara[21] of the World Bank has at least spoken out (Notre Dame University, 1969) and it is significant that World Bank projects will in future have ecologists at the reconnaissance stage. The United Nations Development Program will probably follow suit, belatedly.

All efforts to feed, help, or develop backward populations should be subjected to a close scenario technique such as was brilliantly developed by the Hudson School with Herman Kahn.[22] Till now all these relief efforts have smacked of strong missionary zeal and Sunday School teaching. The dangers of uncritical aid and development, observing a present situation without grasping future consequences, could lose the day for civilization. Famine, war, pestilence may strike quickly at the underdeveloped countries as their populations seethe, but in our Western cultures there would be slower increase, more environmental buffering, with a steadily decreasing standard of living till the defeatism of anarchy takes over. Recent events on the western and eastern seaboards of the United States point to this.

Britain, Sweden, and the United States are taking their pollution problems very seriously and are acting for the future. It is becoming obvious that pollution control will be an international task. Population control must also be. There will be some harsh words returned for the most humane intentions, and we shall have to be prepared for them. There will be no thanks.

Chapter Five

THE POPULATION PROBLEM OF THE UNITED STATES

CONRAD TAEUBER

THE American population problem is less a matter of numbers pressing on resources than of the distribution of the growing numbers, the quality of life which is available, and our willingness to allocate our resources in such a way as to provide a desired level of living to all rather than to only a favored few. There undoubtedly is pressure on certain resources; there are shortages of raw materials as nations which are not suppliers develop their own industrial base to the point where they become active competitors for resources which are now being devoted to our use. A continuation of recent trends in the distribution of our population leads to predictable consequences, many of them undesirable.

There are important gaps in our knowledge of current population trends, but there is an even more significant absence of knowledge of the longer run significance of these trends for our society and economy. As a nation we have been so accustomed to growth that we have taken it for granted. Very little is known about the role of sheer population growth in our economic development, of the consequences of different rates of growth, or of the means by which we might influence population growth or distribution. Goals in this field have not been formulated to the point where there is general consensus. Some of the more vocal proponents of a zero growth rate, or some other rate, are not prepared to state what effective methods might lead us to that point, or what the broad range of consequences would be.

We think of ourselves as a pluralistic society, but there has been evidence recently of some marked tendencies to develop groups or enclaves which feel themselves significantly cut off from the mainstream of our society. Their isolation is reflected in part by their divergent demographic trends. There are currents toward divergence and others toward convergent demographic trends among different groups in the population.

There has been a growing amount of demographic research, but much of it remains isolated and fragmentary. The few efforts to define the broader picture, to evaluate determinants and consequences of population growth, or to formulate desirable population policies for this country are rather badly scattered. Some voices have recently been raised urging the desirability of a reduced rate of growth, perhaps a zero growth rate, or even a decline in the national population. In the main, however, economic and social policies are formulated without much regard to the demographic variables which are essential. Important exceptions are advertising and marketing where there have been recent energetic efforts to take into account the demographic variables. Some local and state planning bodies have also become aware of the same elements.

It is hardly open to argument that planning for the future requires information about the size of our population, its characteristics, distribution, and growth rate; but there is not now any organized approach to analysis of these matters in relation to the whole spectrum of economic and social development. A center which could marshall the resources of related disciplines to an analysis of the American population could make a significant contribution to the formulation of policies for this country. From the standpoint of the world as a whole, the major problem continues to be that of inadequately controlled population growth. However, that is not the problem for the United States or other industrially developed countries. Nonetheless, even we have important population problems deserving major research efforts.

Profound changes have been occurring in the population of the United States and more are expected in the coming years. As a result of the large numbers of births shortly after the end of World War II and through the 1950's, the 1970's will witness an especially rapid increase in the number of young adults (young people in their twenties and thirties). Increases in these age groups lead to increases in the rate of family formation, and presumably increases in the number of births. They also imply increased needs for employment opportunities.

More than three fourths of the nation's growth since 1960 has occurred in metropolitan areas, most of it in the suburban parts which now include more people than the central cities. Although some cities have grown to metropolitan status since 1960, there has not been any significant development of "new cities." The virtual stabilization of the population of our large cities has been accompanied by a significant change in the characteristics of their residents—an increase in the number of their black residents and a decline in the number of their white residents.

Migration from rural to urban, and from the South to the North and West was less in the 1960's than in the 1950's, but there continue to be large movements between the states. It is not clear to what extent the reduction in the rate of migration reflects increasing opportunities in the former areas of outmigration.

Our birth rates have fluctuated considerably in the last twenty years. The continuous decline during the 1960's seems to have been halted, at least temporarily, with births in 1969 at a level somewhat above those for 1968. Marriage rates and the number of marriages have increased, and further increases are expected as a result of the changes in the age composition. The current birth rate is a highly controlled and apparently quite self-imposed rate. Nonetheless, there are large numbers of people who are in the need of family-planning services.

Immigration has recently contributed about one fifth of our annual population growth, an absolute and a relative increase in comparison to the early postwar years.

Overall population growth, and especially rapid growth in the metropolitan areas, is accompanied by population declines in some parts of the country. The effects of past migrations have left such a distorted age composition in some areas that there are now more than three hundred counties which have so many old people and so few young ones that they have more deaths than births, and the number of such counties will increase. Since 1960, approximately one half of the counties in the United States have lost population through outmigration or through an excess of deaths over births. About three fourths of all counties had a net outmigration between the years 1960 and 1966. The farm population has continued to decline and in many rural areas there has been a consequent decline of the total population.

The growth of the states has been very uneven since 1060, as it has sometimes been in the past. California continues to lead all other states in net gain in population, having added about four million persons between the years 1960 and 1970. This is more than three times New York's gain of 1.2 million. One state, West Virginia, has continued to lose population in the 1960's. North and South Dakota also lost between the years 1960 and 1970.

The Negro population accounts for about 22 million persons or about 11 percent of the total. Its rate of increase has recently been about one third faster than that of the white population. Birth rates among Negroes have gone up and down as the rates among whites have, though the former have consistently been at a higher level. The Negro population is now more urbanized than the white, with more than half living in the central cities of our metropolitan areas. There the share has gone up from 12 percent in 1950 to 20 percent at present. In a number of cities the 1970 Census is expected to find that they are in a majority. Only 53 percent of Negroes now live in the South— as recently as 1950 that percentage had been 68. Because of their higher birth rates, the Negro population includes a larger proportion of young children and youth than the white population.

More whites than blacks live in poverty, but the chances of being in poverty are greater for blacks than for whites. Educational attainment for whites and blacks has reached the point where half of those who have recently completed their schooling have had at least a high school education. Yet there are large differences in the quality of that education, in the level of school dropouts, and in the ability to make education count toward better paying jobs.

These shifting, perhaps transitory, aspects of our domestic population problem deserve major research efforts if we are to handle intelligently the distribution of the people in this country.

Chapter Six

THE FUTURE POPULATION OF THE UNITED STATES

HERMAN P. MILLER

FORECASTERS have never been liked. In ancient Rome, the Emperor Constantius made a law forbidding "anyone to consult a soothsayer, a mathematician, or a forecaster. . . . May curiosity to foretell the future be silenced forever." He prescribed the penalty of death for forecasting, but there is no evidence that even so severe a punishment could stop the practice.

In his *Inferno,* Dante reserved the Eighth Circle of Hell for forecasters, diviners, augurers, and sorcerers because they endeavored to foretell the future which belongs to God alone. They were condemned to Hell, with their heads twisted completely around so that they were unable to see where they were going. Perhaps that is the reason forecasters to this day continue to have their heads screwed on backward. It is only by looking at the past that they can foretell the future.

Let me start with a caveat that is usually put in a footnote and then forgotten. The views that I will express are my own and are in no way associated with the Bureau of the Census or any other part of the Federal Government. We shall be talking today about major directions of public policy. I do not set this policy. I am merely a government statistician who provides the data which I hope are used to formulate policy. I am, however, also an informed citizen in a democracy and it is in that capacity that I speak here and not as a government employee.

All of my remarks today will relate to the United States only and not to the rest of the world, particularly the underdeveloped part of it. Our fate may be tied to what happens in the

Note: Paper prepared for meeting on Policy Planning for Alternative Futures at National Bureau of Standards on March 9, 1970, sponsored by the Institute of Management Science, the World Future Society, and the National Bureau of Standards.

rest of the world. We do, however, have population problems that are independent of the world problem. We can influence what the people do in Arkansas and Alabama; we have little, if any, influence over what the people do in Algeria and Afghanistan. We elect our own representatives who make our policies; we have no such control in foreign lands. We can and do supply other nations with financial and technical aid to help them control their population growth. In the end, however, we can serve only as interested bystanders in all countries except our own.

There are some who argue that we must reduce our population growth to zero to set an example for others. Paul Ehrlich is one such advocate. In *The Population Bomb*[23] he states, "Our first step must be to immediately establish and advertise drastic policies designed to bring our own population size under control." This move would accomplish two things in his estimation: "It improves our chances of obtaining the kind of country and society we all want and it sets an example for the world." Utter nonsense. It is time we stopped setting examples for others. We are not that virtuous or wise. Like any true believer, Mr. Ehrlich sees the light not only for himself but for the entire world and he is prepared to take drastic action on the basis of these beliefs. Here, for example, is how he would help India solve its population problem:

> While we are working toward setting up a world program of the general sort outlined above, the United States could take effective unilateral action in many cases. A good example of how we might have acted can be built around the Chandrasekhar incident I mentioned earlier. When we suggested sterilizing all Indian males with three or more children, we should have applied pressure on the Indian government to go ahead with the plan. We should have volunteered logistic support in the form of helicopters, vehicles, and surgical instruments. We should have sent doctors to aid in the program by setting up centers for training paramedical personnel to do vasectomies. Coercion? Perhaps, but coercion in a good cause.

Where have we heard that before?

To avoid the danger of misunderstanding, let me say at the outset that I think it would be desirable for our population growth to slow down. It would be particularly advantageous to reduce the supply of unwanted children. Such children often become problems to themselves and to society. At some point we will undoubtedly have to stop growing. The only real question is when, and should we be greatly concerned about that problem now. My own feeling is that we have more pressing population problems.

The threat of overpopulation looms large in many American minds today. Even poor old Charlie Brown cannot escape the problem. In a recent *Peanuts* cartoon he is asked by one of his little friends, "So you have a new baby sister, huh, Charlie Brown?" "Yes," says Charlie, "and I'm so happy." At which point Lucy retorts, "Happy! I suppose it's never occurred to you that overpopulation is a serious problem."

As usual, the cartoonist Schulz is using his delightful little characters to lampoon the foibles of our society, in this case, the flood of anti-natalist propaganda that hits us almost daily in the press. There has been much of it in recent years. Here, for example, is a selection from an article that appeared in the December 1969 issue of *Reader's Digest* by Representative Udall of Arizona. In this article the Congressman states:

> Suppose I told you that I have a plan which would guarantee to every area of the country: reduced local, state and Federal taxes; less crowded highways, freeways, and hospitals; single session schools and shortened waiting lists at colleges; some genuine hope for lower crime rates; measurable progress against pollution. This plan would cost almost nothing in public spending and involve no government controls.[24]

What is the plan? Here it is:

> Americans voluntarily and openly must face the fact that many of our tensions and failures are due to a spiraling population growth. Every family with two or more children would make a personal, voluntary decision to have no more. Every couple with one child or more would agree to stop with the second.

This article is a very clever piece of propaganda. The first part of the statement is carefully worded. All it promises is *some hope* for the reduction of crime and *measurable progress* against pollution. These are meaningless phrases without further quantification. The second statement is much less guarded and attributes "many of our tensions and failures . . . to a spiraling population growth." This statement implies, without saying it in so many words, that crime, pollution, and traffic jams are due to population growth. This is very doubtful. Many European countries are far more densely settled than we are and do not suffer any more than we do from pollution, crime, or traffic jams. Crime, pollution, and transportation problems may be aggravated by population growth, but neither their cause nor solution is necessarily related to a change in the size of the population.

Before going any further, we might first examine the evidence regarding our future population. How much are we likely to grow in the next fifteen years and what will be the distribution of the population by residence, age, income, and other important characteristics? On the basis of this evidence, we might then try to develop some conclusions regarding the importance of the expected increase in our numbers.

EXPECTED POPULATION GROWTH: 1970 TO 1985

In 1967 the Bureau of the Census prepared four series of population projections. Underlying these projections is the assumption that completed fertility will range as follows: 3.35 children per woman for Series A; 3.10 children for Series B; 2.78 children for Series C, and 2.45 children for Series D. Mortality is assumed to decline slightly and net migration is assumed to continue at its present level of about 400,000 per year. Recent trends in fertility suggest that the two higher series are no longer reasonable possibilities for 1985. The current level of fertility is at Series D. Between 1940 and 1957, average age at marriage declined, the proportion of women who were married increased, birth intervals became shorter, and fertility rose sharply, especially during the postwar years. As a result, population growth between 1947 and 1957 averaged 1.7 percent per year, which is a very high rate for an industrial nation to sustain. Since 1957, age at marriage and the spacing of births has increased slightly and fertility dropped sharply. As a result, the growth rate dropped to 1.1 percent during the past few years.

One of the main reasons for the drop in fertility in recent years is the fact that more young women are now having fewer children than women in the same age groups had during the 1950's. Since most of these women still profess a desire to have an average of three children, it is possible that they are merely postponing childbirth, just as their mothers accelerated their fertility immediately after World War II and then stopped having children relatively early in life. Many demographers, however, believe that this postponement will result in a reduction of completed fertility for these women. This uncertainty is one of the factors that complicates the problem of forecasting the population fifteen years hence. Another factor, which is even more important, is that many of the women who will begin to have children fifteen years from now are still playing with dolls. There is no way of knowing how many children they will decide to have, but they are likely to have better control over the number of children they bear than their mothers.

In view of the fact that the recent level of fertility is at the Series D level in the census projections, and the outlook for the immediate future appears to be in the direction of still further reductions in fertility, I would hazard a guess that the population will be between 240 and 250 million in 1985, representing an increase of 35 to 45 million people over the present level. The number of births should run between four and five million per year and the rate of population increase should be between 1.0 and 1.5 percent per year. The growth rate will start at relatively low levels in the early seventies and rise for the next decade because the proportion of women in the childbearing ages will increase. In making this "prediction" we must bear in mind that population forecasters have a notorious record for accuracy. Even a brilliant man like J. M. Keynes,[25] the father of modern economics, made the mistake of proclaiming in 1937, "We know much more securely than we know almost any other social or economic factor relating to the future that, in the place of the steady and indeed steeply rising level of population which we have experienced for a number of decades, we shall be faced in a very short time with a stationary or a declining level." Within a decade, Keynes not only proved to be wrong, but badly wrong. With the end of World War II most countries of the world embarked on an unparalleled increase in population growth.

EXPECTED CHANGES IN GEOGRAPHIC DISTRIBUTION: 1970-1985

Detailed statistics are available showing expected population trends for each state and for each metropolitan area. This is neither the time nor the place to attempt to analyze these very detailed figures. I do want to point out, however, that states have grown and are expected to grow at widely different rates. Since population growth in most places is primarily attributable to the excess of births over deaths rather than to net migration, it is not surprising that the greatest absolute growth is expected in the most populous states—California, New York, Texas, New Jersey, Ohio, Illinois, and Michigan. If we examine gains due to net migration only, we find that the states which can expect to attract the greatest number of migrants are California and Arizona in the West, Florida and Maryland in the South, and New York, New Jersey, and Connecticut in the Northeast. Most of the North Central States can expect to continue to experience outmigration of their population to other parts of the country.

Although most attention is directed to places which have been gaining in population, it is important to recognize that there are many areas which are losing people, and which have been losing them for a long time. About 1,100 counties—approximately one out of every three—had a net loss in population between 1960 and 1966, and about 1,800 counties had more outmigrants than inmigrants. There is a great band of counties in the Midwest from the Dakotas and Minnesota to Texas and Louisiana and across the South to Georgia and South Carolina which lost population between 1940 and 1950 and again between 1950 and 1960. In addition, there are areas in South Appalachia and in the section adjoining the northern Great Lakes which have a long history of population decline.

From a national policy point of view, the most significant geographic shifts in population are those which have taken place and which are expected to take place in the central cities and the suburbs of the metropolitan areas. People throughout the world have long shown a decided preference for city life. In the United States, two persons out of every three live in metropolitan areas today. Since 1900, the Nation's population has more than doubled. In that same time, the number of people in our metropolitan areas has increased much faster (about three and one-half times). Between 1950 and 1960, when the Nation as a whole grew by about 19 percent, the metropolitan areas grew by 27 percent. Since 1960, when the national growth was about 11 percent, that of the metropolitan areas was about 13 percent. This change is particularly striking and it bodes well for the future. It indicates that although metropolitan areas are still growing more rapidly than the rest of the country, the differential is narrowing and the result should be a slowdown in the metropolitanization of the country. If the trends of the past decade continue, the proportion of the population living in metropolitan areas is expected to increase by 1 percentage point between 1965 and 1975 as compared with an increase of 4 percentage points between 1940 and 1950 and an additional 4 percentage points between 1950 and 1960.

Although nonmetropolitan counties as a whole are growing below the national average, those nonmetropolitan counties that are crossed by a freeway and have a moderate-sized urban center (between 25,000 and 50,000 people) are growing more rapidly than others. Since 1960, these counties have grown at the same rate as the national average. These data do not suggest that a population explosion is taking place in these areas, but neither do they suggest that population growth is restricted to large urban centers. The growth in these counties contradicts the popular belief that the Nation's population is heading blindly toward smothering itself in a few huge, densely packed urban centers.

In recent years practically all of the growth in the metropolitan areas was in the suburban rings. Since 1960, the central cities as a whole grew only 1 percent; the suburban rings by 28 percent. In 1960, the suburban areas had shifted, and today more than half the people in our metropolitan areas live outside the central cities. There is every indication that this fraction is likely to grow.

There have been significant shifts in the characteristics of the residents of the central cities of our metropolitan areas. As a group, the central cities gained about three quarters of a million persons between 1960 and 1969. This net change was the result of an increase of 2.7 million in the Negro population and a decline of 2.1 million in the white population. About three fourths of the growth in the Negro population since 1960 has occurred in the central cities of the metropolitan areas. The Negro population is now more heavily concentrated in cities than the white population.

Most of the increase in the population of the metropolitan areas was the result of the fact that they had more births than deaths. For these areas as a whole, only one fourth of the total increase between 1960 and 1966 was the result of net immigration; three fourths was due to natural increase.

If past trends continue, nearly half of our population will be living in the suburban parts of our metropolitan areas in 1985 and only one fourth will be living in central cities. Virtually all of the white growth is expected to take place in the suburban ring, whereas the nonwhite growth is expected to occur primarily in the central cities. One third of the central-city residents are expected to be black in 1985 as compared with one fifth at present. A word of caution is appropriate here. These projections of the population in metropolitan areas are based on trends observed during the 1950-60 decade which may be out of date. We should be able to make more reliable projections using data from the 1970 census.

THE EXPANDING METROPOLIS

The projections of the population in the metropolitan areas described above assume that the land in these areas would be the same in 1985 as it is today. This assumption is unrealistic. Eighteen new metropolitan areas have been added since 1960 and the land area of seven other metropolitan areas has also expanded considerably since that time. Since the metropolitan area is defined as a central city of 50,000 or more plus the adjacent counties which are socially and economically integrated with that city, it is to be expected that the size of metropolitan areas will grow as technology improves and as new highways and other transportation systems are built which make it possible for people in the outlying areas to travel to nearby large cities to work. This expansion in the size of the metropolitan area makes it possible for the proportion of the population living in the metropolitan area to increase without causing any increase in population density. Computations show that population per square mile in these urbanized areas declined from 6,580 in 1920 to 4,230 in 1960. By the year 2000, when it is estimated that 70 percent of the United States population will be living in these areas, the population per square mile is expected to decline still more to 3,732.

Thus, despite the increased concentration of population in metropolitan areas, there has also been a "decentralization" of the population within these areas—an expansion of the land area in the suburban ring and an increase in the proportion of people living in these outlying areas. In part, this movement to suburbia represents a flight by middle-class white families from the problems of the city. More important, however, is the fact that advances in technology, such as electric power, automobiles, trucks, highways, and telephones, have made it possible for people to move farther and farther away from central cities and yet remain within easy commuting distance. In this process, the suburban rings have grown faster than the central cities because they are the only areas in which growth could take place. Most of the central cities have been filled up since 1920 and typically have been unable by law to annex new territory.

One important element of concern regarding the expanding metropolis is the length of the work trip. This concern is by no means new. About a century ago a German observer lamented that the distance people on the outskirts of cities had to travel had reached the limit of what was bearable. There can be little doubt that conversations in many carpools would dry up completely if this favorite topic were eliminated. But what are the facts? The passenger-transportation survey conducted by the U.S. Bureau of the Census in 1963 showed that only about one fifth of all work commuters spend more than half an hour getting to work. According to Hans Blumenfeld,[26] who is a member of the School of Town and Regional Planning of the University of Toronto and a consultant to several municipal and provincial agencies of Canada, "in most metropolitan areas the average travel time to work for the working population as a whole is about half an hour. No more than 15 percent of the workers spend more than forty-five minutes in the daily journey to work."

Another important aspect of the physical expansion of metropolitan areas is the dislocation between jobs and people. When metropolitan areas expand, jobs as well as people move to the outlying areas. There are many reasons for the change. Cheaper land in the suburbs permits the construction of one- or two-story manufacturing plants which are more modern, more attractive, and more efficient than those in the inner city. The suburbs also have far less traffic congestion and they often have a better educated labor supply that is either close at hand or within easy commuting distance. It often takes less time to travel twenty-five miles on the beltway from one part of the metropolitan area to another than it does to travel to the downtown area.

The movement of jobs to the suburbs does not adversely affect large proportions of the middle-class white population who already live in the outlying areas and who have private automobiles to get them to and from work. It does, however, have serious consequences for the residents of the inner city, many of whom are low-income Negroes who cannot afford to buy and maintain automobiles and who do not have access to public transportation which can get them to the new plant locations, or for whom public transportation is far too costly. According to one recent estimate, although one million workers are unemployed in central cities and about two million are subemployed, there are about 250,000 unfilled jobs in manufacturing plants outside the city limits. It is likely that more of these jobs would be filled by Negroes if they could find homes in the suburban areas or if cheap and efficient transportation facilities were available for them to commute to the suburban jobs from their homes in the central cities.

EXPECTED CHANGES IN AGE COMPOSITION AND HOUSEHOLD FORMATION: 1970-1985

The only uncertainty about the age structure of the population in 1985 concerns the number and distribution of persons who will be under fifteen at that time. Everyone else is now alive; so charting their flow through the age structure is just a matter of simple arithmetic. The first of the prewar babies will be approaching his fortieth birthday in 1985, and the last of the great wave of births that began to subside in 1961 will be approaching twenty-five. There will, therefore, be a very dramatic rise in the number of younger adults during this period. As a matter of fact, one third of the expected population increase will be in the twenty-five- to thirty-four-year age group and an additional one sixth will be in the thirty-five- to forty-four-year group. Altogether, we might expect an additional 27 million people—more than half of the total expected increase—who will be in their twenties, thirties, and early forties. On the other hand, there will be virtually no change in the number who will be forty-five to sixty-four years old in 1985, because this age group was born between 1925 and 1945 when the birth rate was low and the annual number of births was declining. Most of the remaining twenty million who are expected to be added to the population during the next fifteen years will be preschoolers (9 million), and school age children five to fifteen years old (5 million); and the number of persons over sixty-five will increase by five million.

Perhaps the most significant fact about the expected change in age composition is the very sharp increase in the number of persons in their twenties and early thirties. Since this is the age at which most marriages take place, we can expect that during the next fifteen years the annual number of marriages will be relatively high. We are also likely to see a fairly rapid rate of household formation and also relatively large numbers of births. During the past few years, there has been an average of nearly two million marriages per year. This number is expected to rise gradually during the next fifteen years and reach a peak of about 2.5 million by 1985. Not all marriages result in the formation of new households. When persons remarry or when single people each give up their small apartments and move into a larger as a result of marriage, there may actually be a reduction in the number of households. During the past few years, the number of households has been growing by about 900,000 per year. By 1985, this number is expected to increase to about 1.4 million per year.

One of the important concomitants of this projected increase in household formation is in the demand for housing. It is likely that we will need about two million new dwelling units per year to accommodate the new families that will be formed and to replace the units that are wearing out. Any appreciable increase in housing standards or an increase in the tendency for youngsters to move out on their own at an early age would increase the demand for housing even more. Since the number of younger households will be rising rapidly during the next fifteen years, it is likely that much of the demand will be for apartments rather than for private homes, because that is the kind of housing newlyweds generally prefer. We can already see tendencies in this direction in many suburban areas. As a result of the rapid rise in land values and the increase in the cost of constructing one-family homes, many new high-rise apartment buildings are springing up just outside the city limits. These apartments are generally close to nearby shopping areas and public transportation facilities. If this trend should continue, it could result in a radical change in present land use and life styles.

The expected trends in age distribution are also likely to have an important impact on future school enrollments. The number of elementary school pupils will probably drop slightly during the next few years, return to its present level by 1980, and then rise somewhat by 1985. High school enrollment is expected to change relatively little during the next fifteen years. This breathing spell should make it possible to divert some of the funds that were going for classroom construction to the much-needed improvements and experimentation in education, particularly in slum areas. The number of college students, however, is expected to rise by over 50 percent from its present level of 7.5 million to about 11.5 million in 1985. About half of the expected rise in college enrollment is due to population increase and an equal amount to a rise in the proportion of young people attending college. Breakthroughs are badly needed in our ability to handle the large numbers of young people who are entering college today and are often inadequately prepared for higher education. This problem may get worse in the future as larger proportions of graduating classes seek admission to the colleges and universities.

The rapid growth in the number of young adults between twenty and thirty-four years of age and the lack of growth in the forty-five- to sixty-four-year age group may have particularly significant implications for the structure of executive management and political leadership in the future. For one thing, it may mean that there will be a shortage of experienced older men available for positions of leadership in politics, industrial management, and government. Those who will be available will be much in demand, and there may be some pressure for them to postpone retirement. At the same time, there will be a large reservoir of young, well-educated men, with great expectations, looking to fill these jobs. As a result, by 1985 we might expect to see more young leaders in politics, private industry, and the upper echelons of government service, than is the case today.

The shortage of mature men for positions of leadership may also provide greater opportunities for women. Although a very large proportion of all married women now work, relatively few attain responsible positions. Many are not trained for such jobs and others with training have family responsibilities which prevent them from capitalizing fully on that training. Young women coming into the labor force today, however, will be far better trained, on the average, than their mothers were and they will have much better control over the number and spacing of their children. Moreover, the crucial baby-sitting problem may be eased for many by Headstart programs, day-care centers, and general acceptance of the idea that many three and four year olds are better off in school than they are at home. As a result of these developments it may be possible for more young women to pursue their careers almost as seriously as men and to be available for responsible jobs when they are needed.

EXPECTED CHANGES IN INCOME DISTRIBUTION: 1970-85

Barring a catastrophe, American families will have far better incomes in 1985 than they have today. A reasonable indication of just how much richer we will be is provided by the projected income distribution which has been prepared. This distribution is based on the assumption that during the next fifteen years, the Lorenz curve (that is the cumulative percent distribution of families and of income) will be constant for each age group and that the level of income will continue to rise at the same rate as it has risen during the past ten years. Overall, this growth rate has been a little over 3 percent per year. The rate was somewhat higher for the younger age groups and lower for the older ones. The figures are all in dollars of 1968 purchasing power and are before the deduction of taxes. The assumption is that taxes are just one of the ways in which we spend our money.

Based on these assumptions, real incomes would grow by over 100 percent during the next fifteen years. In 1968, family money income totaled 500 billion dollars. It is expected to exceed a trillion dollars by 1985, measuring in dollars of constant purchasing power. At present, about one third of total income is received by families with incomes over fifteen thousand dollars. By 1985, families at this income level will receive nearly three fourths of that income. Moreover, because of the combined impact of both income and population growth, the number of dollars (in terms of constant purchasing power) at this upper-income level will be about five times as great as it is today.

Most of the added purchasing power will occur in the twenty-five- to forty-four-year age group and among the higher-income groups. At present, about 42 percent of all the purchasing power is represented in the twenty-five- to forty-four-year age category. In 1985, this age group will account for about half of the purchasing power.

CONCLUSIONS

1. At present, our population is growing at a rate of 1.1 percent per year (roughly 2.5 million per year), and it has been growing at that rate for nearly a decade. According to the judgment of most demographers I know, in the absence of a major disaster or drastic changes in social and economic conditions, this rate may rise during the 1970's and early 1980's as the proportion of women in the childbearing years increases, but it should then recede to its present level or perhaps even go below it. A slower rate of growth would be desirable. It would make easier the task of coping with the many domestic problems we now have which are caused by a variety of factors in addition to population growth. At the same time, however, I do not believe that the expected rate of population growth during the next fifteen years will present insurmountable problems. We have had far higher growth rates in the past with no demonstrable harmful effects.

We must also remember that a stationary population will have problems of its own which may be as serious as those we face today with moderate growth. It was only a little over thirty years ago that the specter of economic stagnation haunted many industrialized Western countries and caused a brilliant economist like Keynes to write about the economic consequences of a declining population. Before embracing the concept of a stationary population too warmly, we had better face up to the fact that such a population would be much older than the present one. It would have an equal number of people under fifteen and over sixty and the average age would be thirty-seven as compared with thirty at present. An affluent society with a stationary population would probably be more resistant to change than our present society because wealth and conservatism tend to increase with age. If the present establishment seems intolerable to the youth of America, imagine how it might be under a stationary population where rich old men would be even more likely to be running things.

2. We do have serious population problems today and they are likely to intensify in the next fifteen years. These problems relate to the geographic distribution and to the values of our people rather than to their numbers and rates of growth. The continued loss of population in the central cities of most large metropolitan areas is making it extremely difficult to provide adequate services for those who continue to live here, the growing concentration of affluent whites in the suburbs and Negroes in the central cities has increased the polarization in our society; the increase in residential segregation within cities and the deterioration of conditions in our worst slums tend to increase racial tensions; although one third of our counties have lost population during the past decade, the crowded metropolitan areas keep gaining people, thereby placing a further strain on the resources in those places. These are some of the population problems that are threatening to tear us apart as a society.

The recent report of the National Commission on the Causes and Prevention of Violence contains a description of the American city of the future which is both realistic and terrifying. The report notes that unless effective action is taken soon to improve conditions in our cities, within a few years

> central business districts . . . will be largely deserted except for police patrols during nighttime hours. Highrise apartment buildings and residential compounds protected by private guards and security devices will be fortified cells—ownership of guns will be almost universal in the suburbs, homes will be fortified by an array of devices from window grills to electronic surveillance equipment, armed citizen volunteers in cars will supplement inadequate police patrols in neighborhoods closer to the central city—private automobiles, taxicabs, and commercial vehicles will be routinely equipped with unbreakable glass, light armor, and other security features— streets and residential neighborhoods in the central cities will be places of terror with widespread crime, perhaps entirely out of police control during nighttime hours.[27]

In light of this prospect, it seems unreasonable to make no distinction between the population problems associated with growth and those associated with distribution. There is no question that we can manage very well for the next fifteen years with a 1 percent rate of growth in population. There is some question whether we can survive as a free society if the tensions we have experienced during the past few years continue or multiply.

3. There is some connection between pollution, high crime rates, transportation problems, and other social ills and the rate of population growth. These problems, however, are more directly related to other factors such as the geographic distribution of people, the customs and morals of the people, the underlying social and economic conditions and the intensity of the effort that is made to cope directly with our social problems. No one really knows what share of our social ills is due to population growth and what share is due to these other factors. My own guess is that the latter are more important. Professor Ansley Coale, in his presidential address to the Population Association of America, pointed out in 1968 that Sydney, Australia, has traffic jams and pollution despite the fact that it is situated in a country which is nearly as large as the United States, but has only twelve million people. Pollution, traffic jams, delinquency, and crime are no worse in France, England, and Holland than in the United States despite the fact that population density in these countries is between five and thirty times as great as in the United States. It seems to me that trying to deal with the social problems we now have by persuading women not to have babies is like treating cancer with a sedative. It might relieve the pain, but it will not make the problem go away. If we attack our social ills directly during the next decade, the way we attacked outer space during the past decade, we might begin to see results. One big difference, of course, is that it cost only five billion dollars per year to get to the moon, whereas it would cost at least twenty billion dollars more per year to clean up some of the mess we have created.

4. If real incomes grow during the next fifteen years at the same rate as they grew during the past ten years—and most economists I know think they will—we will have the resources which may be used to intensify—or to alleviate—many of the problems associated with population distribution. The richer we get

the more we increase our demand for privacy, more spacious living quarters, recreational facilities, automobiles, roads, and other material goods.

Fifteen years from now, half the families will have incomes over fifteen thousand dollars in terms of today's purchasing power. If we continue to use this growing affluence largely to satisfy our private needs, we are likely to be faced with more intense problems of pollution and transportation than we now have, even if our population stops growing. According to estimates I have made, expenditures for housing, transportation, and recreation will double by 1985, using dollars of constant purchasing power. Only about 30 percent of the increase is due to population growth; most of the rise is due to affluence—higher incomes and greater demand for more luxurious goods and services. The great bulk of the rise in expenditures for these items—and the concomitant increase in pollution, transportation, and other problems that will accompany it—would take place even if our population stopped growing tomorrow but we continued our past income growth and we continued to spend our money in the same old way.

There are, however, other alternatives. We are free men in a free society, not robots. Whatever the ad men tell us and whatever the social pressures may be, we still have the power to stand up on our hind legs and say, "Shove it!" That's what some of our children are trying to tell us and perhaps it is time we listened. We can decide through our elected officials to use more of our income to meet more of our social needs. As individuals we cannot purify the air or the water. We cannot buy better jails or police protection on our own. They can be obtained only if we are willing to pay the cost of making the improvements. Some of the cost may come in the form of higher prices and some in the form of higher taxes. It is possible to reduce the smog resulting from the exhausts of automobiles and jet planes; but, the changes will cost money. We can insist upon other methods of disposing of industrial waste, but the changes will cost money. We know how to reduce some of the brutalizing aspects of prison life, but the changes will cost money. We can provide more reasonable minimum incomes for all families and thereby reduce some of the social problems that are associated with poverty, but this change will cost money.

The choice is ours. If we choose to spend our money on wars, our ability to deal with domestic problems will be seriously impaired. If we choose to invest in space exploration, we may solve all of the mysteries of the universe and remain ignorant about man himself. If we choose to give ourselves tax cuts, we will spend the money on things we can buy—more material goods which will intensify many of our problems. If we choose to spend more of our money for public services, we might buy pure air and water, cleaner and more efficient transportation systems, better schools, the elimination of hunger, and the reduction of poverty.

Which will we choose? There is little doubt in my mind. Until conditions grow much worse than they are, my guess is that we will move farther out into the suburbs where we will need more roads, more sewers, more expensive homes, more cars—and more vacations to get away from the headaches we will have made. In England, the fight against air pollution began as a direct result of the disastrous smog that hit London in December 1952, lasting for three days and killing about four thousand sufferers from bronchial and cardiac illnesses. This event led to the Clean Air Act of 1956, which brought gradual creation of smoke-control areas across the United Kingdom. It will probably take a similar catastrophe to produce similar legislation in the United States. Nearly everyone is opposed to higher taxes; everyone professes a desire to clean up the environment, reduce crime, racial tensions, and other social problems. But if the money does not come from new taxes, from where will it come? One source would be a major change in government expenditures—a transfer of funds from military to civilian spending. There have been some small steps in this direction.

Perhaps there was a time when each of us could maximize his satisfaction by spending his hard-earned money as he saw fit, without taking the needs of others into account. If there ever was such a time, it no longer exists. Each of us can only maximize his own satisfaction today by taking the needs of others into account. Each time we land at an airport, the black jet stream we create spoils the air we ourselves breathe. Each time we dump raw sewage or industrial waste into a river or a lake, we pollute the water we drink and destroy the fish we might have eaten. Each untreated emotionally disturbed child is the man who may one day rob us on a city street or kill a President. It is no act of altruism today to favor more spending for the solution of domestic problems. It is merely a matter of each of us furthering his own self-interest.

Unless we change our ways, our rising incomes will result in increased expenditures for luxury goods. More families will undoubtedly buy more expensive homes and rent more luxurious apartments, which will be loaded with the latest gadgets. There will be many more swimming pools in backyards, heated where necessary, and homes with three and four cars will perhaps be common. Increased funds and more leisure time, resulting in part from the increase in the number of three-day weekends, will undoubtedly result in a vast rise in expenditures for travel and other types of recreation. All of these activities will bring a great deal of satisfaction to the individual families that partake of them, but they will also intensify many of the domestic problems we now have. At present, we are paying little more than lip service to the solution of these problems and this is one of the reasons for the difficulties we are having with people in the younger generation. They hear a great deal of pious talk about the need for change, but they see little change actually taking place. They hear constant complaints about high taxes, but they see their parents growing more affluent and less concerned about social problems. The fact that the younger generation shares this affluence only adds to their sense of guilt.

One of the big hopes for the future is that about two fifths of the families that will be in existence in 1985 have not yet been formed. Many of these families will be headed by children who are now throwing stones at their teachers or watching their older brothers and sisters mocking the establishment. In 1985 it will be to an important degree their society, not ours. They may even constitute the affluent majority, and it will be interesting to see what they do with their affluence. I am confident about their ability to channel their libidinous instincts into non-productive outlets. I am not so sure, however, that they will put the lie to John Gardner's prediction that we will "get richer and richer in filthier communities until we reach a final state of affluent misery—Croesus on a garbage heap."

Chapter Seven

THE POPULATION PROBLEM: A FACTOR IN THE WORLD MACROPROBLEM

WILLIS W. HARMAN

TO BE concerned about the determinants and consequents of population change as these relate to the physical and psychosocial factors which contribute to or detract from the quality of life, is literally to be concerned with the whole world. It is to be concerned with the future of the biosphere as well as the design of a work environment, with new technological threats to individual freedoms and rights as well as with inner-city housing. This concern I will term "the world macroproblem," for concern for the whole of the world supercedes a concern for population alone.

How does one go about thinking about the whole world? Clearly new conceptual tools are needed for the tests. Tools are needed which are aimed at illuminating educational policy, population policy and housing policy, law enforcement and justice, health and defense policy, to mention only a few areas of concern. What is our range of available futures? What policy choices would help move us toward the goal of universal access to a high quality of life?

In what follows, we present one framework for thinking about this so called macroproblem, and about the broad policy choices which make up the context of more specific system and design choices. Some of the major findings thus far are also summarized.

The trail of the discussion is somewhat hard to follow, so a preliminary map will help. Let me begin with a description of a method of constructing alternative future histories and with a summary set of such histories for the next thirty years. From these, some broad conclusions are drawn, highlighting the

Note: Adapted from a paper delivered at the First Symposium on Habitability, May 11-14, 1970, Los Angeles, California.

"world macroproblem." This leads to a reconsideration of some very basic premises in the culture which appear to be at the root of the world macroproblem—premises which are so much a part of our way of perception that they largely go unexamined. Two additional indications of a drastic shift in premises and values taking place will be examined. All this, then, becomes the context for a systematic assessment of policy issues relating to habitability—an assessment yet to be made.

PRECIS OF THE METHOD OF CONSTRUCTING ALTERNATIVE FUTURE HISTORIES

The method used to construct alternative future histories derives from an approach originated by Robert Johnson of Johnson Research Associates, Santa Barbara, California.[28] In underlying philosophy it is similar to the powerful relaxation methods of mathematical physics. Its ultimate power lies in the possibility of continued refinement, through systematic iterations, of a field of feasible future histories, considered as a whole.

In this preliminary work, six aspects of U.S. society were selected to comprise a minimal descriptive framework. (More aspects would provide a richer description but be harder to handle.) These were U.S. economics, U.S. internal politics, science and technology, U.S. demographic patterns, world population/subsistence, and U.S. foreign relations.

For each of these, from four to six alternative patterns were selected covering the likely range of variation. Thus, a description of the state of society comprised, in its skeletal form, a choice of one pattern in each of six aspects. Sparse though such a description may seem, this listing leads to well over 20,000 possible combinations.

The next task was to reduce these by eliminating those which are not self-consistent or do not seem feasible by the year 2000. Reduction of approximately fifty internally consistent descriptions proved relatively rapid. Next, these were examined to see which could plausibly occur in sequence, working forward from the present state and working backward from various assumed end (year 2000) states. Continued reexamination of the set of plausible sequences as a whole, to eliminate remaining inconsistencies and to uncover missed possibilities, resulted in the tree* of alternative future histories shown in Figure 7-1.

Examination of the descriptions of the various "year 2000" alternative states showed that they tended to differ in two especially significant dimensions. One has to do with the degree to which the society is adept (both competent and motivated) at achieving its undertaken goals. The other relates to the degree of "openness," implying flexibility, accessibility, and decentralized decision-making. A suggestive representation of the "year 2000" slice of the tree of Figure 7-1, with the alternative future states arrayed in these two dimensions, is given in Figure 7-2.

* The use of the word "tree" is based on the shape of the graphic. "Tree" has no technical meaning. The author explains the graphic in subsequent paragraphs, showing the reader the alternative paths which might be open to mankind, depending on his choices.

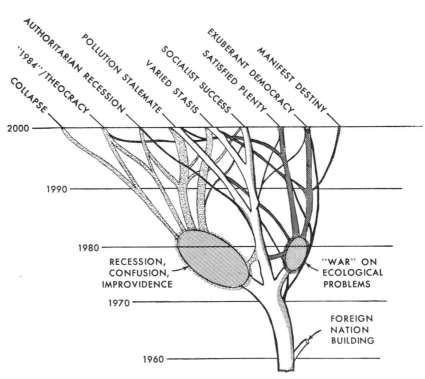

Figure 7-1. "Tree" of alternative future histories.

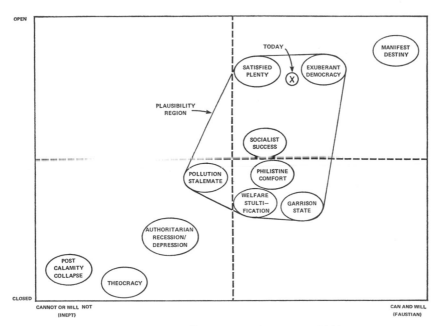

Figure 7-2. "Slice" of Figure 7-1 at year 2000.

These results, to repeat, must be considered as tentative and preliminary. The alternative future states need to be fleshed out in various ways to provide richer descriptions. Prevailing value-belief systems in the different paths need to be examined, and stakeholder-group dynamics at the branching points assessed. The whole needs to be recycled and adjusted until overall consistency is assured. Nevertheless, to the extent that the major features of the present futures map seem dependable, important policy implications follow.

A PRELIMINARY GENERAL CONCLUSION

The abbreviated names assigned to the different paths in the map are too concise to convey much detail, and may even be misleading. More complete descriptions of the paths are being made available for serious examination of these findings. One should be hesitant about concluding anything on the basis of the brief remarks above and these two diagrams.

For example, the path labeled "Exuberant Democracy" is characterized by a mood of exuberant expansiveness, a high degree of confidence in the economy and the political system, a U.S. ability to project its influence throughout the world, an actively questing science, and an expanding technology. Identifications with the culture and the nation are positive and proud, and horizons are seen as unlimited. Americans and their Government are extroverted and confident in their dealing with other nationals and nations. However, it seems very unlikely that this state of affairs could come about without an all-out national effort on ecosystem problems (including amelioration of poverty within and outside the nation) of a magnitude approaching that of World War II and with similar unification of national will, launched no later than 1975-80. It is also probable that the solution to these problems would have involved considerable encroachment on individual freedoms, and these would be impingement on quality of life in significant respects. Furthermore, if this state has been reached through a successful "Green Revolution"* in agriculture, thus avoiding widespread famine in the underdeveloped world, population levels are likely to be such as to have resulted in a very fragile ecosystem balance; the prognosis for the decades beyond 2000 involves probable catastrophe within another half century.

From Figure 7-1 it appears that unless some such overriding goal as a "war on ecological problems" serves to unite the increasingly fractionated nation, a path representing an undesirable future history is all too likely. To be successful in pulling the people of the U.S. over into the more desirable stem of the tree, such an effort would have to have a sufficiently large scope to touch the lives of most Americans (beyond its reflection in their taxes). It would need to focus public action for a sustained rather than a spasmodic effort, to mobilize resources enough to make obvious progress, and to engender sufficient mutual trust and commitment to enable joint action on a mass scale.

---

* "Green Revolution" is a term referring to the discovery and use of high yield grains which have greatly increased the food production in the world. Future "Green Revolutions" might involve new discoveries and means for increasing other forms of vegetations and even animal protein for food consumption.

In overall outlook, it appears that of some two score of feasible future histories there are very few which manage to avoid one or another kind of time of serious troubles between now and 2050. The few that do, require a dramatic shift of values and perceptions with regard to the "world macroproblem."

THE WORLD MACROPROBLEM

This macroproblem will be the predominant concern of the forseeable future, for all the alternative paths. It is the composite of all the problems which have been brought about by a combination of rampant technology application and industrial development together with high population levels (in turn, a consequence of technology-reduced mortality rate):

1. Problems of the ecosystem (ecological imbalances, fouling of the environment, resource depletion; overpopulation and consequent famine and plague in underdeveloped regions).

2. Intrinsically expanding have/have-not gap (domestically and between nations, with resulting internal and external dissension).

3. Technological threats (weapons of mass destruction; vulnerability of a complex society to sabotoge; new powers to "engineer" the human body mind, foetus, and genetic transmission; threats to privacy and individual rights; mental stress of complex living).

Although terms like "environment" and "ecology" have entered the political rhetoric, Americans have not yet begun to take this world macroproblem seriously. Even among the informed public there is a pronounced tendency to believe the following:

1. New technological breakthroughs will be achieved which will enable us to control pollution.

2. The green revolution in agriculture will solve the world's food problem.

3. Technological breakthroughs in contraception will take care of the population explosion.

4. The deterrence policy will continue to preserve the world from the horrors of nuclear warfare.

5. International controls will adequately protect against small-nation development and the use of biological weapons.

6. The right programs for urban problems will begin to reduce the severity of the problems of racism in the nation.

7. The drastically fallen world image of America, from the hope of the oppressed to imperialist oppressor, is a regrettable consequence of our involvement in the Vietnamese conflict, and can be righted by finding a satisfactory way to extricate the United States from that situation.

8. As soon as the Vietnam war is over, America will begin to make steady progress on the serious social and environmental problems which beset us.

9. By supplying capital and American know-how to the underdeveloped nations, the gap between the haves and have-nots will begin to close, thus reducing the continuing threat to world peace, or making it possible to safely disregard the issue.

10. As available supplies of physical resources—fresh water, fossil fuels, minerals, etc.—are used up, technological breakthroughs will provide substitutes.

11. As per capita energy usage continues to rise and conventional power sources (hydroelectric, fossil fuels) approach limits, technological breakthroughs will result in new energy sources (efficient solar cells, nuclear fusion processes with no side radioactive contaminants) which will fill the demands.

These expectations looked less and less credible as one studied the data from whence this research was generated. Rather, the various aspects of the world macroproblem looked more and more like surface manifestations of a pathogenic condition much more fundamental. This showed up in the projections of alternative futures, wherein it appeared that desirable "future histories" were hard to come by, and furthermore, involved significant changes in operative values. It appeared again as analysis was attempted to determine how the world had gotten to its present state. The suspicion arose that hard-to-come-by future histories suggested that implicit in them were the premises of present forms of the technological-industrial state, awaiting only suitable levels of population and technological application to become intolerable. This surface manifestation of a pathogenic condition showed up once again when the significance of contemporary revolutionary forces was studied and it was apparent that the crucial gap is not that between generations, nor between liberals and conservatives, but between those who rely on a continuation of present trends and those who insist that a drastic change is absolutely necessary.

PATHOGENIC PREMISES

Admittedly, the concept of pathogenic premises is a loose one. It is meant to connote that certain aspects of the prevailing (whether explicit or implicit) premises are problem-generating; in other ways they may produce useful consequences. For example, at one time the premise that blacks are subhuman contributed significantly to a thriving agricultural economy in the South. Few today, however, would doubt that it was also pathogenic. Similarly, premises which contributed significantly to present industrial and technological accomplishments in this society may have pathogenic aspects with present population levels and technological powers. Among these might be listed the following:

1. The premise that the pride of families, the power of nations, and the survival of the human species all are to be furthered (as in the past) by population increase.

2. The "technological imperative," that any technology that *can* be developed, and any knowledge that *can* be applied, *should* be.

3. The premise that the summed knowledge of experts provides adequate operative strategies for dealing with problems of the South.

4. The reductionist view of man: a premise associated with the development of contemporary science and which lends sanction to dehumanizing ways of thinking about and treating men.

5. The premise that men are essentially separate, so that little intrinsic responsibility is felt for the effects of present actions on remote individuals or future generations.

6. The premise that man is separate from nature, and

hence that nature is to be exploited and "controlled" rather than cooperated with.

7. The "economic man" image, leading to an economics based on ever-increasing GNP, consumption, and expenditure of irreplaceable resources.

8. The premise that the future of the planet can safely be left to autonomous nation-states, operating essentially independently.

9. The belief that "what ought to be" is a meaningful concept and is achievable.

The reason that these premises are pathogenic now, whereas they were apparently fairly workable in the recent past, lies in the way in which the future is profoundly different from the past. From now on, *everything* in man's environment, in his physical makeup and behavior, and in his future development is subject to human meddling, interference, and "control." But Americans have not developed the responsibility for making the momentous choices which face them.

If this judgment is sound—that the various aspects of the world macroproblem, while they may be ameliorated or postponed by certain technological achievements, are intrinsic in the basic operative premises of present industrialized culture—if this is correct, then it follows that *self-education toward changing those premises is a paramount and urgent task for the nation and for the world.* This involves at least the assumption of responsible stewardship of life on earth, and the associated changes in values and premises. It probably includes adaptation to a new and evolving metaphysic which will support these changes (since values are always rooted in an implicit picture of man-in-relationship-to-his-world) and probably calls for a new alliance between education and law enforcement to help not only Americans, but all mankind through a coming time of troubles.

A CONFLICT IN PREMISES

A conflict exists between the basic premises of a democracy—that man is, by virtue of his transcendental nature, endowed with reason, will, and a valid sense of value—and the reductionistic, deterministic, physicalistic premises of the prevailing be-havioral-science and sociopolitical theories. Sociology has shifted from its earlier emphasis on techniques and empirical studies, with the implication that man is a creature of his drives, habits, and social roles, in whose behavior reason and choice play no de-cisive part. In psychology courses this point of view is likely to be made even more explicit, with consciousness considered to be an inconsequential accompaniment to behavior governed by ex-ternal stimuli and instinctive urges. Contemporary political sci-ence tends to focus on the processes by which public policies are made, and to be relatively little concerned with their con-tents. Amid the measurement of attitudes, population move-ments, organizational trends, and political behavior, and the modeling of society and governments, little attention is given to the historic questions relating to man, his condition, and his destiny.

On the other hand, the concept of a transcendental, choosing, ultimately responsible self is essential to the entire theory of democratic government. It underlies the assumption that the criminal is responsible for his act (while recognizing in provid-ing rehabilitation opportunities that his antisocial traits may have their roots in environmental conditioning). It is basic to the assumption in the judicial process that the judge can mean-ingfully make a normative judgment. It is essential to the work-ability of "government of the people, by the people, and for the people."

This conflict in basic premises is directly related to the future of the planet. Arguing from essentially the same standpoint as the "world macroproblem" discussion above, Victor Ferkiss[29] as-serts that nothing short of a new guiding philosophy is required to meet the challenge of the years just ahead. He outlines three basic elements which such a new philosophy would have to in-corporate. First is what he terms a "new naturalism," which af-firms that man is absolutely a part of a nature, a universe, that is always in process of becoming. The second element, "the new holism," recognizes that "no part can be defined or understood save in relation to the whole." The third, "the new immanentism," sees that the whole is "determined not from outside but from within." It follows from these that meaningful social policies must be ecological in character, that is, they must be based on a recognition that any decision, any change affects everything in the total system. Men's actions and the forces they set in motion are all part of the developing whole; "every part of the whole has power and influence; every living particle is a source of direction and life." If man is to acquire the necessary sense of responsibility for the impact of his own actions on the shaping of the whole, he "must so internalize these ideas and make them so much a part of his instinctive world view that they inform his personal, political, and cultural life."

As will be shown below, two other forces in society appear to be suggesting similar premises and values, toward a new image of man. One is an aspect of the dissent of youth; the other a development within the realm of science.

The kinds of educational system and educational goals a society sets up, the way it handles the problems of environment and social injustice, the priorities it gives to aesthetic considerations, the extent to which it considers its citizens' need for easy access to communion with the nature, the uses of leisure it fosters—all these aspects and many more are affected by the image of man held by the society. Currently in this society these potent emerging forces push for a change in that image, in the direction of transcendent man. Thus far the power is on the image side of reductionists.

THE GREAT REFUSAL

One of these two forces, a component of the youth revolution, is what Mendel[30] terms "the Great Refusal" to go along with the old values, a protest "against that pitiful caricature of man created by five centuries of urban, technological, and scientific progress—*homo economicus*. The essential accusation of the Great Refusal is directed against the subordination of human experience to the economic processes of the consumer society and its increasingly more absurd products, to the aggressive militarism that, at least in our case, has become so tightly interwoven with this society, and to the gigantic, impersonal organizations through which it all functions."

Is it not only among the youth that such sentiments are found? Increasingly, business executives are heard to include, sincerely to some extent, high in the list of corporate objectives that of providing opportunity for the fulfillment of members of the organization, and of contributing in some fashion to the welfare of mankind.

It is, of course, an oversimplification to the point of risking distortion to lump all the dissent together as the Great Refusal. The situation is a good deal more complicated than that. Let us comment on one aspect of the dissidence of youth which is particularly relevant to our discussion here. At least four distinct movements can be discerned which, by around 1968, had coalesced to form one rather powerful thrust. As a consequence of these four tributaries, the present movement has a unique character stemming from its use of what might be termed "person-changing technology."

The first of these converging streams is the new political activism starting with the civil-rights movement which enlisted idealistic youth in increasing numbers for the dozen or so years following the Supreme Court decision *(Brown v. Board of Education)* in 1954. Later causes included the Vietnam war, the draft, "nonrelevance" of higher education, university involvement in weapons research, etc. A second stream, the psychedelic or hippie movement, could be said to have begun in 1963 with the founding by Harvard's Timothy Leary of the International Foundation for Internal Freedom (IFIF), promulgating the ethic "Turn on, tune in, drop out." A third tributary did not start with the young so much as with the psychotherapists—the human potential movement, which takes 1961 as its birthday, with the founding of the first of the growth centers, Esalen Institute, at Big Sur, California, and also the founding of the American Association for Humanistic Psychology. The fourth component is much older, the left-wing political group which was finding its new heroes in Fidel Castro and Mao Tse Tung. As these four movements began to join forces for some purposes (although this is not meant to imply the existence of a unified political movement) and especially as it became more common to assert that the real revolution is not in the ghetto or on the campus, but in people's heads, the use of the person-changing technology became more deliberate.

Some of the elements of this change technology are listed in Table 7-I. Emphasis is on increased awareness in two directions: (1) of the higher consciousness nature of man, and hence of the demeaning quality of the prevailing images of behavioral-science man and economic man and (2) of institutionalized hy-

TABLE 7-I

Elements of "Person-Changing Technology"	Typical Outcomes
Meditation Yoga Psychedelic drugs Hypnosis, autohypnosis Psychosynthesis	Awareness of spiritual dimensions of transcendental self, of the "hypnotic" or "encapsulated" nature of ordinary life
Sensory awareness	Sensitivity to feelings and emotions, beauty
Self-awareness exercises Psychotherapies Group therapy	Sensitivity to human closeness, self-honesty, realization there is nothing to hide
Sensitivity training Encounter groups Gestalt therapy Group nudity, marathons	Spontaneous response to experience, self-expression, individual autonomy, emotional freedom
Psychodrama	Removal of guilt and fear stemming from early training regarding morality and sin
Synanon games New Theater (ridicule of Establishment, crudity and nudity, audience encounter)	Ego-reducing experience, awareness of ego-defense nature of social institutions and customs
Forceful disruption of normal social process	
Underground press	
Radicalizing confrontations	
Deliberate provocation of "instructive encounters" such as police confrontations, black-white confrontations, etc.	Perception of oppressive nature of social institutions

pocrisy, inequity, and inhumanity in the social system. The techniques near the top of the list tend to aim more at expanded self-awareness, and those near the bottom at heightened social awareness.

Young people's concern with awareness-expanding and consciousness-exploring activities is intimately related to their reformulated value convictions. If materialism was the philosophical base for the Old Left, it appears that some form of existential transcendentalism may be coming to play that role for the New Left. The far-flung network of rock stations broadcasting revolutionary messages in the lyrics of their songs and in their parodies of news programs, intersperse material on religious, metaphysical, psychic, and esoteric topics. As Roszak[31] notes in one of the most penetrating analyses of the youth revolt, "If one scans any of the underground weeklies, one is apt to find their pages swarming with Christ and the prophets, Zen, Sufism, Hinduism, primitive shamanism, theosophy, the left-handed Tantra. . . . At the level of our youth, we begin to resemble nothing so much as the cultic hothouse of the Hellenistic period, where every manner of mystery and fakery, ritual and rite, intermingled with marvelous indiscrimination." Notwithstanding, he notes, there is a unifying theme. "The world view of Lao-Tzu, of the Buddha, of the Zen masters . . . has become one of the strongest strains of the counter-culture. . . . The counter-culture is, essentially, an exploration of the politics of consciousness."

A NEW SCIENCE OF CONSCIOUSNESS?

Such indications of a shift in the metaphysical premises of the public at large, or the younger part of it, might appear to be a mere fad. More significant, in a way, are indications that scientists—persons with recognized scientific training who are on the staffs of research organizations and universities with high standards and who hold membership in recognized scientific associations—are manifesting more and more interest in developing a science of ordinary and extraordinary subjective experience. The study of altered states of consciousness is not completely new, of course. The phenomena of hypnosis have been studied in a scientific way, off and on, for at least a century and a half. Phenomenology has been a sporadic influence in psychology. Freud's psychoanalysis and its offshoots have attempted to probe the unconscious processes. But the present thrust is toward a more basic shift in implicit premises and root metaphors.

A list of pioneering works in the systematic exploration of consciousness would include William James' *Varieties of Religious Experience*, F. W. H. Myers' *Human Personality and Its Survival of Bodily Death*, Richard Bucke's *Cosmic Consciousness*, Pitirim Sorokin's *The Ways and Power of Love*, and the writings of numerous Vedanta, Sufi, and Zen scholars. Among modern psychotherapists whose works fit into this same category are C. G. Jung, Roberto Assagioli, and Hubert Benoit. Several new scientific journals serve the field, in particular the *Journal of Transpersonal Psychology* and the *Journal of the Study of Consciousness*.

Research activity is currently significant in at least three approaches to altered states of consciousness: feedback of EEG signals, psychedelic chemicals, and classical (by which we mean sensory deprivation, yoga, autohypnosis, hypnosis, meditation, etc.). It should be noted that there are two recent and significant advances in this area. One is increased access to and voluntary control of diverse states of consciousness making them more available for exploration. The other is the appearance of physiological correlates to altered states (EEG, EMG, GSR, REM, etc.[*]). This latter is of extreme importance in a philosophy-of-science sense. The scientist of subjective experience is now much more in the position of the physicist studying an electron, or the astronomer studying a galaxy, in that he can observe a phenomenon (dream, satori state, etc.) which defies strict definition, but which can be studied through various correlates (alpha waves, rapid-eye-movement, verbal report, observable behavior, etc.). In effect, it means that the barrier between objective, public data and subjective, private data is gone for good and the legitimated boundaries for scientific scrutiny are thus extended.

---

[*] These abbreviations refer to electrical measures of physical processes: They stand for, respectively, electroencephalogram, electromyogram, galvanic skin response, and rapid eye movement.

The science of consciousness is in its infancy. Even so, some of its foreshadowings are evident. With the reclassification of man's subjective experience into the realm of empirical inquiry, we can anticipate an acceleration of research in this area. Consequently, there is new hope of consensus on issues—especially value issues—which have been at the root of conflict for centuries (just as earlier there came about consensus on the place of the Earth in the universe, and on the origin of man). The new science bids fair to incorporate the most penetrating insights of psychology, the humanities, and religion. These developments will have profound impacts on goal priorities in society, on our concepts of education, on the futher development and use of technology, and perhaps (as in the case of the Copernican revolution) on the distribution of power among social institutions and interest groups.

The real significance of a science of subjective experience and altered states of consciousness is that it is in this area that our individual and social values are rooted in experience and history. The development of such a science would redress what in retrospect is a puzzling discrepancy between the audacity with which man has pursued the physical, biological, and social sciences, and the timidity with which he has contemplated the possibility of developing a moral science. Already in the field of clinical psychology several scientists are proposing to formulate through their researchers "a natural value system, a court of ultimate appeal for the determination of good and bad, of right and wrong" (A. H. Maslow),[32] with "universal human value directions emerging from the experiencing of the human organism" (Carl Rogers).[33] What may be in the offing is new means of obtaining consensus on value questions, by submitting them to the test of what is ultimately wholesome for the whole man.

THE NATURE OF THE EMERGING PREMISES

Thus there appear to be in the present situation (1) a *need* for drastic change in the pathogenic premises which have generated the world macroproblem, (2) an emerging *force* for change in the Great Refusal of youth, and (3) an emerging *supportive metaphysic* coming jointly from the nascent science of consciousness and from the collective inner explorations of millions of more informal investigators, particularly among the youth. What is this new metaphysic or, if you will, new religion? It would seem premature to attempt to describe the end state of a conceptual revolution which, if it is taking place, is certainly only in its beginning stages. Yet the signs seem clear enough to warrant a prediction.

Aldous Huxley[34] was one of the first modern writers to suggest that an age-old set of basic assumptions about the nature of man was showing new strength. We shall borrow his term "the Perennial Philosophy":

> Philosphia Pereniss—the phrase was coined by Leibniz; but the thing—the metaphysic that recognizes a divine Reality substantial to the world of things and lives and minds; the psychology that finds in the soul something similar to, or even identical with, divine Reality; the ethic that places man's final end in one knowledge of the imminent and transcendent Ground of all being—the thing is immemorial and universal. Rudiments of the Perennial Philosophy may be found among the traditionary lore of primitive peoples in every region of the world, and in its fully developed forms it has a place in every one of the higher religions. A version of this Highest Common Factor in all preceding and subsequent theologies was first committed to writing more than twenty-five centuries ago, and since that time, from the standpoint of every religious tradition and in all the principal languages of Asia and Europe.

The basic proposition of the "Perennial Philosophy" is an experimental one, that man can under certain conditions attain to a higher awareness, a "cosmic consciousness," in which state he has immediate knowledge of a reality underlying the phenomenal world, in speaking of which it seems appropriate to use such words as infinite and eternal, Divine Ground, Brahman, Godhead, or Clear Light of the Void. From this vantage point, one's own growth and creativity and his participation in the evolutionary process are seen to be under the ultimate direction of a higher center (Atman, the Self of Vedantic writings, the Oversoul). Ordinary perceptions of one's life and of one's environment are likened to the perception, precognition of future events, levitation and other psychokinetic events, instant diagnosis and healing, etc., are only extraordinary, not *a priori* impossible.

The basic assumptions of positivistic science stand in relationship to the "Perennial Philosophy" much as Newtonian mechanics relates to relativistic physics: They are in no way invalidated for those aspects of human experience to which they are appropriate, but comprise a special case, a limited form of the more general theory. Similarly, the philosophies of materialism and idealism are to each other as the wave and particle theories of light and matter; each fits the world as seen with a particular mode of observation, and a complementary relationship holds between them.

Of course the "Perennial Philosophy" is not new to Western culture. It is present in the Rosicrucian and Freemasonry traditions. Its symbolism in the Great Seal of the United States, as it appears on the back of the one-dollar bill is testimony to the role it played in the formation of this country. It also appears in the Transcendentalism of Emerson, the Creative Evolution of Bergson, and the extensive writings of William James.

Whether one ascribes its recent popularity to increased intellectual openness and tolerance or to anxiety brought on by the nuclear threat, indications abound that increasing numbers of persons seem to be taking its premises seriously. Rising book sales in metaphysics, transcendental philosophy, Eastern religious philosophies, and parapsychology indicate growing interest in these related areas. Metaphysically oriented churches, societies, and study groups are much in evidence.

Part of society's thus-far negative reaction to monistic and Eastern kinds of beliefs as they have appeared in the hippie culture, the drug scene, the numerous cults, has been due to the fear that they would lead to quietism and withdrawal and, therefore, would undermine the social structure. Although it is true that these beliefs have been associated with the Eastern world, there is in fact nothing in the Perennial Philosophy which is contrary to virile and active participation in economic and political affairs. Neither are these premises in any way contrary to a high-technology society; they only say something about the ends to which that technology would be put.

Should these forces prevail and some sort of transcendentalist premises come to dominate the culture, the consequence would be a social and historical phenomenon of magnitude comparable with the Protestant Revolution. It might well be accompanied by as pervasive and varied changes in the whole sociocultural system—organizational forms, roles, norms, traditions, power concentrations, and social processes—as accompanied the rise of the Protestant ethic.

ALTERNATIVE FUTURES AND POLICY CHOICES

Now let us return to the alternative future histories. If the shift in basic premises which was postulated in the preceding section takes place, it would be congenial with a future history tending somewhat to the right in Figure 7-1, and aiming toward the upper center of Figure 7-2. Whether or not it is accompanied by such a change in the underlying metaphysic, such a path is about as favorable a one as can be found.

To approach such a favorable future history with a good level of habitability, and to avoid the clearly undesirable futures, seems an eminently reasonable aim. Assuming this, from the preceding discussion, at least six major societal tasks emerge:

1. Make a concerted direct attack on the most urgent aspects of the world macroproblem.

2. Establish mechanisms for control of technological development and application, and for extent and rate of industrialization.

3. Alter prevailing values, perceptions, and premises from those which have pathogenic aspects to others which are more conducive to maintenance of a habitable environment.

4. Establish a new sense of national purpose to put forth the effort which will be required to prevent serious further degradation of the habitability of the environment.

5. Meet the habitability demands of diverse groups, particularly poor, working class, and minority groups.

6. Ensure continuing habitability of various specific environments.

Each of these tasks may require new conceptualizations; for example, long-range analysis of the world macroproblem requires the concept of a homeostatic ecology for the entire bio-

ASPECTS OF THE HABITABILITY OF SOCIETAL TASKS

Societal task	a. New conceptual- izations	b. Research and development	c. Institu- tional changes	d. Programs and resources	e. Change processes
1. Make direct attack on aspects of the world macroproblem					
2. Control technologi- cal application and industrial development					
3. Alter values, perceptions, and premises					
4. Establish a new sense of national purpose					
5. Meet the habit- ability demands of varied groups					
6. Ensure continuing habitability of various specific environments					

Figure 7-3. Matrix of social tasks and habitability components.

sphere, and especially for the urbanized parts of it. They may require research and development, institutional changes, various kinds of programs and change processes. The matrix of Figure 7-3 suggests a systematic way of examining these tasks for specific policy implications. We are a long way from having adequate studies for the boxes in this matrix, let alone having started appropriate action. If the foregoing analysis is at all on the mark, the time is very late.

CONCLUDING REMARK

In this paper it has been suggested that the most crucial issues bearing on the world macroproblem are not necessarily the most obvious ones. If the wrong issues are addressed, the policy which emerges will inevitably be faulty. The most important issue in this nation may well not be one involving radicals versus conservatives, or youth versus middle age, or haves versus have-nots but rather one between those who assume that the future can be more or less like the present, versus those who are convinced that the pathogenic premises and values in the culture are going to have to be replaced by more constructive and humane ones.

The macroproblem which the world faces, and which is rapidly and ineluctably becoming more serious, is at root a problem of value and basic premises—in short, a moral problem. Thus the kind of leadership required in the world is moral leadership. The United States could reassert its role in this domain, but only if we first eliminate our own confusion. It would seem to follow that the paramount task for the nation is the fostering of a unifying national purpose, the development of a will to build toward a nation with liberty and justice—and a habitable environment—for all and to take the lead in the stewardship of the future to ensure continued habitability of spaceship Earth.

Chapter Eight

THE NATURE AND SCOPE OF
POPULATION RESEARCH

ARTHUR CAMPBELL

THE population problem cannot properly be viewed in isolation. The very importance of changes in the size, structure, and distribution of populations derives from the pervasiveness of their effects. Rising numbers and concentrations of people threaten not only levels of health and nutrition, but also affect the prevalence of poverty, the rate of economic development, the possibility for increasing levels of education, the prevention of crime and social disorganization, and many other derivative social problems. In other words, population variables constitute one set of factors in nearly all major social problems. Obviously it would be wrong to pretend that the solution of population problems would automatically solve all other problems, but it would also be a mistake to assume that problems involving public health, economic development, environmental quality, and social organization could be solved without major attention to the effects of population change.

Another reason for giving special and urgent attention to research that will modify population changes in our own country and throughout the world is that the effects of those changes tend to be cumulative and irreversible. The population of the world is now about 3.5 billion and may double by the end of this century. Even if it were possible to cut the rate of growth in half right now, there would still be almost five billion people by the year 2000. At least in the short run, changes of this order of magnitude are irreversible, assuming the continuation of our present moral standards. In other words, we cannot deliberately cancel high birth rates with high death rates. In fact it is pre-

Note: Presented at the Conference on Management of Consolidated Research Institutions for Population Research, Washington, D.C., February 12-13, 1970.

113

cisely this situation that we are trying to avoid by hastening reductions in birth rates. Eventually it may be possible to bring about reductions in birth rates that will cause populations to decline, but this is nothing that we can expect to happen in the near future.

The pervasiveness of the effects of population changes throughout social and economic systems and the cumulative and irreversible impact of these changes emphasize the need for rapid and massive efforts to understand the ramifications of population changes and to develop ways of influencing population growth and distribution that will hasten efforts to improve levels of living.

One of the major components of our efforts to bring about solutions to population problems must be to better understand the consequences of population change for social and economic systems and for the physical environment. It is only through the improved understanding of these consequences that we can formulate rational population goals. Just how poorly we understand the consequences of major population changes is illustrated by the recent experience of the United States. In the fifteen years between 1947 and 1962, birth rates in the United States remained at relatively high levels, compared with those observed in the prewar period.

This brought rapidly increasing numbers of children to public school systems throughout the country and is now having a heavy impact on our colleges. It is also severely testing the capacity of our economy to absorb young workers. The economic and human costs of this period of inflated fertility have never been counted, although we are all aware of their general nature. The present trends of fertility rates and of numbers of couples of reproductive age indicate that we are on the threshold of another increase in annual numbers of births that will again have severe consequences for various institutions in our society. In other words, in the United States, during the twentieth century we have structured fertility in such a way as to bring about successive waves of children and young people and, eventually, of mature adults and old people. The social and economic consequences of this patterning of fertility will be with us for many years to come.

An even more serious deficiency is our understanding of the relationship between population growth and improved levels of living in developed countries. For example, if we were asked now to determine the optimum timing for reaching a zero rate of population growth in the United States, we would have to admit that we do not have the research base needed to provide an answer. Obviously all countries of the world will eventually have to reach a zero or negative rate of population growth because no positive growth rate can continue indefinitely. The major questions are when to try to reach a zero rate of population growth and how to do so.

The exploration of the various effects of changes in population growth, structure, and density requires an interdisciplinary approach. This means that investigators in the fields of social, economic, and environmental change must take population explicitly into account in their research. Also, population specialists must learn more about the relevance of population change to other aspects of the social and economic system. How to bring the various disciplines together is, of course, one of the questions that we hope population research centers can help solve.

Population research must also help us learn a great deal more than we now know about the determinants of population change in order to provide a basis for the formulation of effective policies and programs to influence population change in desirable ways. Most of our recent research efforts have concentrated on the determinants of fertility partly because of the urgency of the need for reductions in growth rates in developing societies. A great deal of additional research must be done on the determinants of fertility because it is becoming increasingly obvious that we still do not know how to influence reproductive norms rapidly in societies where prolific childbearing is highly valued. It is apparent that for many women in such societies, the bearing and rearing of children provide important means of social recognition and personal fulfillment. Understandably they are not willing to modify their reproductive roles quickly.

In addition, children are often regarded as sources of labor and of economic support in old age. These attitudes are proving difficult to change in peasant societies, although major progress has been made in countries, such as Taiwan, where economic development and social change have been rapid.

An important element in the search for ways to moderate birth rates is the development of methods of contraception that are more satisfactory than those now in common use. Although the contraceptive pill is highly effective in preventing conception, it may also produce deleterious side effects which make administrators reluctant to use it in massive programs. The IUD also has major drawbacks—particularly the high rates of expulsion and of voluntary removal because of real or imagined side effects. It is important to find methods of contraception that are superior to these and to conventional methods because many of the people that must be reached in massive birth control programs are not sufficiently motivated to use methods that require frequent administration. Therefore, an important component of population research must be concerned with the development of new knowledge about the reproductive system that will lead to improved methods of fertility control. Along with this research there must be continuing attention to the side effects of physiological methods of fertility control. At the present time in the Center for Population Research, most of our funds are spent on these biomedical areas.

There are a number of interfaces between biomedical and behavioral areas of research that could take advantage of an interdisciplinary approach. For example, I think we have much to learn about the reaction of husbands and wives to particular kinds of contraceptive methods. Perhaps for some couples a modern male method would be more acceptable than a modern female method. Also, more work should be done on the perception of side effects of various methods of fertility control, including conventional methods.

An interdisciplinary approach is also needed within the social sciences to better understand the various social, psychological, and economic factors affecting fertility.

Childbearing patterns are closely related to couples' aspirations for themselves and their children and the values of the social groups to which they belong. But these personal goals and social values are not immutable. They are subject to modification by changing social and economic circumstances, by the presence or absence of personally fulfilling goals that may be viewed as alternatives to childbearing, and by the individual's increasing comprehension of his responsibility to future generations. Research is needed on methods of influencing reproductive choices that do not involve compulsion or penalties, although the latter possibilities have been seriously proposed. As populations grow it will become increasingly difficult to preserve humane and democratic values and at the same time reduce rates of population growth, but the effort must be made and can be accomplished only on the basis of research on the personal and social determinants of childbearing patterns. Such research could involve a number of disciplines; for example, psychology, sociology, anthropology, and communication.

Research is also needed on the determinants of migratory patterns inasmuch as many of our more serious social problems are related to overcrowding in central cities, urban sprawl in the suburban areas, and inadequate transportation between home and work. Many of these problems are intensified, if not caused, by patterns of migration that might be subject to the influence of government policies. As is the case with fertility patterns, migratory patterns result from personal aspirations and social values about which little is known at the present time. If we are ever to be able to influence the choices people make without the use of compulsion, we shall have to understand these determinants better than we do.

In addition to the kinds of research described above, efforts must be made to improve programs that are designed to bring contraceptive measures to couples who want them both in this country and abroad. Although responsibility for research on operational aspects of family planning programs within the United States has been assigned to the National Center for Family Planning Services rather than to the Center for Population Research, I believe that population research centers can contribute greatly to research on this important aspect of the population problem.

In summary, we hope that population research centers will contribute to our understanding of both the determinants and consequences of population change and that they will provide and continually improve the bases for formulating policies and programs to solve population problems throughout the world within the context of a humane and democratic value system.

IS THE UNIVERSITY DEALING WITH THE POPULATION PROBLEM?

Much of the research in the field of population, especially in the demographic area and in reproductive biology, is being done in the universities. But the universities themselves are being subjected to wracking pressures.

Against this background, eight chapters of this section are devoted to the question of whether the universities are capable of coping with the problem. L. K. Caldwell, Ronald Freedman, William Liu, and Ansley Coale go into the strengths and weaknesses built into the idea of having universities as hosts to such centers.

In what might be called a projection, W. W. Harman, D. W. North, and I. J. Weinstein describe the sort of center that might be able to deal with the kinds of questions we assume will be involved in meeting the population problem head-on. William Linvill follows with a provocative chapter on what part a center might play in a university, in a turbulent and unpredictable world.

The section concludes with the penetrating but perhaps cynical view of a professor, Arnold Nash, and the view of a much-too-ignored group, the student. The student, James Pepper, cannot be considered in any sense a radical, except perhaps as he expresses the views of the vanguard of tomorrow's leaders, and except as these views conflict with establishment convictions.

Chapter Nine

THE UNIVERSITY CENTER:
ITS REQUIREMENTS AND PROBLEMS

LYNTON K. CALDWELL

A CONTINUING and widely pervasive problem of higher education has been the accommodation of studies that cross
disciplinary lines. Characteristically, these studies are directed
toward the solution of social problems or toward development
of skills and understanding that require multidisciplinary inputs. Among the more common of them are urban studies, environmental studies, public administration, public policy for
science and technology, and population dynamics. These fields
of study are not always organized under these particular names;
and they are sometimes attached administratively to a single
school, department, or division of the university. But they have
a separate identity that is usually distinguished by their designation as programs, institutes, or centers.

The relationships between these centers and their immediate
hosts are not always happy. The tasks and orientations of the
centers virtually mandate a multidisciplinary character. Thus
they are often seen from the viewpoint of any single discipline
as prejudicial to the commitment and values of the discipline,
and as competitors for personnel, loyalty, and funds. Yet because some faculty members and administrators see advantages
to themselves or to institutional convenience through enforced
association with a department or school, a center is often held
captive by its host. Academic administrators have been known
to insist on assigning multidisciplinary efforts to the department
or school of the university most apparently concerned.

A common argument for this departmentalizing of centers is
the alleged need to simplify the "reporting" structure of the
university—to reduce the number of separate units reporting directly to deans or chancellors. There have been instances in

121

which programs, institutes, or centers failing to fit a discipline-oriented structure were abolished or driven to seek hospitality in other universities. As administrative aptitude has not historically appeared to be a major consideration in the selection of university administrators, the effort to simplify structure may in these instances be more in the nature of concessions to administrative incapacity or convenience than to any soundly conceived theory of university organization.

Opposition to centers has developed a rationale that usually includes some combination of the following points:

1. *The functions of the university include teaching and the advancement of knowledge (research), but do not extend to problem-solving or to the analysis of policy issues.* The line between the traditional functions of higher education and the training, problem-solving, and policy-study activities of the multiversity is difficult to define. It is a largely theoretical proposition if one examines what actually happens in universities—in "private" institutions such as Harvard and Stanford as well as in the great state and land grant universities. Nevertheless, the argument for scholastic purity, in principle, continues to be made.

2. *When extensions of university activity beyond its traditional functions cannot be avoided, they must be firmly tied to the disciplines, or incorporated within their departmental structures;* otherwise, these activities will be unable to obtain the respect or cooperation of the departments, and will be cut off from the knowledge and wisdom alleged to reside therein.

3. *Centers increase administrative overhead, and are therefore uneconomic.* This argument sidesteps the possibility that a cost-effectiveness study of a center might justify increased overhead; and it equally overlooks the overhead of center-type programs that may be hidden in departmental expenditures.

4. *Centers are unnecessary because there is nothing that prevents individual faculty members or students from informal cooperation and joint efforts.* In fact, almost every-

thing in the conventional organization of the university discourages the collaboration except for relatively short-term, clearly focused efforts. This argument is premised on the unexpressed assumption that the proper place for the scholar is in his discipline (as presently defined). It is a counsel of intellectual conservatism, uncongenial to the emergence of novel configurations of knowledge and of hybrid-disciplines. The interdepartmental committee (used sparingly) is seen as the appropriate mechanism for obtaining multidisciplinary cooperation.

5. *Centers more often reflect discontent or "empire-building" among faculty members than a genuine commitment to multidisciplinary problem-solving.* They perpetuate faculty antagonisms that could be resolved in some less cumbersome and expensive manner. Once created, the center may lose its vitality when the personal needs of its sponsor have been satisfied; it may linger on as an academic derelict no longer useful, but difficult to abolish. This objection may be valid for particular centers, but it is hardly less applicable to university committees. Moreover, the exploitation of organizational structure for personal ambition or grievance has been known to occur *within* departments and even at the highest levels of academic administration.

Nevertheless, centers exist. Despite biases and presumptions against them, they continue to be created. Their establishment has frequently been encouraged by Federal and foundation funding. The desire of the funding agency to have a clearly designated, responsible, and continuing recipient for its money has commonly been a factor in the establishment of centers. University presidents, deans, and department heads have sometimes reluctantly acquiesced in the establishment of a multidisciplinary center in order to obtain outside funds or, as a concession, to attract or retain a scholar of note.[35] But the basic problem of centers is not made fully explicit in this list of difficulties and objections. It is embedded in conflicting interpretations of the functions of the university, in assessment of priorities among those functions, and in the structuring of the university to serve its varied missions with equal effectiveness.

WHY CENTERS?

With all their attendant hazards, the compulsion to create and maintain centers must be strong. They are numerous and many are long-lived. It is difficult to generalize about the circumstances leading to their establishment. Some of the reasons suggested by the critics of centers may be valid in particular instances; for example, personal or pecuniary motives have, in fact, played a part in the establishment of some centers. The principal reason for centers, however, is that they are necessary to carry on work and to attain objectives that would not be feasible under the traditional subdivisions of the university. We have already alluded to some of the reasons for creating centers in discussing the arguments raised against them. It may be useful at this point to summarize these reasons so as to see more clearly the nature of the problems they present:

1. The urge to apply knowledge to socially relevant ends prompts some scholars to seek institutional means conducive to the attainment of these ends. There is a "moral imperative" behind the formation of many of the action-oriented centers.

2. The inputs required to attain these social objectives transcend the arbitrary scope of any single discipline. Thus goal-directed or problem-solving institutional means must be multidisciplinary, interdisciplinary, or supradisciplinary in scope.

3. Because departmental organization is normally designed only for teaching and individual research within the discipline, it is not adaptable to multidisciplinary or group efforts. The discipline-oriented department serves a set of values that cannot easily be combined with a social-action, problem-solving focus. Some academic departments have established centers within or attached to the department to enable members of the same discipline to focus on problem-solving or action-oriented efforts more effectively.

4. The logistical and procedural difficulties of interdepart-

mental collaboration tend to force the creation of centers as a way out of the complexities and frustrations of trying to work through departmental machinery and departmental jealousies aroused in the allocations of faculty salaries, time, and research assistance.

5. A center facilitates the coherent definition of a goal or mission without conformity to the parameters or perspectives of a particular discipline.

6. A center provides for continuity of attention to an area of concern going beyond the temporary involvement of particular individuals. It thus affords a continuing facility capable of building upon previous work and experience and of maintaining a focus on problems or phenomena that present continuing challenges to society.

If the foregoing reasons afford cogent and plausible explanations for the creation of centers, why does their existence create a problem? Why cannot centers be looked upon as normal, logical extensions of the functions of the university to new types of intellectual efforts called forth by exigencies of the times? Many people do view them in this light, but many others see them as exceptional or incidental to the true function of the university. To the extent that this view prevails, there is "a problem of centers."

WHAT IS THE PROBLEM?

The problem is how to redefine the mission of the university and to restructure its organization so that among its missions it may serve the purposes for which centers are created. Expressed another way, the problem of centers is that the contemporary university has not found a generally accepted way to incorporate the new tasks of problem-focused education within its regular structure.

This problem, as most problems, is subdivisible into component parts. Incongruities and incompatibilities among the parts have added complexities to the total problem. To resolve the problem, one must not attack the general attitude or point of view that constrains the university, but the detailed aspects of the problem in academic policies and procedures must also be considered. The tendency to treat centers as exceptional and probably ephemeral has frequently resulted in denying them the status and facilities that would greatly enhance the prospect of their success. The criticism of centers often assumes the character of self-fulfilling prophecy—the centers fail to achieve full effectiveness because their critics are in position to deny them the resources or status that would increase the probability of their success.

We have already cited several major objections raised against centers. Now let us look at the actual difficulties that most centers encounter in trying to fulfill a function in the university that influential members of the faculty and administration tend to view with misgiving or condescension.[36]

1. Lack of influence in the academic system of rewards and penalties is a major handicap. The power to reward and to punish lies almost wholly in the disciplines (represented by departments) and in the professional schools. In the absence of strong institutional support, the scholars and staff associated with a center are almost wholly dependent upon their departments with respect to faculty status, compensation, teaching load, and academic duties and privileges generally.

2. Closely related is the frequent lack of an autonomous faculty or administration in the center. This places the center almost wholly at the prerogative of the department on personnel matters. When, as often happens, university policy requires an appointee to a center also to obtain appointment in a department, the departments are given a *de facto* veto over center appointments.

3. Unless similar centers exist in other universities, a center may suffer from lack of external psychic support. The regular disciplines and professions being organized in all major universities afford their members career mobility and support for common academic goals, expectations, and values. Centers need an interuniversity "critical mass" to obtain this mobility and psychic support. In brief, centers need strengthening through the presence of minimal numbers of their own kind.

4. Centers frequently are denied a teaching function and

have no way to influence effectively the university curriculum. Departments tend to be jealous of encroachments upon their academic territories. Multidisciplinary centers may impinge upon many territories and thus arouse anxieties in many places.

5. Centers often are dependent upon sources of funding external to the general university budget. This dependency reduces their ability to make long-range plans or commitments, and to this extent makes them less attractive than the regular departments when career opportunities are considered.

6. Because of their presumed *ad hoc* and exceptional status, they are seldom equipped with means to redirect and revitalize their efforts. To an extent much greater than the regular disciplines, the centers need flexibility to deal with the evolving phases of the problems that they attack. Not all centers are intended for permanence, and for these some appropriate means of termination should be provided.

7. Centers frequently lack philosophic justification for their objectives. Their founders have too seldom addressed themselves to their roles in the total functions of the university. Their opposition usually relies upon the so-called classic definition of the meaning of a university which can be presented with literary eloquence and the sanctions of long and respectable tradition.

The organization of universities has changed; the contemporary university has moved a long way from its medieval ancestor. And yet it seems evident that the university has been unable to reorganize itself to keep pace with the new knowledge that it largely creates. Bernard Berelson concluded in his study of graduate education in the United States, that an entirely new university was needed every fifty years to assist in the reintegration of knowledge.[37] Possibly Berelson would agree, in assessing the present expansion of knowledge, that his remedy alone might be too little and too late. The obsolescence that is invading nearly every institution of contemporary society has been especially insidious in the universities. A considerable degree of student unrest and faculty disaffection may fairly be attributed to the failure of the universities to be relevant to the real problems of the world.

RESTRUCTURING THE UNIVERSITY

The problem of centers is therefore really a problem of the functions of the university and of the adequacy of its guiding concepts and organization to its missions in the modern world. The centers are overt symptoms of the slowness of universities to redefine their missions to meet the circumstances of a rapidly changing environment. Some imaginative new designs for university structures have been proposed,[38] but little innovation has actually taken place. An obvious but often overlooked and widely resisted reason is that the university is poorly constituted to reform itself; it needs help from without.

The mobility of faculty and students in American universities imposes a practical restraint upon innovation. No institution can afford to depart very far from the organizational norm of other universities. There is danger in becoming incongruent with the rest of American higher education. When this happens, faculty cannot be easily recruited, credits will not transfer, students will be reluctant to enter nonconforming institutions, and graduates will not easily be placed. The myth of university self-governance does not stand-up well under realistic examination of the constraints on structural change. Major innovations such as those induced by the Morrill Land Grant Act, have resulted from outside interposition, usually through federal funding (as in the National Defense Education Act) or in area studies promoted by private foundations as well as by federal action.

To obtain the critical mass of interuniversity involvement required for the viability of new or multidisciplinary programs, sufficient nationwide action must be induced to provide career mobility and meaningful communication among workers in the field. In most of the center program areas, this critical mass has not been reached and the field of studies is amorphous, unbalanced, and sometimes duplicative, with major aspects of the subject matter area neglected. The advantage of additive or complementary studies is largely lost in the absence of any central clearinghouse or communication network or center for the research field. Concerted attack upon urgent social problems of population, environment, public health, science policy, or public administration cannot be made with the present disparate and *ad hoc* organizational structure.

In those areas of social policy where the national need is most urgent, an adequately funded national program of assistance to university efforts is required. But the program would fall short of needed effectiveness if it proceeded on the assumption that the universities could unilaterally restructure themselves to do the job. It would be naive to suppose that a federal agency could restructure American universities without their consent and cooperation; it would be equally naive to believe that the universities can or will do so without outside inducement.

The most fruitful Government-university relationship might be almost the opposite of the pattern that prevails today, which is for the federal agency to defer to the university on how a program is organized and situated within the structure of the university, but to be niggling over details of expenditure and procedures.[39] Federal funding often falls short of the help it is intended to bring to the university center, because the funding agency prefers to overlook some of the most apparent facts of life upon university campuses. Federal resources to promote multidisciplinary collaboration on socially relevant problems are thus often allocated where they are the least needed, or prove ineffective where needed because the agency has had no strategy to reinforce the efforts of the center to establish an academic climate conducive to multidisciplinary work.

A significant number of studies on problem-focused research have concluded that universities are not the best places to do this work. New corporation-types of institutions are being proposed to deal with problems of environment, population, and technology. Proposals are being discussed to redirect the work of the National Laboratories (e.g. at Argonne, Brookhaven, Oak Ridge) toward these purposes. Action along these lines may be taken and may be fruitful, but it ought not preclude the possibility that the universities themselves may be changed—and with benefit to their traditional missions.

In brief, the problem of centers is the problem of the suitability of the contemporary university to serve the relevant needs of the society that supports it. Social needs that are relevant to the mission of a university or a university-like institution are those requiring the inputs of knowledge and skill that are largely generated and localized in these institutions. This knowledge and the needs that it could serve have grown more rapidly than the organizing and delivery machinery of the university. The restructuring of the university has been retarded by conceptual obsolescence and by institutional constraints inherent in the system of higher education in America. Centers have been an *ad hoc* answer to the organizational problem. A better answer is needed, but to obtain it the concerted action of the Federal Government, the universities, and perhaps of the foundations will be required.

Chapter Ten

SOME NOTES ON UNIVERSITY CENTERS

RONALD FREEDMAN

IN THE United States most of the significant research on the social and economic causes and consequences of population trends has been done at a smaller number of university centers or by students trained at those centers. Despite some recent expansion, the total number of people working or trained in these university centers is small in relation to the magnitude of the research problems and programs to which attention has recently been directed. Any significant growth in the next five years or so in this part of the population field will require either expanding these centers or drawing personnel from them for the socio-demographic component of the work. Large new programs elsewhere are likely to be understaffed or are likely to wreck the going research and training organizations built over the years in the existing centers.

Without making invidious comparisons, I think I can say that most of the significant work has been done at no more than five or ten first-rank universities. Work in population is going on at many more universities, but this usually involves teaching, and less often, research by one or two men. This extension of population work in many more institutions is extremely important in putting population into the curriculum of large numbers of social scientists and of educated citizens. However, these dispersed activities are unlikely to provide a sufficient critical mass either for significant research or for major training programs in the next decade.

There seems to be a prima facie case for strengthening existing centers as a matter of high priority, without ruling out establishment of a few large-scale, radically new kinds of institutions.

The existing centers provide a range of size, history, and emphasis. Most of them are attached to departments of sociology or economics or of public health, or combinations of these. With the exception of Johns Hopkins University and scattered earlier work in departments of biostatistics, the participation of the schools of public health is of such recent origin that it is too early to evaluate their research product. The work in established centers, like Princeton, Chicago, Michigan, and North Carolina, goes back twenty years or more. There is a substantial record that can be evaluated for its contribution to the field and relevance to current concerns. Past performance is the best predictor for the future, in my judgment, so evaluating these centers and their future course should be much easier than deciding whether new centers will be viable.

These university centers do not fit any uniform pattern. Few attempt to encompass the field, and none does. Their differences in emphasis are a valuable resource. I deplore any attempt to move them toward a uniform multidisciplinary format. Of course, any university centers in which holistic, interdisciplinary approaches are feasible and desired by competent participants should be encouraged, if they are promising of productive results. However, to insist, for example, on a public-health involvement for the sociologically or economically oriented centers would rule out such universities as Princeton and Chicago which have eminent records and capabilities.

So far as I know, no one of the existing population centers has essential core financial support for more than a few years, at best. Except for the direct costs of formal teaching, it is completely unrealistic to expect the universities to provide the financing, in view of current pressures on them to meet the instructional costs for rising enrollments.

Building a center of excellence requires a critical mass of people, experience, data-accumulation, and a tradition of intellectual interaction, which are not feasible without substantial long-range support for infrastructure from outside the university. Contracts and project grants are an important supplement. But they can be the basis for research and training of quality only if there are basic supporting funds for the facilities and framework for continuing work and commitment of a staff. Current programs for large-scale research contracts in the social-science aspects of the field are ill advised, in my opinion, unless there is support for centers in which a significant proportion of such contracts and grants can be accepted, with reasonable prospects of useful results.

Our Population Study Center at the University of Michigan is not necessarily either typical or a model. However, as a concrete basis for discussion, perhaps it will be useful to describe some of its features and problems.

1. We operate on an apprenticeship principle for training. Graduate students have the opportunity to learn how large-scale population research is done by involvement in ongoing work aiming to meet professional standards. Our graduates are in demand because many of them know how to produce.

2. Almost all professional staff members have academic appointments in sociology and economics. They teach courses in population studies, ecology, urban studies, methodology, stratification. The departments pay for all teaching. Such staff members get a fraction of their time released for research at the Center from the Center's basic support funds on a rotating basis. They also receive services from the Center which supports work on small projects or on the initial development or completion of larger projects. For projects requiring large field operations or other large expenditures, the staff member is expected to get a research contract or grant. In recent years, such additional project funds have constituted about 30 to 40 percent of the total money administered at the Center.

3. The formal teaching by staff members involved graduate and undergraduate students from many departments. During the most recent twelve-month period the basic course in population studies was taught in four different forms from different audiences and enrolled about three hundred students. The basic graduate course had as many students from other departments as from sociology and economics.

4. The Center's research emphases are defined by the interests of the individual staff members, rather than by a central mission-oriented research program. However, informal processes inevitably result in selected lines of emphasis.

5. The recruitment of staff and the admission of students are

much affected by the requirements and standards of the University. This means that potential staff members who may be quite adequate for a field or research mission sometimes have a difficult career line in the University. For students, our problem, shared by other universities, is that motivated applicants, especially from abroad, may not be able to meet the high admission standards of a first-class university or to compete with this generation's bright students in the general basic social and economic curricula. There have been special nondegree programs for such students, but, increasingly, they compete with enrollment pressures on the regular degree programs. In any case, many foreign students want or need degrees as part of their career line at home.

6. In our particular Center there is a regular close connection to sociology and economics. Further, we are linked with centers in public health and medicine in a University-wide Program on Population, which has a principal operational mission making small grants for research to people not in the three centers. So far, this has involved people in history, anthropology, southeast Asian studies, geography, psychology, the Chinese Center, and political science. Apart from such formal arrangements, we have had informal associations for research and teaching by our staff members with the Chinese Center, Center for Research in Economic Development, the Japanese Center, Anthropology, Psychology, the Survey Research Center, Public Health, the Institute for Public Administration, and the School of Social Work. The two other Michigan centers have had interaction with a range of other units. All of us depend, of course, on the University Computing Center, the business offices, and similar central facilities.

7. Our continuing work in Taiwan (begun in 1961) represents one kind of model for intensive cumulative population work.[40] It has as an explicit orienting framework the idea that the family-planning program is an unprecedented attempt at organizing intervention in reproductive institutions deeply rooted in the social and economic institutions of the society. In Taiwan, as in many other places, the whole system of relationships is changing. We are trying to study major aspects of the system, its

changes, and effects of the intervention in changing the rate of change. While this is our guiding general framework, the system is too large and with too many unknowns to study it in a holistic fashion. Besides, this would make it difficult to study and serve the current needs of the planned program of change which is both our entry and our obligation. Our cooperative work with the Chinese has involved the following:

a. Strengthening the statistical systems which record social and demographic indicators for the 362 local areas as well as for the whole island.

b. Developing data systems for collecting program inputs and outputs for the units which serve as the basis for the on-going general statistical series.

c. Developing a local research capability which is used for periodic sample surveys of the general childbearing population, the population of program clients, and for *ad hoc* surveys and experiments on a large variety of problems which emerge over time.

d. Providing training for about a half-dozen key Taiwanese research staff members at Michigan and for several others elsewhere.

e. Developing data resources cumulatively both in Taiwan and at Michigan, which have served as the basis for a large number of research publications both in Taiwan and at Michigan, including at least a half-dozen dissertations.

f. Continuously giving priority to data-based answers to the questions the program people ask. At least as important has been our role in bringing to the attention of the administrators pertinent data-based answers to questions that they should be asking.

g. Probing progressively into a very large number of variables on the individual, local, and national levels, which are only a sample of what is involved. To list a few we have dealt with: mortality, migration, education, population density, urbanization, many measures of fertility and the family life cycle, fecundability, lactation and amenorrhea, savings and investment, traditional versus modern consumption, contraception, abortion, sterilization, birth-spacing, age at marriage, values, and aspirations for children and family and self, and program inputs at various levels. We do not have for any country, for any time, knowledge of the interactions among what we guess now to be some of the key variables in fertility change. Beginning to approach that in one population is our modest but complex goal in Taiwan.

h. Serving as continuing consultants to the outside funding agencies as well as to several key groups in Taiwan. After an initial two-year residence of a member of our staff, this has involved about sixteen short-term trips. An invaluable resource has been our capacity through a limited flexibility in our funding mechanism to make small grants of money to facilitate work that is either too small in scale or too urgent in time to bring to the attention of major funding agencies.

i. We have concentrated most of our research and consulting work abroad in other countries near to Taiwan (e.g. Korea, Hong Kong, Malaysia, and India). This permits combining trips to save valuable time of scarce professional personnel. It limits an already wide range of cultural contexts. It facilitates developing essential and time-consuming knowledge of local people and resources, because regional centers and conferences are likely to link people from these areas. Nevertheless, individual Center members of our staff have done or are planning to do work in such other places as Turkey, North Africa, Europe, and Mexico. We have no Center dictum limiting work to Asia, but there is a natural informal gravitation to this area. We usually advise students from Latin America and Africa, for example, to go to universities with field experience and programs in those areas. I am skeptical at this stage of efforts to serve all countries and continents from any university center. The overhead investment in developing knowledge of the regions is simply too great.

8. While our work in Taiwan involves a major set of projects, the work at the Population Center covers a wide range of other topics. For example, another important line is on the nature, causes, and consequences of the process of social stratification in the American population, centering on the work of my colleague O. D. Duncan.[41] This relates, for example, to the barriers

and channels for educational and occupational achievement and mobility in our changing population.

9. The Center also serves as a base from which our staff can serve as consultants or members in a wide variety of organizations, committees, and programs in the field. These include the United Nations, our Census Bureau, AID, the foundations, the population programs of a number of countries, professional organizations, etc.

10. The Center is oriented to basic research and to providing freedom for capable researchers. However, it is the fact that much of our work has in the long-run been policy oriented or had policy implications that have brought it into the public arena. Thus, for example, clusters of research projects in Taiwan, Hong Kong, and Malaysia have related to population and other programs in those countries, but they have also been used in quite a few other countries and in teaching and consulting both by our staff and others. The work on U.S. social-stratification processes is receiving wide attention with reference to the problems of educational and occupational opportunity in this country. Our work on fertility, family planning, and the reproduction norms of the American population over the last fifteen years has been one basis for policy recommendations, debates, and discussions in a wide variety of contexts, although it was hardly oriented to that purpose in 1955 and earlier when the issues about population now being discussed were hardly considered fit for public discussion.

11. Members of our staff, like those at other centers, are trying simultaneously, to be research workers, administrators, teachers, consultants, and to handle policy-oriented assignments. This imposes considerable strain especially where the work involves foreign travel. At first-class universities the desire to do all these things at a high standard increases the burden. More specialization and a larger number of people together with a small number of professional generalists and/or nonacademic administrators seems to be a rational way out. But, I think this option will be accepted only with anguish and doubts by those now in the field.

I am not in the position to generalize about the university centers which specialize on the social and economic aspects of demography. Therefore, I have taken the easy path of describing the one I know well. I hope that questions, criticisms, and comparisons arising from this concrete example may provide some useful points of discussion. Full discussion and careful consideration certainly should precede any radical change in course away from the university centers, whose records are available, and into new research structures whose effectiveness can only be conjectured.

Chapter Eleven

REFLECTIONS OF A UNIVERSITY
POPULATION RESEARCH CENTER DIRECTOR

WILLIAM T. LIU

THOSE of us interested in population, in terms of numbers and distribution, and in terms of its potential for good or evil, its probable progression, its perplexities and paradoxes, have sometimes been considered scientific dolts because we can produce so few precise answers to the wide assortment of philosophic, ethical, moral, and social questions. We have moved ahead, but we have a fearful distance yet to cover; I will attempt herein to give at least a rudimentary verbal map of some of the routes I think we should follow.

So far as research is concerned, our progress has been encouraging. This is especially so considering the fact that the problem has been fully recognized only recently in the broader historical sense, and considering also the fact that the people themselves are only now beginning to concede that population growth deserves their deep concern, and a more intensive application of highly advanced techniques.

We have some idea of what a major center for population study should be. There are many fine and well-established centers in this country, each with a remarkable record of significant contributions in research and training. We also have some idea of what a population planning center should be. Applications of existing knowledge about reproductive biology in the field of conception control have been made in many parts of the world; results have been fed back to these centers for evaluation; field workers have been trained, the data collection apparatus has been refined, and statistics evaluated. More significantly, we have seen in recent years the combination of population programs with public-health training which gives family planning impetus and more effective programs. The injection of public health into family planning gives maternal and child health, nutrition, cancer detection, sanitation, and even sex education their proper roles in the total and comprehensive effort to curtail births and enhance economic opportunities for millions. It seems to me that all that needed to be done has indeed been *done,* and done rather well so far. The expansion of the field from the almost exclusive concern of the demographic experts to include behavioral scientists, educators, physicians, and even biologists within a short span of one decade seems remarkable indeed. I think that the present trend of such expansion and integration of problem-centered and application-oriented multidisciplinary centers is going to continue and, for every conceivable reason, should continue.

There are, however, some disturbing thoughts about the way we perceive a program and the way to solve problems. These uneasy feelings have been expressed by many people in different words. I shall now take up some of these issues on hand and attempt to articulate some that may be controversial at this time.

In an attempt to examine the utilization of resources and ideas to solve problems of enormous magnitude, we have become accustomed to turning to science and technology. In the context of a technological culture, the measures of success or failure depend upon keen minds and skills working together to bring about desired results. In the field of reproductive biology, we shall soon have the capabilities to control the sex of our offspring and to influence the genetic characteristics of future generations. We have been able for quite some time now to separate completely sex from procreation, by a variety of means. We are able to control not only birth but aging, infectious diseases, and even biological death. It seems, however, that even with high confidence in science and technology our creativity falters when we come to project the economic health and population pressures of many of the developing countries. The idea of merely increasing, even doubling the technological effort when the goal of such effort is unclear, raises in the gravest form the question of the responsibility to accept the consequences of man's relentless effort to conquer nature and his environment. There is, it seems to me, a real dilemma between the concept of technical efficiency, on the one hand, and the sense of responsibility, on the other. And the ultimate question remains as Robert Hutchins asks: "Who is to conquer whom?"

Hence the dilemma of our effort here is not to be dismissed lightly. There has never been a *moral neutrality* in science. From what I could read on population efforts in recent years, no one has yet denied the moral consequences of these concerted efforts. Serious as these thoughts may be, there has been remarkably little discussion on the possible consequences of some of the best-engineered programs. Social sciences, like medical sciences and biology, have made tremendous inroads into the policy-making apparatus of our National Government. Social research has become an increasingly important factor in our social and political life. The social scientists, like the biological scientists, are therefore confronted ever more sharply with the question of what kind of social force their research represents. What is the nature of the social processes that research is helping to foster, the trend of social values that it is helping to promote? What is the human good?

At the risk of being subjective, I would like to recall a series of conferences held at Notre Dame a few years ago beginning in 1964 and extending through 1967. The initial interests at Notre Dame on population began when a small group of theologians and social and biological scientists met in almost total seclusion. The group started out by asking questions on the responsibilities of the State and the Church on problems of increasing population. These discussions covered many broad questions. What is the family in our time? What is the obligation of human love and the responsibilities of the couple with respect to children brought into the world? The group was concerned with the most fundamental issues of morality or ethics which, until recently, have been dealt with on a most practical ground. Obviously not one of these queries is easy to answer. In short, the problem of population growth with which we are dealing has profound and troubling implications in the basic value references of man. These discussions at least began to identify problems far beyond the cold facts of statistics on human growth patterns. It is on the basis of these understandings of the problems that Notre Dame began to move into practical areas of scientific research on family and fertility.

We should speculate on what seems to be lacking in current efforts to establish sufficient criteria in evaluating population policies. This is a ticklish issue and I shall try very hard to articulate the essence of my argument. In a recent thought-provoking article on the family planning programs, Berelson[42] asks for a population program which will be "scientifically available, politically acceptable, administratively feasible, economically justifiable, and *morally tolerated depending upon people's perceptions of consequences.*" (italics mine) We have practically no knowledge—save large scale KAP* studies, which deal primarily with attitudes toward family size, family limitation, and the use of contraceptives by individual couples—concerning the attitudes of peoples toward population policies and how changes in procreation may alter the family life of men. We have no reason to believe that the failure to convince many couples in economically underdeveloped countries to limit family size is caused primarily by their ignorance or by their indifference to hunger, sickness, and suffering. It is perhaps more accurate to think that the reluctance to prevent unlimited conceptions is an indication that their interrelated systems of social organization and motivation, traditionally geared to what appears to us to be a relatively large family size, have not yet been affected sufficiently by socioeconomic change to make a smaller family size desirable.

I would like to suggest two general guideposts in our search for causes of problems with which we are concerned. First, that the instance of high fertility and other dynamics of demographic behavior can only be fully understood in terms of a host of interrelated factors which are parts of the social and value system of a society; some of these are undoubtedly more important than others, as they are closer to the family life. Second, that these factors are themselves structured differently in any two societies.

---

* Knowledge, Attitudes, and Practices (popularly referred to as KAP studies).

A corollary to these points is that an oversimplified answer to such complex problems is not only factually doubtful but also logically unacceptable; for example, man everywhere at all times desires to improve his lot; this is a psychological constant. But the degree of demand for the control of family size differs from time to time, from one country to another, from one cultural and social area to another. This is a variable. In order to explain the varying degrees of demand for a more effective conception control, we must study other variables, probably in the structure of traditional values and institutions. The pace of change in some instances creates great strain on and under the traditional system. In others, the changes are buttressed by the traditional institutions and values.

These and many other concerns bring up the need for some centers to assume a responsibility to take up the whole spectrum of legal, economic, social, and moral issues related to the policy of population. Though this is a long and painful task with seemingly only indirect bearing on the action level, it may be regarded as no little gain to be able to achieve an understanding in depth so essential in evaluating policies and consequences of actions. When dealing with problems involving nonpostponable human wants, however, there is a particular desire to bring such information to bear upon the specific forces resulting from calculated and conscious policy decisions, as well as from drift and inertia. I think that it is important to identify both the *inertial* and the *directive* forces that have caused the lack of concern or the lack of visible results in depressing population growth. It is important to identify, for example, which force or combination of forces serves as resistance; which buttress the change of population behavior. This does not imply that in our concern to discover a solution we must declare a moratorium on moral beliefs. The argument is that we should find a clearly defined and practically creative set of normative or moral principles which is now lacking.

Second, there is a conspicuous absence of research work done on the psychological aspects of family planning. Added to this is the lack of concern of the psychological consequence of users of one method of contraception over the other. We know little, for example, about the psychological effects of the rhythm method, so widely used by couples in this country and elsewhere, with respect to the conjugal relations vis-à-vis the female controlled methods such as the pill, IUD, and injections. What are the effects of these two psychologically different systems on the finer feelings of the woman as the wife and the man as the husband, their sex-role identity and their feelings for each other?

Undoubtedly, how husband and wife are adjusted to each other depends upon the social context within which the conjugal unit functions. We have a dearth of research reports dealing with micro-details of conjugal interactions both in developed countries and in developing countries, yet little has been done to collate even these materials in a systematic way to focus on reproductive behavior. Four years ago at Notre Dame we made a special attempt to bring the "family" back into "family planning," to borrow Reuben Hill's phraseology, with research and training efforts directly steered toward this end in both Latin America and the Philippines. It is my deepest conviction that we need more efforts in these areas.

Third, with respect to the public health aspect of family planning, the importance of designing a kind of highly technical and functionally specific discipline or medicine to fit into a cultural environment requires particular consideration. When we move from the cultural belief system to the institution of health and medicine, it becomes crucial to find the proper role of medical practices and training which is culturally appropriate rather than technically sophisticated. Leaving aside for the time being the uneven distribution of medical and paramedical personnel between urban and rural areas of developing societies, even if a crash program on family limitation is introduced, there is no health distributive mechanism to promote such a program when the training of the majority of practitioners does not include experience in dealing directly with people in their natural environment. In areas where modern doctors and government midwives are available, oftentimes the training of highly sophisticated personnel increases the distance between the professionals and village women. This presumably could be true in some parts of any country, including the United States.

The interplay of the culturally defined belief system and the professional-client relationship is of particular importance in promoting the public-health concept of family planning. The complex pattern of insufficient use of modern medicine, the need for midwives and folkhealers and many of the latent social functions they perform, and the interpersonal influence of older women on younger women are all significant in the planning of maternal and child-health clinics. The argument further asserts that the employment of modern medicine in some of the underdeveloped areas must overcome some cultural resistance. This requires first of all, the change of the cognitive system with respect to the causes of infecundity, high fertility, and problems related to childbirths; and secondly, a conversion to, or the establishment of faith in, modern medicine. These are two separate processes.

All of these experiences, gained in work with cultures other than our own, point to the necessity of introducing more social science training in family planning. They point also to the need for program planners in nontechnological cultural environments to do more practical work in order to overcome some of the resistance to modern medicine and Western medicine men. One additional point is that such training will enable indigenous professionals to practice in their own countries, in cultures consonant with their practical training and within their moral and ethical frameworks. Because of the lack of medical facilities and the folk beliefs in conception and childbirths in rural villages, indigenous medical students not only do not wish to practice in rural areas, they often cannot do so—a point which shows up in our studies in the Philippines. It seems to me that rural medical practice needs a special kind of training not ordinarily obtainable in medical schools. This is where some of the best-equipped training centers failed.

In the same vein, when it comes to evaluating a centers program, we need better defined criteria which are lacking mainly because we often confuse the ultimate goals of the center. The organization of collective and interdisciplinary efforts in solving problems needs the following ingredients: (1) the procurement of skills and resources, (2) the coordination of available skills and resources, (3) the operational effectiveness primarily in terms of the capabilities to perform certain manifest functions, and (4) the measure of success or failure in terms of stated objectives. It is my feeling that the criteria of success or failure are focused on the first three types of "effectiveness," since it is easy for us to see the budget, the output of work in terms of published papers and statistics on program output. It is when we come to judging progress toward the eventual goal that we are somewhat uncertain as to what constitutes success.

Perhaps the problem can be analyzed from different viewpoints: First, there is the objective of an academic community with regard to the contribution of a center to the growth of the university in the modern world. The effectiveness of a center in this sense is measured by the relative contribution of such a center to the research and teaching of members of the academic community, regardless of whether such contribution is visible as measured against the program created by a legislative act. Second, there is the objective of the legislative mandate of Congress with respect to a certain problem. While these two sets of objectives may not necessarily require conflicting courses of action, the primary emphasis, in a short run, requires the concentration of collective energy in differently structured priority systems. This is perhaps the source of some of our problems in defining a successful center.

Thus, for our purposes, we need to examine the criteria of a successful center with reference to (1) the center itself as an autonomous unit; i.e., how good is the performance of the organization vis-à-vis itself, rather than its contribution to the larger system of which it is a part, (2) the contribution of the center to the academic community and to the understanding of relevant human problems, and (3) its contribution to the national goals as a whole.

My argument then is that the center's performance should be measured against the second and the third objectives. What I am proposing is that we need desperately some concerted efforts to research on policies: policies of the whole dimension of human values which encompass the birth, the growth, the existence, and the death of all mankind. We need to know the responsibilities of planners and the ways and means to implement objectives thus defined. We feel that the solution of one problem sometimes creates new ones; and that it is the hope that we anticipate these consequences. It is in this spirit that I am hopeful that those who are planning the creation of more centers will not continue to duplicate existing programs, but strengthen areas where some of the concerns of human worth are currently lacking.

Chapter Twelve

AN EXAMPLE OF ONE OF AMERICA'S OLDEST POPULATION CENTERS

ANSLEY COALE

THE Office of Population Research at Princeton University was founded in 1936, and as one of the oldest in the country, qualifies as a brave pioneer in the field, if nothing more. Its first director was Frank W. Notestein, who resigned in 1959 to become president of the Population Council.

The principal functions of the office have been threefold: (1) the training of graduates and undergraduates in demography and supervision of student research projects, (2) professional research, and (3) publication of a bibliographical quarterly that provides an annotated guide to current world literature on population.

The research program has been characterized by persistent lines of interest such as international population studies particularly in Europe, Asia, and Africa. One of our major projects is a study of fertility changes in Europe over the past century and a half. Another line of research has been into the economic and social problems associated with population trends in low-income countries. A third is a study of fertility, especially in the United States, which includes field surveys. A fourth area has been demographic methodology: methods of estimation and analysis, methods of detecting errors and adjusting data.

The training provided within the Office takes the form of two graduate courses, an undergraduate course, and individual supervision of separate research projects undertaken by students. The two graduate courses (on world population problems and on techniques of research and analysis) serve three somewhat different kinds of students. The first category includes Ph.D. candidates in economics, sociology, or statistics, and occasionally candidates in biology, history and political science. The

148

Ph.D. candidates may offer demography as one of several fields in which they must be examined in the preliminary examinations for the doctorate. The second class is for students in the Woodrow Wilson School who are candidates for a master's degree in public administration. These students characteristically take only the first semester course on world-population problems, since the remainder, which involves research and analysis, goes beyond their interests. A third category is visiting students enrolled in a special training program. These visiting students are ordinarily from abroad, but occasionally an American with a special interest in population enrolls. Visiting students are usually in Princeton for a year and supplement their course work in population by taking other relevant courses in statistics, economic development, and the like, and also by carrying out an individually supervised research project, which we call our Demographic Workshop. In addition, degree candidates in economics, sociology, or other departments, may write doctoral dissertations on a demographic subject. Fifteen doctoral dissertations in demography have been completed in the last decade, and at the moment there are seven in progress.

The undergraduate course covers (in lesser depth) much of the same ground. In the last decade, enrollment has increased from twelve to fifteen students annually to twenty-five to thirty.

The most important service function provided by the Office is the continuing publication of *Population Index*, which was edited by Irene Taeuber from 1935 to 1955, and since then by Dr. Dorothy Good. *Population Index* contains in each issue brief items written or invited by the Editor on topics of current interest, summary tables of population size, birth rates, death rates, and other important population measures for most of the countries of the world for which statistics are available, and, as the most important part, brief abstracts of current literature in population.

Other services of the Office take the form of advice, consultation, membership on committees and commissions, and lectures at outside institutions.

EXAMPLES OF RESEARCH PROJECTS

In Europe in the past two centuries virtually every region has experienced a substantial reduction in fertility. Widely known generalizations about the typical population changes that occur during industrialization or modernization—the so-called demographic transition—are based to a large extent on an impression of typical European experience. Some demographers question the need for population policies directed at reducing natality, because of the supposedly inevitable effect of modernization in reducing the birth rates.

Because there has not been a systematic collation and comparison of the statistical records of various European populations to providing a thorough documentation of these changes, the Office three years ago undertook such an effort. In order to deal with more nearly homogeneous experience, we decided to analyze the decline in fertility by provinces of which there are some seven hundred in Europe. It might be said that these seven hundred provinces, characterized for the most part by fairly complete and accurate data on population, provide a unique statistical laboratory in which to investigate the decline of fertility. The project should, at a minimum, be an important contribution to the cultural history of Europe; and at a maximum, a major step toward understanding the circumstances under which fertility control begins.

Another project is the longitudinal study of the fertility of couples in metropolitan areas of this country. The basic data have been collected in three interviews with a group of women constituting a random sample of couples who had recently had their second children and who were living in the seven largest metropolitan areas in the United States. They were first interviewed in 1957, six months after the birth of the second child, interviewed again three years later, and a third and final time during the five-year period that has just ended. The last interview was timed as nearly as feasible to occur after each woman had completed childbearing.

The longitudinal design of the study has proven to have many advantages. The first interview included a large inventory of social, economic, and psychological characteristics, and a battery of questions about previous fertility experience, including the circumstances surrounding each of the first two pregnancies. The second interview made it possible to determine the extent to which couples have accurately predicted their own subsequent fertility, to determine changes in attitude, and also to ask additional questions based on the analysis of the first interview results. The final phase will make it possible to trace the consistency of attitudes, the degree to which expectations at an early period of family building are fulfilled, and reasons for discrepancies.

One of the interesting and puzzling findings from the first stages of the project was a positive relationship between the amount of education and desired and achieved family size among Catholic women in metropolitan America. A detailed examination of the data showed that this unexpected relationship resulted entirely from differences in fertility attitudes and performance among women whose schooling had been wholly within church-operated schools, colleges, and universities. An effort to find out more about the reasons for this relationship led to the questioning of a large sample of female college freshmen and seniors of all religions and denominations at various kinds of American colleges and universities (secular and religious, Catholic and other). This study was summarized in a book by Westoff and Father Raymond Potvin entitled *College Women and Fertility Values*,[43] in which it was demonstrated that higher education exerts little or no effect on fertility values and that the high-fertility orientations of women in Catholic schools was mainly a matter of personal choice.

Still another significant project was the 1965 National Fertility Study. It intended to make at five-year intervals, the series of nationwide fertility surveys beginning in 1955. It was repeated in 1960, under the direction of the Survey Research Center at the University of Michigan and the Scripps Foundation for Research in Population Problems at Miami University, Oxford, Ohio. The 1955 survey covered a representative sample of white married women of reproductive age and the 1960 survey added a sample of nonwhite married women. A large volume of information was collected about expected family size, fecundity and sterility, incidence and effectiveness of the voluntary control of fertility, and on the timing and spacing of births, all related to a wide variety of characteristics of American couples. However, neither Michigan nor Scripps was able to continue its surveys. This was regrettable, for in 1965 their continuation seemed especially desirable because of the marked decline of fertility in the United States that began in 1957 and accelerated after 1960 and because of the importance of documenting the early stages of the use of the extremely important new contraceptive, the steroid pills. Some of the preliminary findings of this study have been published by Westoff and Ryder.

Then we have a study of the population in mainland China and in other parts of East Asia. Dr. Irene Taeuber has for many years been assembling data on the population of mainland China as well as on Chinese populations in Taiwan, Hong Kong, Malaya, Singapore, and Indonesia. She has also collected and analyzed material on the populations of cultures closely related to the Chinese, such as that of Korea and Thailand.

Most of the published statistical information on the bulk of the Chinese population is of dubious validity and completeness. Therefore, Dr. Taeuber has found it necessary to make use of the scattered bits of reliable information such as data on Manchuria and the south Manchurian railway zone collected during the period of the Japanese occupation of Chinese territory. It is her hope that detailed analysis of accurate data on peripheral Chinese populations will make it possible to interpret the fragmentary information on the mainland population itself. The extraordinarily thorough and imaginative research that Dr. Taeuber carried out in preparation for her monumental book[13] on the population of Japan provides her with an exceptional background for this major project.

Now brief summaries of other major endeavors during a recent year:

Dr. Pravin Visaria, a visiting research staff member from India was involved in two research projects. One was on the high proportion of males to females in the Indian population. Visaria has shown that this male-female disbalance was primarily the result of unusually unfavorable mortality conditions for Indian females in relation to Indian males. He also analyzed trends in labor-force participation and employment in India.

Professor Tan Goan Tiang of the University of Indonesia was a visiting fellow at the Office of Population Research. Under a fellowship from the Ford Foundation's Indonesian Public Administration Project at Berkeley, Tan Goan Tiang brought from Indonesia tabulations from the 1961 census and special demographic surveys from which he constructed estimates of current fertility and mortality in Indonesia and an adjusted distribution of the population by age and sex. With this basic information he made a new set of population projections for Indonesia, showing the relation between these population prospects and the problems of social and economic development in Indonesia.

Ansley J. Coale has been working intermittently since the mid 1950's on an analysis of human age distribution. The substance of this book is the mathematical relationship between the changing structure of human population by age and the fertility and mortality experience to which the population is subject. Now completed, but not yet published, the book will be the last of a trilogy, the first two of which were *Regional Model Life Tables and Stable Population*[44] by Coale and Demeny, published in 1966 by the Princeton University Press, and *Methods of Estimating Basic Demographic Measures from Incomplete Data,*[45] manual written by Coale and Demeny for the United Nations and published in 1967.

Chapter Thirteen

AN EXAMPLE OF A NOVEL INSTITUTIONAL FORM FOR THE STUDY OF POPULATION AND ENVIRONMENTAL POLICY

W. W. HARMAN, D. W. NORTH, and I. J. WEINSTEIN

THE NEED FOR ECOLOGICAL POLICY RESEARCH

ALTHOUGH the environment has become a major public issue, little general or political attention has been devoted to the obvious need for comprehensive planning on the related matters of population-distribution environmental policy. As has been detailed in this volume, population growth, resource utilization, and environmental quality are extremely complex issues that cannot be dealt with separately; their interrelationships must be taken into account. The environmental macroproblem is one of the most difficult challenges facing the human race. We must learn to live in harmony with our planet. This harmony will not be natural, but rather it will be a creation of man.

This problem merits our best scientific talent, but in spite of all the recent publicity and debate, little has been done to mobilize the necessary resources. The programs proposed within the Government deal with specific issues such as water pollution, air pollution, a population assistance to emerging nations, and other programs lodged in a multitude of different agencies. The need for a comprehensive overview as a basis for high-level policy decision is self-evident. This need is reenforced by the nation's past experience with complex large-scale undertakings, such as the space program and military weapons systems. To deal with environmental problems, we shall need comparable planning efforts, which at present do not exist. As a means for remedying this serious deficiency, we recommend the establishment of one or more centers for ecological policy research.

THE FUNCTION OF THE CENTER—THE MOBILIZATION OF KNOWLEDGE AND IDEAS

The function of the center for ecological policy research should be to provide the information and methodology needed for intelligent, informed decision-making in the formulation of national and regional ecological policy. The center would be concerned with the environmental macroproblem: the interrelationship of population growth, resource scarcity, and environmental quality. It would be multidisciplinary, and serve as a focus for relevant information from many different functional areas. The study of social, legal, economic, and political institutions affecting the environment would be an important aspect of the center's work.

The activities of the center would be twofold: (1) to conduct a general *exploration* of the environmental macroproblem and (2) to provide *analysis* and advice on specific decisions and policy areas of interest to the Federal Government, and possibly state and local governments as well. Both types of activities would be conducted on an ongoing basis.

The goal of the exploration activities would be greater understanding of the physical, biological, and economic relationships that are important to the management of the ecosystem. The center would gather and organize information, recognize and define specific problems in areas of concern, search for creative insights, and identify areas in which crucial policy decisions must be made in the near future. In addition to research on the physical, biological, and economic systems, the center would conduct research investigations on the existing legal-political system and propose new legal structures for managing the environment.

Another important area for exploration is that of human values pertaining to the environment. While nearly everyone agrees that smog or the eutrophication of lakes is undesirable, there is virtually no agreement as to what constitutes the most desirable environment. Society must make difficult and often irrevocable choices between the production of material good (e.g. paper, electric power) and the preservation of natural beauty (e.g. setting aside a forest as a wilderness area). Questions of value assessment are subtle and difficult, and yet values are assigned implicitly whenever these economic choices are made.

In addition to these broad exploratory activities, the center would investigate current decision problems confronting Government policy-makers. These investigations would go beyond providing assistance on the specific issues at hand; the development of new methodology for the analysis of environmental problems would be an important objective. Only in analyzing actual decisions is useful new methodology likely to be evolved.

For the specific analytical activities, the center would require good liaison with the Government policy-makers. However, the center should remain primarily a research organization. It should act only in an advisory capacity, and it should not be charged with the responsibility for operational decisions. In providing advice and consultation on specific decisions, the center would not be intended to supplant existing agencies or groups within the Government. It should supplement them by providing a broad multidisciplinary perspective and fresh methodological approaches.

The center would have to have close contact with researchers active in the functional areas relevant to ecological planning, and it should have a scientific staff of its own, in addition to a staff skilled in the policy research disciplines. Together they would work to integrate the knowledge from the various functional fields and focus it on specific policy issues. These functional fields would include the following:

1. The earth as a physical system: physicists, chemists, geologists, meteorologists, etc.

2. The biosphere: biologists, botanists, zoologists, ecologists, organic chemists, etc.

3. The economic system and human ecology: economists, demographers, argiculturalists, psychologists, sociologists, etc.

4. The legal-political system: specialists in resource law, international law, political science, etc.

5. Environmental values: sociologists, psychologists, philosophers, humanists, etc.

The breadth of this knowledge bearing on ecological policy makes the integration of relevant information a formidable task, but this task is vital to the center's objective of illuminating the consequences of policy alternatives. The policy research methods will provide a structure for the information from the functional fields. The process of structuring information will often consist of building formal models that summarize explicitly the information deemed to be relevant. The skills required will include those of specialists in systems analysis and in econometric and ecological modeling methods.

It is expected that ecological policy research will require a great deal of methodological development. Promising methodology such as matrix analysis, alternative futures, and decision analysis[28, 46–49] should be explored in the context of environmental policy decisions and utilized where these methods were found to be useful and appropriate.

As a complement to these analytical modeling activities the center should develop a data base on environmental problems. This descriptive activity would draw on information-processing technology, with substantial contributions from experts on social indicators and technology assessment and forecasting. An important aspect of the work would be the development of recommendations for areas in which further information is urgently needed.

The center for ecological policy research might consist, at least initially, of a nucleus of full-time scientific staff, with a much larger pool of scientific talent participating only as needed on a part-time basis. The center should have available to it the resources of the scholarly community, a large group of consultants, and a mechanism by which outstanding scholars might visit it for extended periods. The inherent complexity of highly multidisciplinary ecological policy research would make full-time management of the center's activities essential.

THE NEED FOR URGENCY

The ecological problems of population growth, resource allocation, and environmental quality are complex, and decisions taken in these areas may have far-reaching consequences to the economic system and to the biosphere. There is a vital need for coordinated thinking and comprehensive planning in arriving at these decisions. As a society, we cannot afford to allow these decisions to be made according to which special interest group is most vociferous in pleading its cause. We must assess the consequences of environmental policies before these policies are adopted.

No major center for ecological research exists today in the United States. A center is needed for investigating the ecological problems, comparable to the centers that have been established to study the problems associated with space exploration and with national defense.

The ecological problems continue to become more acute with the rapid advance of technology. We concur with the conclusion reached in a recent study by a Congressional Committee: "A well intentioned but poorly informed society is haphazardly deploying a powerful, accelerating technology in a complex and somewhat fragile environment. The consequences are only vaguely discernible."[50]

The center for ecological policy research can be but one element in the massive effort that is needed to bring man into harmony with his environment. The center must build on the knowledge gained in the past, and it must work closely with other institutions. But the solution to our problems of population growth, resource utilization, and environmental quality is unlikely to come from the methods now being used, in which these problems are treated as separable. A broader viewpoint is needed; these problems must be examined together as an organic whole. This comprehensive approach to the environmental macroproblem would characterize the proposed center for ecological policy research.

Chapter Fourteen

A CATALYST FOR SOCIETY'S TECHNOLOGICAL TRANSITION: THE UNIVERSITY ROLE

WILLIAM K. LINVILL

THE world is experiencing a cascade of technological advances which either promises a new era of opportunity for mankind or threatens a chaotic disruption of human values, depending upon how well society can adapt to them. Every projection into the future promises an acceleration of the technological advance. The strategy that society must adopt is one of continual adaptation to continuing technological transition.

Technological transition requires a combination of the exploratory mode of life and the operational mode. The two modes serve very different but vital functions. The object of the exploratory mode is illumination and understanding. The object of the operational mode is productivity and efficiency. The exploratory mode is characterized by open communication and broadly interdisciplinary activity devoted to illuminating a problem area. The operational mode is a highly structured activity characterized by focused leadership, well-established goals, strong competition, a relatively long-term life pattern, and attendant loss of flexibility. Both modes of life are well established but very different and presently isolated from each other. In the past, a new venture started in the exploratory mode and the operational mode evolved on a trial-and-error basis. Because of the present technological pace, transitions are so frequent that great advantages would be realized by making the transitions from exploratory mode to the operational mode more systematic. The new problem is to organize a system for continual effective evolution from exploratory modes to operational modes.

Systematic evolution from exploration to operation requires

159

two elements not generally available: (1) a new language understandable to both explorers and operators and (2) a catalytic mechanism so that effective interaction between explorers and operators can be stimulated. The new language, systems analysis, is being developed as a new professional discipline which combines a set of mathematical and logical concepts to structure problems and a set of problem-solving concepts to provide the color, shading, and tone which mathematical language alone cannot capture.

The exploratory mode and the operational mode of life are basically so different that they tend to become isolated from each other. In times of rapid transition such as we have now, their interaction is so vitally necessary that it must be catalyzed. The mechanism for catalysis is to provide a sanctuary for exploration of new problem areas by interdisciplinary teams, and at the same time to provide multiple coupling means to tie the explorations into relevant operations. The exploration (or the exploratory mode) must be coupled in two places: (1) to academic operations so that long-term future projections can be made and correlated with academic foundations already established and (2) to operations in the practical world, so that useful discoveries can be exploited quickly and efficiently to the benefit of mankind.

A pilot program along these lines has been set up at Stanford University. It combines an academic program to establish the professional discipline and a set of exploratory projects, internships, and senior fellowships to provide the catalytic mechanism.

The first section of this chapter will describe a number of situations which exemplify the present rapidly changing nature of our society. The object of the next section is to characterize and to distinguish between the exploratory and the operational modes of life. The problems of coupling exploratory and operational modes will be assessed along with the catalytic mechanism to promote interaction between these modes in the third section. Systems analysis as the language of transition will be described, in a fourth section, and a pilot program in Engineering-Economic Systems is presented in the fifth section.

A WORLD IN TRANSITION

Technological Opportunities

Revolutionary developments in technology and the accompanying changes in the society that have occurred since World War II are making drastic changes in our way of life. A torrent of developments in television, computers, automation, nuclear energy, high-speed transportation, and satellite communication has come in one generation. Any one of these advances would have had drastic consequences by itself. Collective and interactive effects of their introduction in two decades represent remarkable potential if mankind can exploit them properly. Existing patterns established in the past impose limitations on the human beings living in today's environment. In our present social structure, technological changes impose extreme stress on people to accommodate technology. This whole process should be turned around, with the question to ask being how technology can serve humanity and enable individuals to live a better life.

Because of the radical changes, the options are very hard to assess. The danger is that we will not grasp the opportunities that are afforded and will accordingly live too cautiously, keep too strong ties with the outdated patterns of the past, and have too little appreciation of the functions that are now available for the future. Areas in which technology offers tremendous opportunities may become areas of tremendous threats, if improperly used.

Because of technological advances, the influence of each individual activity is much greater than it was before. If we view each individual activity as a point on a plane, then the scope of influences may be thought of as circles surrounding those points. As the range of interactions increases, the radii of the circles can be increased to represent this increased scope. Significant overlapping results. Overlapping offers great possibilities and at the same time threatens great confusion.

A given company, for example, could cut down its inventory cost by having a high-speed automated delivery system and only one warehouse. The Air Force has made such a system for the delivery of jet engines by air to any place in the world whenever needed, thereby achieving very substantial overall operational savings.

When a private industry tries to do this same thing, many problems arise because so many independent entities have to be coordinated. There has to be a different kind of packaging system, a high-speed ground delivery system on the receiving end as well as the coordination required to cut down the delivery time to the customer.

These entangling interactions could be handled if they were properly coordinated. In many cases such coordination is economically profitable. In other cases, however, the interactions may be too complex.

Multiple Revolutions Are in Process

Technological advances have led our society into a set of revolutions, each of which involves many opportunities and many hazards. If taken creatively and collectively, they offer promise of a better life for mankind.

Automation Revolution

Automation promises to remove a lot of the menial production-line work that has been done by human hands over the last fifty years. It could mean a shorter work week. It could mean that the demand for human participation in many production processes will be drastically reduced. It could mean that goods will be more available to all of us. It could also mean that human beings will be detached from much of the production process. Our old ideas of an individual's worth being measured in terms of what one can produce will have to be drastically changed.

Fortunately, the chores that can be most readily automated are the uninteresting, repetitive jobs in which workers are trapped by the present industrial world. Our problem in this case is to develop a new set of capabilities in the people that now hold these jobs, so they can make the transition to new kinds of life. Their lives will thereby be fuller than they were before. The transition, however, is not an easy one.

Industry and Management Revolution

Many of today's large cities were built in response to the need for a large work force close to production lines and shops in the big industrial centers of our country. As new automated plants are built, and as transportation becomes cheaper and more uniformly available to the population, there is a shift away from the city. There is now no functional reason to have these industries in large, dismal clumps. Rather, the communities can be designed to provide the worker with the most pleasant, enjoyable, and rewarding life. The emerging pattern is to have even the headquarters of large companies move out of the cities, into a more congenial, relaxed atmosphere.

Technical-Training Revolution

In the past, a one-job specialty for a worker's professional lifetime was standard. A person who was interested in power engineering, for example, would expect to spend most of his productive life in that particular industry. The tendency was to train a person in the details of a skill, in which he or she would spend most of the money-making career. The situation now is that the time constant of a person's particular professional career may be five to ten years, and not forty or fifty years as it was in the past. Accordingly, the kind of training needed now does not go into the immediate details of a given situation, but rather must provide flexibility, so that one has the mobility to move from job to job as the situation demands. More important than the detailed training that an individual receives is the ability to make changes when the need occurs.

Communication and Education Revolution

Fifty years ago the main method of communication was reading. A person was either in touch with the society or was isolated from it in its broad aspects, depending upon how well he could read, and whether he had access to adequate printed information. The advent of television and the implications that it brings with it have very greatly changed the impediment to communication associated with the inability to read.

The nature of the new communication capability makes us also reevaluate the role of the teacher. In the past, the teacher mainly taught students how to read and write. Teachers brought a class of twenty-five to fifty students along a certain pathway, all together. They stayed together, not because this was the best way for each to learn the material; but because that was the only way that the teacher could keep in touch with all of them at once. Now, because of the ease of back-and-forth communication using computers, a great deal more flexibility is afforded in the whole educational process. It is foreseeable that students will not even need to go to a central school facility to receive their whole training. It is entirely feasible that small neighborhood units of the school system could be set up and could be kept in contact with the other units by means of audio and television links. Whether this is a good idea depends not only on how usefully the teaching function can be realized with this arrangement, but also on what other functions the educational system is expected to serve. For example, social development is an important part of education in the public school system. Probably the school serves a special social role. How important is it for community integration, for example? How important is it for the individual students to have a sense of belonging? How important is the school system as a vehicle for enlarging the personal contacts of young people?

There is an even deeper question with regard to education. In the past, there was a great deal of emphasis on the cognitive aspects of learning. The ability to read and write and to master arithmetic has always been considered of paramount importance, and will probably continue to be. However, the question now appears in terms of the new broader goals for education, particularly whether or not more time can be spent in developing the human potential in every student. This may be possible, if better training methods produce the same kind of skill development, knowledge, and understanding in less time, allowing more time for additional attention to the individual.

International-Ties Revolution

Many separate parts of the world are now closely tied together by advances in transportation, communication, and the use of high-speed computers. Now an operation can be analyzed carefully before it starts. Significant alternatives can be checked out in detail and evaluated carefully. Planners and leaders can keep closely in touch with the whole operation. Absence of this ability to coordinate has been a severe stumbling block to the development of our own country.

The technology of the next twenty-five years will be vastly different from that available before World War II. We must look at the problems of world economic development with those tremendous advances in mind. The problems of world economic development are the problems of bringing technological advances and the possibilities for economic growth to all parts of the world, through high-speed communications and mutual help. The United States is very much interested in cooperation with other countries. They can profit and we can profit by an exchange of capabilities. Because we have much of the technology already developed, there are certain things we can do better than they. Because they have large untapped resources, both manpower and material, there are many things that they can contribute more effectively than we.

Certainly, in every case, the development of emerging countries will have to be controlled and guided from the homeland in which it occurs. Any effort on our part to guide or control them would rightfully be rebuffed, just as we would have rebuffed a similar effort by any other nation throughout our history. The dilemma posed by the world economic development problem is that intensive interactions are required from several different kinds of independent entities which will bring revolutionary changes in economic, social, industrial, and governmental patterns for several generations. Centralized control of the development process is out of the question; and yet these independent entities must be brought together to develop a more effective joint action.

A Long-Term Plan to Exploit Change

The transition from the past to the present has not been a one-step transition. There will probably always be technological advances offered to our society. The response of the society, therefore, must not be to make one transition and then settle down again into the new pattern of more or less static behavior. A continuing look into the future will be required. The continuing flexibility will be necessary in order to develop the continually emerging new frontiers. Functions which must be performed to aid society in adapting to the future possibilities will need to be in operation continuously; these functions must be performed on many different problems, and over a long period of time. Because of this long-term nature of the prospect for change, a set of long-term solutions should be developed in order to realize the advantages that the changes will present.

Indispensable Characteristics of an Agency to Exploit Change

There are two characteristics of any agency or institution which will be indispensable for its success in developing the opportunities that technology provides our society. The first characteristic is that the agency must combine the two basic drives of our society—the drive *to do* which has characterized our industrialists, our politicians, our managers, our enterprisers, and has made our country as strong as it is today; and the drive *to understand* which has characterized the efforts of scholars through the ages. The present situation calls for a *combination* of the drive *to do* with the drive *to understand*. The revolution that we are involved in is so drastic that *doing without understanding* will be futile. The opportunities are so great that *understanding without doing* is equally pointless.

The second characteristic of the agency is that it must have the capability for regeneration. Though the revolutionary forces of change present today are strong, nonetheless our whole culture has tremendous natural inertia. Therefore, any successful agency designed to foster long-term planning and development must provide sustained guidance and direction for several generations. For this reason, any agency which will last long enough to be effective, in the long run must have the capability to insure regeneration. This is a capability uniquely found in the universities. Among the institutions that exist today, those with the longest history and the greatest sustained or regenerative influence are the universities.

In contemplating an agency or activity to help develop the potential that the new technology provides our society, it is clear that the university or any agency which we can plan, must couple the drive to *do* with the drive to *understand* in order to have a long enough lifetime to be effective.

Academic World and Practical World Must Be Coupled to Exploit Technology

Effective living in the new age requires that we must in some sense combine the academic world and the practical world. The academic world has been almost the exclusive keeper of the drive to understand. Because of the tradition of training our youth in the academic world, it has the built-in capability for regeneration. The academic world has almost completely separated itself from the drive to do, which has been the trademark of the practical world. The practical world has similarly separated itself from the academic world in order to do its job.

Many contrasts exist between the academic and the practical worlds. While the academic world must be comprehensive in its approach in order to take into account the possibility of interacting influences in a given situation, the practical world must take a simple approximate approach in order to have its operations practical, workable. The academic world tends to be contemplative in order to understand. The practical world tends to be decisive in order to be efficient and active. The academic world tends to be philosophical; the practical world tends to be operationally direct. The interests of the academic world are long term; those of the practical world tend to be short term. The responses of the latter need to be immediate. The approach of the academic world is to analyze and to infer; the approach of the practical world is to do and to assess the outcome immediately.

The ways of operating and the organizational structures of both worlds are set up consistent with their basic very different missions. Each has been able to do its individual job more simply by remaining isolated from the other, which makes it all the more difficult to combine the two.

To be successful in bringing society the benefits of the ever developing technology, it is necessary to combine the efforts of the academic and the practical world. Our selection of a dichotomy between the practical world and the academic world has made the problem appear to be more difficult than it is. Actually, the model of the intellectual activity which is appropriate to describe this situation more accurately is not a dichotomy of practical and real, but is actually a "layer" model. Each "layer" has both its practical aspects or external aspects and its academic or internal aspects.

A Model of Intellectual Activity

At this point, it is well to observe a model of intellectual activity (Figure 14-1). It can be characterized in terms of "layers,"

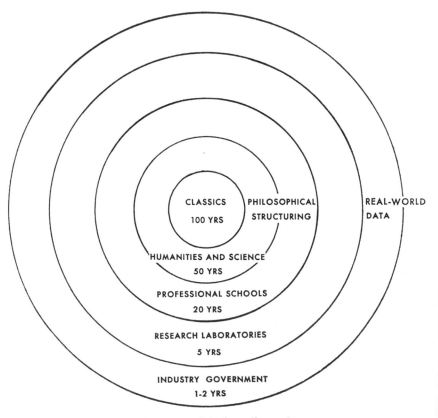

Figure 14-1. A model of intellectual activity.

like "layers" of an onion. In the central core of intellectual activity is the work in the classics; the next layer is the work of humanities and sciences; the next layer is the work in professional disciplines; next comes the work in planning institutes and in research and development laboratories; the outside layer is the layer of the practical world, which involves both governmental and private institutions. Each of these layers is characterized in terms of a time constant. The time constant is the equivalent of a half-life* of an activity. The time constant of the classic core is greater than one hundred years; the time constant of the humanities and science program is about fifty years; the time constant of the professional schools can be derived on the basis of the function that they serve: a professional school must train its students in such a way that their training will remain meaningful to them when they are at the peak of their careers, which is about twenty years after they leave the university. Accordingly, the programs that we give them have to have time constants of twenty years. Planning institutes and research and development laboratories have time constants on the order of five years. In the operational world, the time constants are about two years. The time constant for a politician is limited by the period between election during which he must collect persuasive evidence of his value in office.

Each layer is influenced very strongly by its adjoining layers. Generally, the drive to do (from the real world) is fed in from the outer layers toward the center, and philosophical structuring is supplied from the inner layers to the outer layers. Thus, the basic drive to understand comes from within and the basic drive to do comes from without. In a time of high stress and rapid change, which are characteristics of the present time, there is a tendency for these adjoining layers to become detached from each other. It is often painful for the academician to try to structure the new and ever-changing situation of the real world. A researcher's whole observing, measuring, and evaluating mechanism is upset by the tumultuous changes that are occurring in the outside world. Thus, such an investigator tends to ignore the

---

* The time required for an activity to reach a level of output or efficiency of one-half that of its original strength. The author derives this concept which is used in measurement of radioactivity and applies it to the present context.

outer layers. The opportunities to the operator on the outside are so great as to offer temptation to take on projects which in the short term look very meaningful but which may in the long term not serve any very useful function, thus, ignoring the inner layers.

In the present environment of great technological opportunity these layers should be closely coupled or, under ideal circumstances, even merged. The humanities and sciences programs in the university can be greatly aided in getting signals from the outside world by a proper collaboration with the professional schools. Any good operation within a given layer should involve at least the two adjoining layers, and possibly the two outside of those.

The organization for operations in a given layer is very dependent upon the nature of the function performed by that layer. Any layer which is real-world oriented generally is focused toward some rather immediate payoff in the practical world. Within a group, the leadership, the organization, and the performance are each associated with fairly short-term payoffs. Generally, the goals of practically oriented groups are externally generated. If a group is more academically oriented, then its structure is more closely tied to the completion of a philosophical structure and the goals are internally generated. The evaluation is done very much more on a philosophical basis. The payoffs are long term, the drives are internally generated, and the objectives generally are to complete a philosophical structure or to answer philosophical questions.

A SYSTEM TO OPERATE IN THE ENVIRONMENT OF CONTINUING TECHNOLOGICAL TRANSITION

The import of the previous section has been to indicate some aspects of our rapidly changing technology. A new pattern of operation must be developed which allows society more effectively to take advantage of the opportunities that are afforded it by technological innovations.

Modes of Life

The life of an individual as well as the life of an organization is often characterized by being in one of two very different modes. The two modes are the *exploratory mode* and the *operational mode*. As we have indicated, these two modes are so radically different and their operations, aims, and outcomes are so radically different that it is well to recognize them as two necessary components to a whole life and organize them in such a way that they are mutually supporting and effective in themselves. We next consider the mode of exploration and the mode of operation *as they apply to an organization.*

The Exploratory Mode

The object of the exploratory mode is to illuminate some specific problem or specific situation. The exploratory mode is characterized by being multidisciplinary or interdisciplinary. The organization of the exploratory mode is circular. Figure 14-2 indicates the nature of the exploratory mode. Each unit of the organization around the circle represents a different background, a different set of interests, and a different point of view. Each of the participants is then focused upon the same specific problem which is represented by the center of the circle. In order that the problem be properly illuminated, it is necessary that the attention be focused on it from all sides. The nature of the exploratory operation is such that it is very important that all of

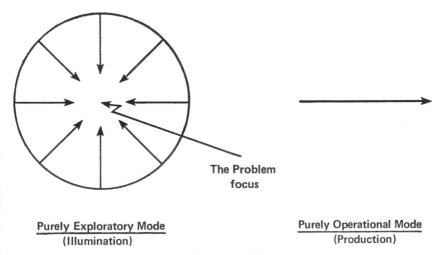

**The Problem
focus**

Purely Exploratory Mode
(Illumination)

Purely Operational Mode
(Production)

Figure 14-2. Two modes in the life of an organization.

the participating specialists illuminate the problem, each from his point of view. The exploratory mode of life is a temporary mode. The group of people come together to explore a problem on a term basis. There is no permanent leader for the group. As a result of the illumination of the problem, it is likely that one or more operational modes will emerge. Because of the multi-disciplinary nature of the exploratory mode, it is important that the attention of the various participants be focused on to a specific problem or a specific situation. Generally, the objective of the chairman of the exploratory operations is to guide the group in the illumination process. It is important that the chairman not force a change from the exploratory mode to the operational mode.

The Operational Mode

The objective of an operational mode is to perform some specific function or to carry out a specific operation. The operational mode is characterized by an arrow. It has a well-defined direction, it has an hierarchy of leadership, it has a very strict discipline, it involves substantial constraints on the direction of action of the members of the operational group. As was indicated at the end of the first section of this paper, the life of an individual in a given layer of intellectual activity will be characterized by being largely in the operational phase. Both the academic world and the practical world have their operational modes.

In the academic world, the goal of the operation generally will be internally generated and the structure will be that which is appropriate to a long time-constant situation. The organization will be structured along philosophical lines.

An operational mode in a practical-world situation generally will have its direction externally generated. The objective will be to serve a specific function or to make some specific product. The time constants will generally be short. The effectiveness of a practical-world operation will be judged on the basis of its efficiency and productivity.

The Combination of Exploratory and Operational Modes

Generally, an individual or organization carries on its exploratory mode in a layer of intellectual activity different from its normal operational layer. If the exploration is a philosophical exploration, it generally goes on in the adjoining layer to the *inside* of the operational layer. If an exploration is a practical exploration, it generally goes on in a layer *outside* of the operational layer. Often any single exploration involves participants from at least three layers of intellectual activity. Those from the outermost layers provide the philosophical structuring, the practical inputs and the drives from the outer layer representing the real world; generally those from the operational layer are exploring some new aspects of their normal operation.

Questions should arise about the balance between the exploratory mode and the operational mode in the life of an organization and an individual. Generally, the major part of the life of an individual is in the operational mode, with a small fraction, a quarter or less, of this effort being directed toward exploration. This ratio is dependent upon the nature of the organization or the nature of the individual. Some organizations or individuals are more exploratory by nature than others. Also, the nature of the world situation strongly determines the ratio of effort on the exploratory mode to that on the operational mode. The greater the rate of change of the world situation, the more difficult it would be to keep up with those changes, and the more exploring would be needed. Another dimension to this relationship is the duration of the exploratory phases as compared to the operational phases. Generally, the exploratory phases are short, perhaps a few months or at most a few years. The longer the time constant of a situation, the longer the time necessary for exploration.

An exploratory mode can be followed by an operational mode either in the practical world of the outside or in the philosophical world of the inside. Generally, as one changes from the exploratory mode to a practical operational mode, the immediate productive objectives are settled upon and a transition takes place. It is as if a few of the arrows represented in the exploratory mode were found to be extremely important, as indicated in Figure 14-3. They, then, determine the direction of the practical operational mode that follows. Each time a change is contemplated in an operational mode, some exploration is necessary

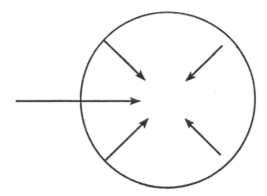

Figure 14-3. Emergence of a dominant factor (exploration is now limited). Several dominant-factor situations can emerge from a single exploratory process.

in order to assess the nature of the changes possible and to evaluate which ones are most promising. Again, the more static an operation becomes, the less frequent are explorations called for.

If an exploratory mode of operation is to be followed by a more permanent operation of a philosophical sort, then the philosophical direction is chosen as a result of the exploration, the directions are established, organizations are set up, and the operational mode in the academic world is then initiated.

The transition from exploratory mode to operational mode must be made by one or more individuals who gained insight from the illumination process in the exploratory mode. Maintaining continuity during this transition is vital.

For an operational mode to retain its vigor, it is necessary that it be buttressed both on the interior and on the exterior by effective exploratory modes. In a large organization, of course, the organization's funds must be committed at the same time to an operational mode and to several exploratory modes.

Support comes from participants on the basis of expected return. Initial exploration is almost uniformly supported by the participants. In the transition from the exploratory to the operational mode, support shifts to the main direction and the constraints increase on exploration.

Organizing to Serve Transition Between
Exploratory and Operational Modes

The problems of transition from exploratory modes to operational modes are difficult but solvable and have great similarity over a wide range of problem areas. Developing an efficient mechanism to aid the transition is essential. Again, as previously noted, two separate components must be developed: (1) a mechanism to catalyze the interaction between exploratory and operational modes and (2) a system language which captures the common elements of the exploratory and operational modes.

The catalytic mechanism suggested here is (1) a sanctuary provided for exploration and (2) a mechanism to couple the explorations with appropriate operational modes. The sanctuary away from operational pressures is needed to stimulate and support interdisciplinary explorations and a multichannel coupling mechanism is needed to couple both to academic operations and to production operations. Coupling to academic operations should (1) help to build a broad projection into the future and (2) provide the practical focus and real-world involvement, which is an essential ingredient in the broad education of our youth appropriate and necessary to the projected future. Coupling to the practical world of production operations should (1) provide for implementation of the discoveries of the explorations and (2) provide a basis for reorientation and retraining of practitioners in mid career to allow them flexibly to adapt to new opportunities and challenges.

The systems language may be developed as a new professional discipline. This discipline should establish strong ties with the humanities and sciences and with existing professional schools, on one hand, and with the practical world, on the other. Its primary business is to evolve a common language so that all entities can communicate more effectively.

THE CATALYTIC MECHANISM

The exploratory sanctuary and the coupling mechanisms to couple exploratory modes to operational modes are the two components of the catalytic mechanism. The exploratory sanctuary should be established in the university neighborhood but separated from the regular academic operational structure. It must be interdisciplinary in the broad sense developed below.

Interdisciplinary Requirement for the Exploratory Sanctuary

Coupling of exploratory to operational modes is vital for the effectiveness of both. Several specific mechanisms are suggested to make the exploratory sanctuary and its coupling to operational modes successful.

The exploratory sanctuary provided as a companion part of the catalytic mechanism must attract a wide spectrum of disciplines. The several senses in which it must be interdisciplinary should be examined.

The Academic Sense

Many academic disciplines must be simultaneously involved in many of the problems to be explored. Physical sciences and behavioral sciences are jointly involved, for example, in planning transportation systems, or in planning communication systems, or in planning educational systems. Very often it is important to understand the political and human issues involved before one undertakes any technological innovation that seems promising.

The Professional-Discipline Sense .

The artificial barrier that has been raised in the past between management and engineering is very troublesome in working on broad problems in these days. Generally, the manager knows what is technologically available, but he does not know what is technologically feasible. Analogously, the engineer very often knows what is technologically feasible, but he does not know what is operationally feasible. Similarly, many problems require interaction among doctors, engineers, educators, lawyers, and managers.

The Sense of Providing Collaboration Among Independent Private Institutions

In dealing with high-speed transportation systems it is necessary that computer companies, transportation companies, packaging companies, and many different manufacturers who would use high-speed ground transportation get together much more closely than they have in the past. In planning educational systems, no longer may the textbook manufacturers, manufacturers of audiovisual equipment, television manufacturers, and computer manufacturers operate separately.

The Sense of Providing Collaboration on the Same Project Among Different Public Institutions

One example encountered recently is the need for people in the State Department and the Department of Defense to be working jointly on the problems of limited war. We see that the distinctions between military activity and economic activity are very artificial these days. In another area, there must be equal consideration given to budgetary, educational, and communication involvement in educational television.

The foregoing examples have indicated the necessary broad scope of interdisciplinary activity. The problems of getting interdisciplinary activity started are very great indeed. There must be some set of special mechanisms in order to make various different agencies or different groups work together effectively. The establishment of a sanctuary insulated from, but aware of, the day-to-day operational pressures appears to be a vital requirement for effective exploration. Figure 14-4 represents the integrated nature of the exploratory study center which serves as a sanctuary. Obviously, not all components would be involved in each exploration.

Mechanisms to Facilitate Interdisciplinary Work

There are four specific mechanisms to ease the difficulties in interdisciplinary work.

Any Interdisciplinary Program Must Be Focused on Specific Problems

The fact that one has the specific set of issues on which to focus in a given problem makes it possible for an economist and an engineer to work together, for a manager and a planner and a politician to work together. The fact that these individuals

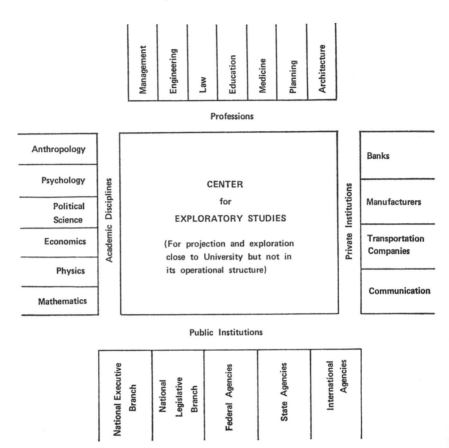

Figure 14-4. Integration provided by center for exploratory studies.

have different backgrounds will lead to an enriched illumination and understanding of the problem. The differences in their backgrounds would be great impediments to mutual understanding without the focusing that is provided once a problem has been made specific.

The Pressure to Do and the Pressure to Philosophize Must Be Alternated

It is important to distinguish these pressures. Any individual or any group or team has to be motivated at some point by a pressure to do. Specific decisions must be made; specific plans must be carried out; specific delegations of authority have to be made; resources have to be committed. This is the pressure to do. Alternating with this pressure to do is the pressure to understand. Each time a long-range plan is studied, it must be reviewed in breadth and detail. There must be an understanding of the deeper issues involved.

A Sanctuary or Neutral Meeting Ground Must Be Provided

Competing or contending real-world elements need a sanctuary where integrative planning can illuminate issues before the competition necessary for efficient operation raises barriers between potentially competing elements. The detachment of the exploratory study center would be a great aid to communication in the exploratory mode among the contending elements from an operational system. The strategic plans of our society need to be integrated and interdisciplinary. The practical aspects can oftentimes be made much more efficient if they are competitive. By allowing competition to be exercised freely in the operational aspects, and by providing a neutral meeting ground in the exploratory studies center where the integration can be brought about, we can capture the benefits of both integration and competition.

The exploration must be done in a sanctuary away from the pressures of the operational world. One reason why there is a great hope for a combination between field agencies and university agencies is that the university environment provides some essential capabilities for philosophical structuring. By having professors and students from the university working for an extended time in the field, they can be involved in the pressure to do. When they come back to the university, the philosophical issues are much more clearly drawn than before. Similarly, senior fellows can come from the practical world to the exploratory study center near the university to restructure new problems at the beginning of new projects. Yet, when they are in the field, their ability to carry out specific operational responsibilities is the component which has the highest priority with them.

A Training and Regeneration Facility Must Be Provided to Business, Industry, and Government

This training and regeneration facility is a component that is becoming increasingly necessary in the lives of practitioners in the field, as the rates of technological progress drastically increase.

Coupling Aspects of the Catalytic Mechanism

The sanctuary appears necessary to insulate the interdisciplinary exploration from the operational pressures on each of the participants. However, the explorations would lead to no useful outcome if they are continually isolated from operational elements of our society. Such coupling will be feasible if it is mutually beneficial to both the exploratory sanctuary and to the operational units. There are two kinds of operational units to be coupled to. First is the academic operation whose function is to collect, organize, store, and disseminate knowledge. Second is the productive operation within the society whose function is to provide those goods and services which improve life for us all. The nature of couplings from the exploratory sanctuary to the two operations is different and needs to be distinguished.

Coupling the Sanctuary to the Academic Operation

The exploratory sanctuary is coupled to the academic operation to provide a projective surveillance of the future which is vital to both the academic operation and the explorations done within the sanctuary. Universities will supply both professors and students to the exploratory sanctuary. This involvement with interdisciplinary exploration is an essential ingredient in a complete academic experience for the students.

Any long-term exploration must involve a projective surveillance of the future. Such a projection obviously requires participation of the academic community for philosophical structuring. The interdisciplinary interactions provided by the explorations within the sanctuary would be very difficult to obtain solely within the constraints of the academic operation. The inputs obtained within the sanctuary from the industrial and governmental fellows who are in from the operational world will be indispensible for practical aspects of projective surveillance. In other words, the academic community must be adequately coupled to the world of affairs. Involvement with the interdisciplinary exploratory center will initiate such coupling to the practical world. The life of the students, especially those in professional schools, is vitally enriched and broadened by such experience.

Coupling the Sanctuary to Production Operations

Implementation of discoveries and plans derived from exploration will have to be made in the operational mode, either in industry or government. Industrial and governmental fellows within the sanctuary will bring a practical realism to the explorations and at the same time will be able to carry discoveries back to the practical world for implementation.

Involvement with the sanctuary can provide the broadening and reorientation experience which is so vitally important to keep practitioners in industry and government up to date in a time of rapidly changing technology.

The Overall Coupling Operation

As of now, nothing is, or can be, standardized in the ways in which one moves from the exploratory work to the academic course program and to the practical world. Substantial differences should be expected resulting from different interests and different areas of practical experience. The whole field is in such a fluid, developing state that any program must be viewed as experimental and subject to substantial modification. To make the university role meaningful and productive, the university parts must be coupled to the world of affairs so that continuing interchanges can take place.

The plan of operation is schematically represented by the diagram in Figure 14-5. The activities toward the left are closer to the intellectual core. The activities toward the right are closer to the world of affairs. The left-most column represents the foundation academic disciplines with which the professional schools must have strong connections. The most important of

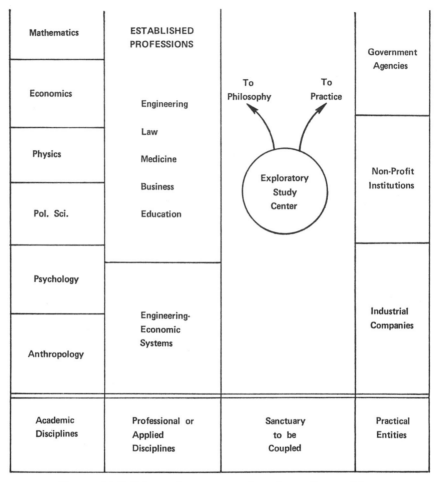

Figure 14-5. Schematic representation of coupling problem.

these is mathematics. Economics, physics, political science, psychology, and anthropology are areas that are relevant.

The second column represents professional disciplines. The upper part represents established disciplines, while the lower part represents the new activity that has been added in systems. Since it is new, it will be described in more detail in the next section.

The third column represents the coupling activity to the

world of affairs done at the Exploratory Study Center described as the sanctuary. The exploratory studies will be involved in exploring specific problems of society and will form a strong coupling link between the academic activities, represented by the left-hand two columns, and the field agencies, practical entities, which are represented by the right-hand column. The right-hand column is divided into three parts: government agencies, nonprofit institutions, and industrial companies.

Exploratory projects done as short-term studies will develop and test new systems concepts and thereby will feed into the Engineering-Economic Systems program. They will also explore and test new practical activities and thus will move into the operational modes in the practical agencies.

THE LANGUAGE OF TRANSITION—ENGINEERING-ECONOMIC SYSTEMS

The concepts of systems analysis have been developing over the last decade or so. As the problems of transfer from exploratory to operational modes become more prevalent, the systems language becomes more universally needed. The field has been referred to by several names. Here we will use the term Engineering-Economic Systems to imply a systems analysis program concerned with a broad scope of issues and a strong quantitative base.

The field is still evolving and will continue to change as new issues are brought up in new problem areas. By gathering insights from several exploratory activities and their implementations, and by making comparative studies of them, the concepts of Engineering-Economics are being built up. If the range of practical situations studied is kept broad enough, the generality of the system concepts can be tested.

Nature of Engineering-Economic Systems

The language of the systems is built on two sets of concepts: mathematical concepts and problem-solving concepts. Mathematical concepts provide the structure, and problem-solving concepts provide the shading and tone. Figure 14-6 pictures the two sets of concepts.

Mathematical Concepts (Methodology)	Problem—Solving Concepts (System Analysis)
MODELING	EXPLORATORY STUDIES
OPTIMIZATION	DECISION ANALYSIS

Figure 14-6. System concepts and methodology.

Mathematics is the mother language of systems analysis. A system is characterized by its structure. Mathematics is pure structure. The two primary mathematical activities for systems analysis are modeling and optimization. Modeling is associated with description and analysis of existing systems as well as those which are projected. Models are classified as static or dynamic, single-variable or multivariable, and as deterministic or stochastic. Optimization is essential as a component activity in design. It is involved with picking the best or most attractive among alternatives.

While mathematics as a language is sharp, clean, and precise, it alone lacks the color, shading, and tone to represent situations in the real world. Those who would be useful in the real world must be problem-solvers. The language of problem-solving must be added to mathematical language to make system theory complete.

The two aspects of problem-solving are exploratory studies and decision analysis. Exploratory studies involve determination of scope and objectives in a given situation. A decision is the irreversible commitment of resources. Under the usual practical conditions of uncertainty and dynamic interaction, risk and time preferences must be accounted for. Usually in strategic situations, or macrosystem problems, having large scope in both time and space, policy issues dominate. In tactical situations or microsystem problems involving detailed constraints and multiple interactions, decision problems dominate. Every practical situation involves policy, issues, and some decisions. Exploratory study describes the process of describing issues, discovering key relationships, inventing alternatives, and clarifying objectives. It is the *inductive part* of problem-solving. Generally decision analysis and policy analysis are the *deductive* parts.

Application Areas

In all practical areas, system activities must serve man. Human needs, human goals, human potential must be realized. Technology and the various institutions of society are man-made instruments whose only justification is to serve man. The outreach of the systems profession is through the applications areas. Work in humanities and sciences provides a foundation for technology and the study of social institutions and, hopefully, a deep appreciation of the basic needs of man. In addition to the basic physical needs for food, shelter, and clothing, there are the limitless possibilities for human development. Not only is an individual important, but mankind as a group or groups must be considered.

When actions are to be taken to achieve specific goals, the connection to the world of affairs is obvious. Actions in the various technical areas are integrated through social, political, and industrial organizations into a coordinated unit. Interaction between theory and application is even more critical for systems than it is for the more established professional disciplines. The systems concepts and methodology are meaningful only to the extent that they apply generally to a wide variety of substantive areas.

Many workers will very much prefer to continue to have a substantive focus on their work rather than a systems focus. Such a focus tends to capture the rich localized context of the problem at the same time that it fails to highlight the systems aspects. A combination of systems focus and substantive focus is probably preferable to pure substantive focus. Figure 14-7 represents the primary existing paths involved when a substantive focus is taken.

In a period of transition much appears to be gained by taking

Foundation Disciplines	Existing Profession	Substantive Focus
Science Mathematics Economics	Engineers Managers	TECHNOLOGY
Psychology Philosophy Religion Art Literature	Artists Writers Musicians Clergy Educators Psychiatrists Medical Doctors	MAN
Political Science History Sociology Anthropology	Public Administrators Lawyers	SOCIETY
Foundation Disciplines	Existing Profession	Substantive Focus

Figure 14-7. Classification of substantive focus for existing professions.

a functional focus and by utilizing the systems language. The objective of the systems discipline is to bring together the previously separate substantive foci so that a coordinated approach to the broad new opportunities can be taken. The systems discipline will *unite* existing disciplines. It will in no sense replace them.

PILOT ACTIVITIES ESTABLISHED AT STANFORD UNIVERSITY

When one attempts to understand the scope of the issues that are involved in long-range planning today, he runs a risk of being misunderstood, as being too ambitious or too arrogant or too self-assured. It would be unrealistic for us at Stanford University, in the small program that we have, to claim a really meaningful long-term plan or an existing institutional structure, which can carry it out. Our aim has been to understand our assumptions about the state of the world. Our program has been going for about five years. A number of combined practical and analytical projects have been completed. About a dozen academic courses have been developed.

We have had about fifty interns working on problems in the field; we now have about eighty doctoral students involved in our program, of whom about fifty are enrolled in the Engineering-Economic Systems Department. Most of our effort over the last five years has been devoted to the development of an analytically focused program.

With regard to applications of systems analysis to the substantive areas, an increasingly stronger connection with humanities and sciences is needed. If Engineering-Economic Systems is to be really meaningful as a profession, it must be built to serve the needs of man. At present, society has far too little understanding of what man's needs are; we hope to join professors from humanities and sciences to explore and define the needs of man in practical situations.

At present, a number of practical projects involving Stanford University's faculty are under way in the field. The first is a project for long-range educational planning. Second is a problem on long-term medical care planning and hospital operation. Third is a fairly extensive set of internships in Washington, including work with the Department of Commerce and with the Department of Transportation on long-term transportation planning.

The effort of professors and graduate students in the Engineering-Economic Systems program is divided into three parts: systems concepts, substantive application areas, and field work. Something more than a third and less than half of the activity in Engineering-Economic Systems is devoted to developing core concepts for systems analysis and doing research on basic concepts and methodology. Between 20 and 40 percent of our effort is put into substantive areas, and between 20 and 40 percent is put into field work.

Comparative studies on the usefulness of the various analytical concepts and methodologies among problems in the various substantive areas is an indispensable part of the program. It is important to try concepts of operation on both tactical and strategic problems. Generally, we think of strategic problems as being those which are involved with the long-term planning. Tactical or microsystem problems are concerned with more specific design and operation.

If the systems language, methodology, and concepts are meaningful, they should be applicable to many areas. Study of a problem and its various phases that might occur in private industry, as opposed to the same problem occurring in long-term government planning, provides a rich field in which comparison can be made.

With regard to field work, usually a project is started because some professor or some set of workers from the outside is interested in going into a given area. One of the functions of our exploratory program is to provide support for investigations into new areas. The investigators consult with practitioners who are working in relevant areas and with government officials who have responsibilities or potential responsibilities in the area that is represented by this work.

After the initial exploration has been made, oftentimes study seminars are set up within our institute for graduate students and visiting fellows where further exploratory work is done. Very often at this stage, experts are brought in on a visiting basis for a short time for exploratory work on the university-centered exploratory projects.

Work of our graduate students (as interns) and our professors (as consultants) in the field follows and allows more specific evaluation of assumptions made and conclusions reached in the exploratory phases. Often the field projects will be led by practitioners who were involved as government or industry fellows in the exploratory project.

This is but a small step toward coupling the exploratory and the operational modes of life, at a time when incredibly rapid technological developments and sometimes lagging university progress seem to be widening the gap between the two. But something must be done, and time is of the essence.

Chapter Fifteen

SOME THOUGHTS ON PROFESSORS AND POPULATION CENTERS

ARNOLD S. NASH

PROFESSORS are, traditionally, difficult people with which to deal. The difficulty lies not so much in their—generally speaking—intellectual superiority over the normal run of the populace perhaps as in their apparent stupidity in using their knowledge and intelligence. There is a vivid description of what I have in mind in a speech by C. P. Snow which he made a few years ago at alma mater where I learned my science, the University of Liverpool. Snow had been asked to make the dedication speech at the opening of the new laboratory which had been formed in memory of the late Sir James Chadwick, a Nobel Prize winner for his work in discovering the neutron. On the death of Chadwick, the University had called back from Cornell, Herbert Skinner, Chadwick's previous younger collaborator in Liverpool, to head the new laboratory. Skinner, alas, had died before the new laboratory was dedicated, and so Snow's sad words were as much about Skinner as about Chadwick. He commented as follows:[51]

> The two of them brought the reputation of the physics department of the University to a place extremely high not only in this country but in the entire Western world. And Skinner played an immense part. But I am going to say what I would have said even more had he been present, that it could be a torment for anyone involved in administration because he was a man of blazing sincerity who knew precisely what he wanted and what in his view everyone ought to want. With immense vigor he was capable of suspecting one—if one happened to be an administrator who got in his way—of competence at the best or probably ill will or conceivably treachery.

What C. P. Snow said was uttered not in malice but in admiration, for during World War II he had worked intimately with

189

Skinner and developed quite an affection for him as well as an admiration for his abilities. But what this quotation brings out is something most puzzling about professors that all of us sooner or later who deal with them have to reckon with. Perhaps the explanation, as has often been remarked, lies in the notion that the choice of a man's profession is often an index of his particular neurosis. This is a plausible thesis, for how else can we explain why a man decides to be a lawyer, knowing that he may become a judge with all that that means. How else can we explain why another man becomes a soldier, knowing that the degree to which he is successful will mean a rise in rank to the point where his orders will increasingly commit his own soldiers as well as their enemies to death. And so we could proceed, asking similar questions for surgeons, for politicians, for ministers, for accountants, and the like. Each profession seems to exhibit its own "mind set" and neurotic character. It is a specific feature in the mind of the professional thinker, like a scientist, to which C. P. Snow draws our attention. And this is no trivial consideration: There is a certain kind of egoism about a professor which, if not understood, will mean that those of us who seek to relate the professor's expertise to practical problems will repeatedly fail to understand what we are up against.

Perhaps the most vivid expression of this kind of egoism is that of the king of France who said: "The State, it is I." But that was a long time ago. Surgeons do not say—at least boldly—"We are the hospital." Lawyers do not say—at least overtly—"We are the law." Generals do not say—at least publicly—"We are the army." Yet professors, like priests speaking of the church in the past, have said and still do say—and with deep conviction—"We are the university."

It is true that students today challenge this claim. Indeed, they have a precedent. The original universities in far away Italy began under student control. But that did not last long. The students today may be asking for their very ancient rights, but the university, as we know it today, is what it is because of the fashion in which professors down the ages—more than anyone else —have molded those strange institutions which we call universities. The professor's role, we must agree, has been the central one. He knows that administrators are not really necessary: There have been universities (indeed, most of the time) without full-time presidents and without full-time deans. He knows that there have been universities—and good ones—without trustees; for example, at Oxford or Cambridge the tenured faculty are the trustees. There have even been universities without buildings; the treks from Paris to Oxford in the Middle Ages or of the Chinese universities from the coastal cities to Chungking a gen eration ago during World War II were universities on the move but still universities. Incredible though it may sound, the professor can truthfully record that there have even been excellent universities without full-time football coaches.

But, leaving out historical accidents like All Souls College, Oxford, we can say that the bare-essential necessity for a university is that it should have students and faculty standing in a learning relation to each other such that, after the professors have finished, the students can go out into the world and serve their day and generation. But the professor sees himself as doing this in terms of serving two loyalties, one to his learning and the other to society. As we seek to understand the role of a professor in a population center we shall have to remember again and again his dual loyalty.

In the tempestuous times in which we now live, it is worth looking at the history of this process whereby the professor has served this second loyalty by relating his knowledge to society, and not just restricting himself to enjoying (for his own self-satisfaction and esteem) what he has discovered and what he has learned from other people.

From his counterpart in the medieval universities (most notably Bologna, Salerno, and Paris) the contemporary professor has learned that he should prepare students to serve as members of the learned professions. Traditionally, they were, of course, medicine, the ministry, and the law. But Oxford and Cambridge, influenced by Renaissance thinking, slowly modified the classical picture so that by the middle of the nineteenth century the universities in the English-speaking world were being asked to produce the scholar-gentleman who would become an administrator or a statesman. On the European continent, notably in Germany, another aim developed: The university was to become primarily a center for research and the professor's task was to produce scholars and scientists like himself. When we come to the twentieth century, an American ideal begins to dominate the entire world: The professor now becomes the key figure in a system whereby the university becomes a service station for the production of scientific experts and technologists to aid governments and corporations in solving their problems.

All these different roles of the professor are the result of the effort by the university to adjust itself over the centuries and in different national contexts to the call of social needs. However, in responding to the call of the present, past answers are not always repudiated. Their embodiment in institutional form is simply modified and the professor has acted accordingly in pursuing his various roles. Moreover, the new Western-type universities in the developing countries, each in their various ways, are considered to exhibit these functions and to serve these needs, and so the professor in these countries, too, carries on his activities accordingly.

But through it all, in any culture, the professor, sometimes clearly but often vaguely, knows that he is the key figure in the process whereby the university seeks to transmit learning, to conserve learning, and to advance learning. But he knows, too, that he does so within the context—even if veiled—of two main features. On the one hand, the university is the primary institution within society which trains people for the old and the new learned professions and for service (to use the ancient phrase) in Church and State. On the other hand, it is more than this. The professor does not like the word "train." He knows that what distinguishes his institution from merely a training institution is that he "educates." And that means two things. The first is that he bases his work with the future doctor or lawyer or scientist upon "a liberal education" construed not as the accumulation of bits of knowledge from many fields but as a particular attitude of mind operating within the context of a comprehensive view of human existence. The second is that the "educated" mind is never satisfied. It is critical of what is known and believed and so it seeks always newer methods and newer truth.

Here we can perceive one source of the most serious issue facing a professor in the contemporary university as he listens to the calls on him for help from his government and its agencies. He does not know when he should look upon his university as a rock standing for a truth and a wisdom which are not necessarily in line with the political loyalties of the outside world and the economic needs of the university, and when he should see it as an instrument serving the causes and satisfying the needs of the country. The traditional danger for the professor is that he tends to view his university not as a rock in the world but as an ivory tower away from it and he forgets that the university, being of the world, must serve it.

Thus, if the professor is to be true to his full mission as he sees it, he must be willing to pay a heavy but inescapable psychological cost. However difficult his task, he must somehow seek to hold simultaneously three convictions about his institution* and his role in it. The first is that if the university is to be true to its mission, it must be in one sense an ivory tower pursuing the truth for its own sake. But it also must be a service station which ministers to human need. And the third is an even more difficult role as it seeks to serve the world. The university must be a source of prophecy in the sense that standing in one sense away from the world it will seek to serve the world not at the point of its *wants*, but at the point of its *needs*.

I make no apology for this lengthy introduction to my subject: the professor and the population center. Indeed it is not really an "introduction." It is the essence of the situation, for if we are to deal adequately with the place of the professor in a research center or a service center—and all population centers are both—the above considerations which we have just presented must be understood if we are to understand the ambiguities and problems which now face us. It is because these considerations

---

* And this will include, of course, any part of it, such as a population center at his institution.

are not understood and so cannot be accepted by the public mind that political leaders and university administrators, being molded in their thinking by the public mind rather than the academic mind, tend to oscillate in their attitude toward professors between two positions. The first is that they are impractical "theoretical" eggheads who do not understand trustees, legislatures, money raising, etc., etc., and the other is that somehow they are the saviors of the world.

It is in this latter role that national governments, international organizations, and foundations, as they struggle with the problems, have naturally called upon professors in universities to help them share their burden. On this side of the Atlantic, influential voices at the highest levels have plainly put their case and challenge in no uncertain terms. Thus Mr. McNamara said in a recent address at the University of Notre Dame:[21]

> This university, over the years, has become a catalytic center of creative thought. It does what universities do best: it probes. It probes the past for what is most relevant to the present. It probes the present for what is most formative of the future. And it probes the future for what will most enlarge man's freedom and fulfillment.

So, too, Mr. McGeorge Bundy, in a recent annual report to the Ford Foundation,[52] said: "Whatever we set as our targets, we cannot hit them without the help of the universities."

But in the midst of these hopeful calls from Macedonia "to come over and help us," there is a deepening disappointment about the measure of success achieved by those of us who are working in universities on the population question. The professor can ignore the political right wing when he is dismissed as a liberal egghead, and he may forget the left wing when it castigates the professor for being the voice of the white establishment. But when a leading friend in Congress, Senator Joseph Tydings,[53] tells us that "the academic community in this country has completely dropped the ball in providing leadership on this relationship between demography and the dynamics of population planning . . . ," professors can hardly continue to sit at ease in their academic Zion.

But this kind of challenging rebuke immediately raises the

question of what are the limits beyond which the professor cannot or ought not to go. Any attempt to deal with this important question raises some far-reaching issues because no institution embodies more vividly, both in its own chaos and in its wider relations with the outside world, the crisis of our own day than does the contemporary university. Universities, as the recent worldwide disturbances indicate, have serious limitations when, regarded as agents of necessary social change, they seek to find ways in which they can serve their day and generation. The professor is faced with a painful paradox. On the one hand, he is being assailed by students (and parents, too) from Mexico to London, from Paris to Tokyo, because he does not really cater to student needs as they face the problems of the modern world. Yet the professor's energies are repeatedly being drained away from student care and other responsibilities within the universities precisely because he has listened to the call from the outside for help in dealing with the population question and the other problems which modern science and technology have precipitated for modern man—with nuclear energy, space research, organ transplantation, urban renewal, and the like.

This dilemma is worldwide, for outside the Communist countries, the liberal democratic university of the Western tradition is now the dominant model for all the countries of the world. Thus the weaknesses of this university pattern overshadow Asia and Africa as well as Europe and America. There seem to be two major shortcomings (for which the professor can blame no one but himself) in this pattern. The first of them is a view of the relation between knowledge and action whereby the highest evaluation of the former is regarded as having no relevance to the latter. Thus knowledge is estimated most highly when, free from all contamination from political and religious loyalties, it is pursued for its own sake. And so it is forgotten that informed action without a proper awareness of the significance of these ultimate loyalties cannot be but vain. The result is that the traditional liberal democratic university teacher seeks enlightenment in terms of the dispassionate study of problems rather than in terms of action which will solve them. In fact, many of our shrewdest thinkers would go much further. Thus Wilfred Cantwell Smith[54] of Harvard rightly bewails the fact that much of our

> modern academic life, especially among the social sciences, has seemed at times in danger of succumbing to a new scholasticism that under the concept of "discipline" would consider only those parts of a given problem, or indeed of all problems, that are susceptible to treatment by the established categories of that particular discipline; rather than beginning with the subject matter [i.e. the problem itself, A.S.N.] and giving one's total loyalty to it, and bringing to bear on it all the categories that are, or can be amended to be, relevant.

The second shortcoming is that in its own organization (which is in terms of a "departmental" approach to knowledge based upon the hoped-for autonomous disciplines) a university is the institutional—as the professor is the personal—expression of the view of knowledge which I have just described. That is why when called upon to contribute to the solution of the problems which outside agencies thrust upon it, a university has been forced to gear its efforts to activities *outside* the ordinary departmental structure of the schools and colleges. And so there has arisen a plethora of centers, institutes, and the like; but they are traditionally expected to operate under a severe limitation: A center or institute usually has no *teaching* responsibilities or rights. These are the monopoly of schools and departments.

What this means is that all its difficulty can be seen by raising the following questions which are relevant for any subject matter and then by applying our answers to population studies:

1. What should be taught about the subject at the undergraduate and graduate levels in our universities?

2. What kind of research should be done there?

3. What kinds of training should be offered by a university?

4. What measure of aid for ongoing services or for starting new ones should be furnished by a university?

As soon as we seriously pick up any one of such questions we run into the fact that the contemporary university is baffled again and again by a very simple but far-reaching consideration:

It is that the traditional patterns of thought and the academic structures of the liberal democratic university are dominated by the notion that a problem is best understood by breaking it up into its constituent parts. Thus, if we take the population issue, the following occurs: The demographers among us seek, for example, to ascertain accurately the quantitative changes in the size and structure of the population of an area, while the biologists in the field of human reproduction wish, for example, to predict the sex of a human fetus. But the political administrator or the statesman is called upon to act in terms of as exhaustive an understanding of the problem in its entirety as he can achieve. Thus, for him, the contributions of the economist, the sociologist, the biologist, and the like, along with awareness of such repercussions as the political implications of, for example, legal, religious, and ethical judgments, have to be brought together into a synoptic whole before he can make a wise decision.

It is for this reason that some are urging that those of us working in the universities should encourage the realistic departure from a state of affairs where population research, like teaching in this field, is only too often subsumed under the academic separatism of a threefold division into demographic studies, the biology of human reproduction, and public-health administration. We welcome the increasing awareness of three important facts. The first is that these studies should be more intimately related to each other. The second is that the bearing of the wider issues of economic development and rapidly changing political organization on population questions should receive increasing attention. A most encouraging third sign of advance in this country is that the National Endowment for the Humanities (an independent agency of the Federal Government) is now showing its concern by awarding a research grant to a law school, not for empirical research in what the law courts have said, but for light which jurisprudence throws on the human issues arising from population planning and research. In short, this wider movement in population studies has now gone beyond the natural sciences, the social sciences, and the health sciences in their relevance to the population question, to the point where the remaining major division of the intellectual life of our universities, the humanities, becomes relevant. It is significant that when Gunnar Myrdal[55] chose a title for his recent massive three volume "Inquiry Into The Poverty Of Nations," he took his metaphor not from the social sciences or medicine or engineering or production management but from the humanities. And so, *Asian Drama!*

But to indicate the need for recruiting help from the professors who profess the humanities is immediately to raise the theoretical question of how the humanities are relevant and the second is how the professional humanitists can be recruited to make their contribution. Here, I can pick up only the first of these two questions.

All issues of social policy involve calculations of consequences of the different possible courses of action before one of them can be recommended for adoption. Whether a course of action will be effective as the means toward the end required is in each case a problem for the social sciences. *But* the prior question of what end is to be achieved is not a scientific question in the usual Anglo-Saxon sense of the term. At this point one has to bring in ideas from law, ethics, religion, etc. And by the latter I do not mean the factual (i.e. empirical) aspects of this kind of data but rather the willingness to commend one goal rather than another one. That is why it is policy and that is why it goes beyond the social sciences to the realm with which the humanities are identified. And "policy" is not just the basis for that which governments do. It is that in which all of us are involved as soon as we recommend one course of action over another. For example, we all take it for granted that too rapid an increase in population is not a good thing. We all believe that rational spacing of children in a family is a good thing and that individual decision by parents is a good thing. But what is involved (in the sense of what is implicit) in all this is what requires most thought and attention. In short, I suppose that I am asking for a serious critical study of what we are doing at the point of the relation between our "science" and our "action."

I have just been studying the report by Reuben Hill *et al*,[56] entitled *Needed Social Science Research in Population and Family Planning*, which Dr. Hill and his colleagues did for the Ford

Foundation last year in India. What puzzles me most about this kind of report is the underlying notion that the kind of research projects which would be initiated, if this report were adopted, will somehow automatically be its own connection between the actual research on a topic done and the point where that research becomes politically effective. In other words, it is somehow believed that if sufficient social scientists work upon sufficient unrelated problems, there will be a kind of invisible hand (a la Adam Smith) which will produce the required social good. And this implication is not justified by experience.

I do wish that all of us in universities, in foundations, and in government who are engaged in population studies at the point where we are indentified with policies (and in some sense we all are) could seriously spend some time, money, and energy comparable on this sort of issue to what we are doing under the rubrics of "the social sciences, or training of administrators for running family-planning programs or the biology of human reproduction. The snag is that what I have in mind is not called research among the social scientists, who dominate the research-grant-awarding establishment. To an old-time physical chemist like me, this position seems to be just too naive for words. What in heaven's name do such people think that theoretical physicists and theoretical chemists are doing when they sit at their desks or stand by a blackboard and use nothing mechanically more complicated than a pen or a piece of chalk. One thing I do know they do is that they make revolutionary and significant advances and we are certainly not doing that in the population field. And we shall not succeed in doing otherwise, I venture to prophesy, until we see that good theory in the population field will look to the social sciences establishment, like philosophy, precisely because it will involve the humanities.

I recognize that the view of the humanities here being entertained hardly fits the image of them as normally construed either by the professional scholar or the man in the street. The former thinks of the humanities as primarily a field, rivaling the natural sciences in intellectual precision and in logical rigor, for the exercise of his thought and scholarship. He thinks, therefore, that the basic purpose of the humanities is to seek answers to such technical questions as the Latin sources of Shakespeare's knowledge of the moon or the distinction between *episteme* and *doxa* in Plato. The latter, the man in the street, considers the humanities in rather more congenial terms but in two further different fashions. He thinks of them either as an adornment to living, such as an expensive glossy art book on his coffee table, or at a more serious level he thinks of listening to Beethoven at the end of a day's work or of taking his children to an art gallery on a rainy afternoon.

Clearly the role of the humanities assumed in this argument is one that sees them dealing with the problems of human life at a deeper level than that of academic scholarship or happy recreation. To say that, of course, is not to denigrate either the one or the other of these two legitimate human activities, but it is to affirm the need for us to go well beyond either one of them. It is to advance to the point where we raise the question of the kind of life and living in which and from which both scholarship and recreation alike take their meaning.

They are the kind of questions which lie behind a far-reaching statement recently issued by the National Endowment for the Humanities:[57]

> The present crisis of American society leads the National Council on the Humanities to reaffirm that the humanities ideally are always relevant to the condition of man, and of man's society. It therefore wishes to encourage, in addition to significant studies and works in the familiar humanistic tradition of pure scholarship and general knowledge, appropriate project proposals within the various fields of the humanities which are concerned with values as they bear on urbanization, minority problems, war, peace, and foreign policy; problems of governmental decision, civil liberties, and the wider application of humanistic knowledge and insights to the general public interest.

Incidentally, such a view of the humanities, apparently strange, actually is far from new. It is a very old one. It goes back to the Father of Humanism, Isocrates, whose students became the lawyers and the politicians who carried the burden of national reconstruction as their native land, Greece, sought the restoration of democracy and recovery from her defeat at the end of the fifth century B.C.

Chapter Sixteen

SOME THOUGHTS ON STUDENTS AND POPULATION CENTERS

JAMES PEPPER

IT IS not simply youthful chauvinism which places America's young at the center of this essay. This is the group, after all, which will produce the population which so concerns us. Any program of population control must persuade them. This is the group, furthermore, which must produce the field workers so necessary for the implementation of the program in this country and possibly abroad. Without the support of youth, the finest theoretical program will remain a tragic testimony to what should have been. Clearly, in the area of population, more than any other, the young demand attention.

It is generally recognized that no comprehensive program of social change can be successful unless there exists an equally comprehensive understanding of the ethos of the group primarily involved. Yet no such understanding of the essential spirit and character of America's young people seems to exist, particularly among those involved in population research. This is not surprising, but it is extremely dangerous. It is not surprising, I believe, because we are witnessing today the beginning of a fundamental metaphysical and epistemological change in our world view. At this point in history, it is impossible to predict just what the outcome will be. But the manifestations of this change are everywhere.

A six hundred-year-old conception of man, forced upon us by urbanization, industrialization, and the Protestant Ethic, is slowly disintegrating under the onslaught of its own absurdities and inner-contradictions.

Stern responsibilities and duties have begun to give way to hedonism and self-indulgence. We no longer are awed by art; we participate in it. Formal relationships are being replaced by open acceptance of ourselves and others. Concepts of government, family, work, schools, and churches, which once held structure to be of first importance, are now becoming molded to meet the needs of the individual. Structures, therefore, should be organic: They should be the natural outgrowth of human society rather than an imposition upon that society. But recognition of just what "natural human society" is supposed to be, after six crushing, dehumanizing centuries, is a long way off. Those who have accepted the theory that structures should fit the man, rather than the other way around, welcome most social experimentation, contradiction, and confusion as a means of ridding ourselves of our stultifying legacy. Yet even these people have little idea where we are or where we are going.

These are just some of the reasons why the lack of understanding of our younger people is not surprising. That youth, the special province of the population expert, manifests the major impact of the new world view is also to be expected—such is the case in all times of fundamental change. Hence, generation gaps. Already, the emerging attitudes of youth seem to indicate that existing population patterns will be substantially altered. This can hardly be expected to soothe those responsible for creating a population program, for clearly, any plan based on a disappearing conceptual structure will be obsolete before it can be inaugurated. Worse, such a plan very possibly will evoke harshly negative reactions which could destroy what little remaining confidence students have in the academic community. This need not happen.

Old institutions and old methodologies cannot be expected to survive unless they can be made to harmonize with emerging world views. Since this is a book about population centers, the remainder of this essay will discuss some of the reasons why old institutions, and old methodologies, especially those in the social sciences, do not now harmonize with the emerging world view, and discuss how they may be made to harmonize with the world view in the future.

The universities and the methodologies, if they have ever harmonized with anything, harmonize with the old conceptual structure. Just as the structure attempted to make man into a statistic rather than an individual, so did the university and most scientific methodologies—everything in its place.

English 101 at 8:30 every Monday, Wednesday, and Friday. No matter if one day at 8:30 you felt like studying genetics, genetics does not begin until your junior year at 10:30 on Tuesday and Thursday. Maybe then you feel like reading a little Keats that fine Thursday morning? The Thrush may have told you that you were right, but Dr. Burns waits for no man. That night you try to bootleg the Keats while you should be reading about objectivity and the social sciences and something called "objectively verifiable data." "Beauty is truth, truth beauty" and "never the twain shall meet." Your roommate tells you not to let your classes get in the way of your education, but if your grades keep dropping, they will take away your scholarship and you will not be able to get a job anywhere without that degree. And so on.

Can a population center, even one founded with the best intentions, thrive in this atmosphere?

Supposedly the liberal arts prepare the student for life. Supposedly the university is a microcosm as dynamic as the real life outside. Perhaps it is exactly that. The zealously guarded departmental walls compare generally and sometimes exactly with those of the corporate and Governmental bureaucracy. The hostilities of the faculty, the students, and the administration—within themselves and one against the other—are closely analogous to what is going on out there in the big world. Needless to say, the individual student is completely prepared for what is to come: He is drained of his imagination so that he will not rock the boat; he is stuffed full of self-discipline so that he will sit uncomplaining at his desk until he is sixty-five or dead, whichever comes first; he is injected with a healthy shot of insecurity, so that he will remain unfulfilled and a constant consumer, joiner, and plugger; he has been given a small dose of paranoia so that he will be sure to cut every throat in sight. He is, in short, a solid citizen.

Youth finally appears unwilling to accept such a fate. Now, it is beginning to look as though the universities must change, must model themselves on the new realities of life or lose their reason for being. Or else, one fine day, there will be no students.

How does this relate to the population center? As we know, the population center, to be successful, must also harmonize with the emerging world view. In an ideal situation—one in which the entire university functions as a microcosm of the new world view (some of the problems with bringing this about will be taken up below under the methodology section)—the presence of the center within the university would be extremely valuable. The university would be as dynamic and as alive as the outside world. If this came about, ideas and innovation would come rapidly and be more eagerly considered. This environment could help invigorate the otherwise isolated people at the center. I would go so far as to suggest that the center directly involve itself, through teaching, with the undergraduates. This way, these students would come to a deeper appreciation of the population problem. Through the normal passage of ideas, the great bulk of students in the entire university would feel the impact of the work of the center. One cannot underestimate the positive value this would have for the program in general. The relevance of the university as such would more closely approach the ideal; it is inconceivable that a center, as a truly interdisciplinary, dynamic facility, would be less than a major influence upon the modernization of the university structure. This process would, of course, work both ways. The teaching faculty at the center would have its understanding of the outside constantly honed and revitalized. It would have available large numbers of at least partially trained students to reduce the work load. Eventually, some of these students would become field workers or members of the center or other centers.

I have referred to a "truly interdisciplinary, dynamic facility." The way this phrase is eventually defined provides, I think, the key to the successful revitalization of the university and the beginning of an effective population center. "Interdisciplinary" means a great deal more than a variety of specialists working together toward the same goal. As an example, at one population center we might find working together a biochemist, an economist, an engineer, a sociologist, a demographer, a physician, a psychologist, and an anthropologist. If each man remained as tightly trapped in his discipline as such specialists often are, chaos and anarchy would result. Little information would actually be shared. Such is the present state of methodology, thanks to present world views. But even should these people finally agree and produce a proposal, I submit that the likelihood that it could favorably alter the population problem would be extremely small. The problem is that few methodologies deal comfortably, if at all, with intangibles. True, there is a very great need for as much concrete, statistically verifiable data as possible. When you deal with human beings, however, a subjective, intuitive, lyrical "feel" for the ethos of the group you are working with is at least of equal importance—and more now, surely, than ever before.

For some time, objectivity has been the great goal of the social and behavioral sciences. When a student picks up almost any one of the textbooks of the trade, he is almost certain to find the first chapter extolling the virtues of scientific methodology as the surest path to truth. Usually the reader will be told that although we cannot quite achieve the certitude of the physical sciences, the very success of the physical sciences in isolating objectively verifiable data is reason enough to emulate their methods.

Yet the certitude, the inflexible accuracy, of the physical sciences is in clear, direct relationship to the degree that those sciences function as closed systems. Mathematics is far more truthful than biology, while history is the dreamiest of fantasies. Implicit in this approach is a very narrow definition of truth. So narrow, in fact, that it often has no application to the broad concerns of the social sciences.

Disciplines which search for objectively verifiable data have no use for intangibles. Yet the ethos of a people, the fountainhead of culture and history, is not only a vast intangible but is the indispensable element in an understanding of the dynamics of human society.

One of the most successful books on a people is Gilberto Freyre's[58] *The Masters and the Slaves*. In many ways, it follows the traditional methods of analysis of the development of a people. Yet it comes alive for an unorthodox reason. The book itself is a microcosm of the ethos of the Brazilian people. At some length, for example, Freyre examines the remarkable sexuality of his people. He discusses its components and its influences and its impact upon Brazil. These things are all valuable. But the amazing, unique thing about the book is that, of itself, it throbs with the same sexuality that the author is attempting to discuss "objectively." The author's turn of phrase, his choice of metaphor, his use of nuance combine to give the feeling that the book itself *is* the Brazilian culture, its complexities and passions. *The Masters and the Slaves* succeeds precisely because it is *subjective,* precisely because it utilizes the insights of the poet along with the scientific methodology. The reader, for a time, lives as a Brazilian; his dynamic understanding is far superior to anything based on objectively verifiable data. The poet has within his grasp truths often unavailable to others.

The much-needed revision of current methodologies will require the concerted, creative efforts of the finest and most sensitive intellects available.

It may be valuable to recognize that the humanities and the arts offer means of uncovering truth not discernable through the physical sciences alone. Human life is far too dynamic and tumultuous to be analyzed by a method which deals uneasily with the transcendental. What light, for example, would the scientific method shed upon the Samurai culture which, as a major means of enlightenment, utilized the Koan? (The most familiar being, "You know the sound of two hands clapping, but what is the sound of one hand clapping?")

This is not to say that the scientific method should be completely abandoned. That would leave us only with an extremism of another sort. Rather, we must recognize that a thorough appreciation of the plastic arts is often more valuable than reams of statistics; at the very least, these statistics have little meaning without the insight necessary to interpret them provided us by our artists. *The Electric Kool-Aid Acid Test* by Tom Wolfe[59] just may have more to offer than stacks of reports by Presidential commissions. And how could anyone possibly understand what is happening in America today unless he submits to the mind-scrambling catharsis of The Who?*

The people of the world are so very proud of what they have done. They learned to utilize fire, they discovered the wheel, they developed agriculture and the nuclear bomb. For the most part, they bolster their sometime-battered egos by applauding themselves. But if they fail to understand what the "Youth Movement" is all about, especially on the population dilemma, they will collectively be clapping with one hand.

---

* "The Who" is a musical group currently enjoying a vogue.

WHAT CAN VARIOUS TYPES OF INSTITUTIONS CONTRIBUTE TO THE POPULATION PROBLEM?

There are seven chapters in this section. The senior administrators from universities, nonprofit research groups, and national laboratories describe the kinds of contributions which their respective organizations can make—and the limitations of each. Reacting to their respective remarks are administrators of similar institutions, thus giving this section the flavor of a symposium, which reflects on the questions raised in *Section Three* as to whether the university can meet the challenge.

Chapter Seventeen

THE PRESIDENT OF A LARGE STATE UNIVERSITY VIEWS RESEARCH CENTERS

CHARLES HITCH

I SUPPOSE in some sense I can speak for university-associated research centers. But I did spend thirteen years of my life and, I think, some of my most productive and satisfying years helping develop a nonuniversity associated research organization called The Rand Corporation. I suppose I know more about the potentialities, problems, and limitations of that type of organization in its conduct of mission-oriented research than I do about the centers within the university.

For many years the National Institutes of Health have had a splendid record of achievement in supporting university-based research, research training, and in helping furnish facilities and equipment. The NIH programs have been well distributed and competently administered by a combination of civil servants.

I think the total Federal effort in this field need not and probably should not follow any single type or style of organization. Every approach, every type of research organization, has its own strengths and weaknesses. The great strength of the American approach to applied research has, in my opinion, been its pluralism. I expect it would make very good sense in a field as new and undeveloped, as diverse and devoid of unifying theory as population research, to back several organizational types, to spend some funds on research and training grants in universities, some on in-house research, and some on nonuniversity-associated centers. Perhaps we need many types of centers with quite different styles.

Universities do have some great strengths as institutions supporting applied research. Let me mention a few points in support of this. I think first, and most important, the university is uniquely qualified to provide training as an integral part of the research effort. In field after field, universities have created a

211

whole new generation of professions in fields where there were only dilettantes before. Population research is desperately short of trained manpower, and attracting bright young minds to population research is one of our most urgent goals. To lure scholars and teachers away from universities only to insulate them from students would be, I think, a great mistake. Laboratories like those of the Atomic Energy Commission do engage in a certain amount of teaching by one device or another. But if you look at the expenditure per student, it is a very high ratio, far higher, I would think, than in the universities where training is traditional.

There are on campus now many of the essential facilities necessary for research and training in the population field. There are excellent library collections, computers, and laboratories. These are very expensive items, and given the existing university equipment, I do not see the need (although it may arise) to allocate substantial funds for building separate large centers in universities or anywhere else.

Further, universities have superior ability to supply research personnel, because faculty appointments in combining research with teaching are highly attractive to many top people and because faculty research can be supplemented by high-quality graduate-student research appointments. We saw the converse of this problem at Rand where we did not have the availability of students and graduate assistants and where certainly in those days we had great difficulty in attracting top people.

Universities contain most of the disciplines relevant to population research: biology, medicine, law, political science, demography, anthropology, sociology, public health, and who knows how many et ceteras at this stage. It is terribly difficult to assemble a critical mass of scholars from all of these diverse disciplines. I should have taken time before I left Berkeley to count the number of research centers, institutes, and bureaus we have in the University of California but I did not; I think it is somewhere between one and two hundred. They range widely in size and degree of interdisciplinary mix; some are mission oriented, some are problem-solving oriented. I suppose the two largest are the Agricultural Experiment Station and the Scripps Institution of Oceanography, both of which have been successful up to a point in achieving interdisciplinary research. This is particularly true of the Agricultural Experiment Station, but even here the range of disciplines covered is not wide. We have biological scientists, engineers, agricultural economists, veterinarians, and perhaps a few others. The Scripps Institution of Oceanography has achieved a great deal of integration of physical scientists and engineers, but the social sciences have been relatively ignored. In other institutes you do have an admixture of social scientists of various kinds, for example, in transportation research, pollution research, and higher-education research.

Of course, there are plenty of things that universities do not do well and should not even be asked to do. By and large, universities are not as good in the development end of "research and development." I think that their public-service activities probably ought to be limited to activities that are closely associated either with their training function or with their research function. The weaknesses of universities in mission-oriented and interdisciplinary research are in most respects the counterpart of their strengths. The independence of the tenured university faculty member which is so desirable up to a point makes him hard to bend in directions that he finds unacceptable. It is a well-known fact, too, that departmental loyalties make interdisciplinary cooperation hard to achieve. The difference between universities and nonuniversity research organizations in these respects is one of degree and not of kind.

Let me express some skepticism about the scope which is desirable in these centers. I am inclined to think that great breadth should not be a necessary qualification for designation of a population center. It is not essential that biomedical research for developing better contraceptives need be carried out in close geographical propinquity to the research being conducted by the demographers and the sociologists. Communication and exchange of information is important, but I expect the best place for medical research is in biology laboratories and medical centers. I frankly do not know whether the present sites for developing contraceptive devices are right or not; but if there is urgency about this development, and it seems to me there is, perhaps more important than where to do the work is a focus on new means for finding the answers.

I conclude with this thought: I do not think that we have here a problem like the development of the atomic bomb. Unlike the bomb project, the problem in the population field is not well defined. Only a few of the disciplines that can contribute significantly to its solution are identified, and even they are desperately short of well-trained professionals to address the problems. In these circumstances, there is everything to be said for a flexible, pluralistic approach, for concentrating on brains, not concrete. At this point I cannot say what proportion of the total effort should be undertaken in the universities, but it is clear to me that it should be a substantial part.

Chapter Eighteen

THE PRESIDENT OF A PRIVATE UNIVERSITY VIEWS RESEARCH CENTERS

KINGMAN BREWSTER, JR.

I AM going to talk about what the inherent structure of some universities seems to be, and the consequences this structure might have for what we might be good at, and what we are not good for. I do not have the competence to zero-in very explicitly with respect to the fitness of universities to work on population or any of its component problems. It is obvious, therefore, that I may run the risk of overgeneralizing in terms of what various institutional forms are able to do. Since I do not care to do this, I make a very strong qualification: I cannot think of any of my colleagues who are presidents of other institutions who would want me to be speaking for them.

I am speaking from the narrow background of my own institution, supplemented a bit by the other two institutions where I have worked, Massachusetts Institute of Technology and Harvard.

I realize that my institution, both in size and tradition, is perhaps far from typical of other major research-intensive universities. But there are certain common denominators. Sometimes they are dealt with in somewhat negative terms by critics.

The university should probably admit that it is the kind of community which is more concerned with the fundamental validity of its work than with the immediate usefulness of that work. In holding that view, it would be expressing the conviction that the validity is seen, in a social sense, as more valuable than current, topical usefulness.

On the research side, generally speaking, the university is more "discipline-oriented," and the motivation of those engaged in research is more "puzzle oriented" than topical problem-solving.

As far as training is concerned, also at the research level, it is quite clear that the training program is intended to stretch a person's capacity in terms of his mastery of the discipline as such. His ability to make a contribution to methodology is itself a more significant mark of educational accomplishment and attainment than is the solution of particular action problems. The primary principle of research organization is focused on the discipline. The organization of departments has some of the attributes of a combination of craft unionism and feudalism. This makes them rather hesitant to change from their long-accepted principles of structure and function.

You may find all kinds of things called "centers" or "institutes" associated with departments or schools, but I do not think that is what we are talking about here.

Also, you might find all kinds of interdisciplinary or interprofessional work which is not structured in the form of institutes or centers, and that *is* what we are talking about here.

Take my own experience. We have at Yale our Center for Mathematical and Econometrics, which I suppose is one of the best in the world and has made enormous fundamental advances in econometrics and mathematical economics. We have also associated with the economics department an Economic Growth Center, financed largely by foundation funds. But I do not think that these are more than research appendages to a discipline, organized as a department.

It does not mean they are not important. It does not mean they are not useful. But they do not become interdisciplinary just because they are called centers or institutes.

Likewise, they are, at our university, collaborative interprofessional, as well as interdisciplinary, activities which draw together different professions and disciplines. On questions of professional ethics, work may join those in practical theology, those in law, and those in medicine to work on unresolved problems of ethics in medicine, on research involving human experimentation, and on certain facets of the problems associated with population. These efforts may occur in the form of a program or a committee, rather than in a center or an institute.

It is perfectly true that as far as dealing with foundations and government is concerned, you do get some extra "Brownie points" if you call these collaborative or clusters of interdisciplinary effort an "institute" or a "center." There is a kind of visibility, fashionability, possibly greater stability, and certainly a status symbolism in calling something an institute or a center rather than a committee or program.

So I realize there are these practical, cynical, but realistic biases which may make a label—a designation—important. But I do think what we are talking about here is the kind of activity, whatever its structure or classification may be, which is transdepartmental.

I would differentiate between that transdepartmental activity which is interdisciplinary on the one hand and that which is problem-solving on the other. This is my own glossary, but I think that quite different things are swept together under the rubric of interdisciplinary activity. You can have that kind of interdisciplinary activity which takes place when the methodology of one discipline is applied to problems of another, such as you have in the application of modern physics to chemistry or modern physics and chemistry to the problems of biology and so on.

This is not mission-oriented simply because it is interdisciplinary, but it is transdepartmental.

No university will, in fact, be able to follow the intellectual curiosity of its most able members unless it has some way of making sure that a person's activity is not confined to the methodology of a single discipline, if his intellectual problems, his puzzles, could be more easily solved by applying the methodology of the neighboring discipline.

But I differentiate that kind of interdisciplinary search for truth, still not motivated by usefulness except on terms of a broader comprehension of the universe, from the problem-solving approach appropriate to the consideration of population research.

I think the question is, Is the university any good at the problem-solving projects? Obviously, in its professional work, the university is doing this kind of thing all the time, for example in law or medicine. In these fields most research is action-oriented; and most research which is action-oriented has to let the problem give the clue to what is relevant to its solution.

Thus, as the problems of law, the problems of medicine defy solutions within their closed systems, you find all professional schools adding inputs from other disciplines, because their problems cannot be dealt with professionally unless the inputs of other disciplines are applied.

Whether in terms of school or interdepartmental programs, action-oriented work at the professional level has deep roots in the university tradition; but as far as interdisciplinary structures are concerned, such work cannot be confined within a single school at the professional level, but must straddle the university as a whole.

Speaking particularly of my own university, I suppose under President Angell, the Institute of Human Relations, vaguely conceived in the 1920's and put to work in the 1930's and 1940's, was one of the first efforts to try to make comprehensible those aspects of human relations which could be understood only if the techniques and data of a variety of disciplines were applied.

We also have the Child Study Center, which for a long time has had both an operational and a research and training function; drawing not only from psychiatry, psychology, and pediatrics, but even more broadly from other political, social, economic, and administrative sciences as they have become more relevant to their work.

We do not have as many centers and institutes of an interdepartmental nature as many universities do, nor do we have a School of Business Administration or Public Administration. But we try to figure out how we can supplement the disciplines in the social sciences with a capacity to attract both faculty, postdoctoral students, and doctoral candidates interested in the professional or problem-solving capacity of the social sciences in contrast to the refinement of the theoretical discipline. And we have set up an Institute of Social Science—or maybe it can be called Institute for Social and Policy Studies—which will have within it what wishfully we think are "collapsible" centers.

The capacity for self-perpetuation of any academic undertaking makes me wonder whether these centers will ever collapse. But the hope, or design, is to have centers which will be staffed in terms of an attack on the intellectual and professional problems peculiar to challenging social issues broadly defined. We will have within this Institute, for example, a Center for the Study of the City; a Center for Educational Studies, focusing largely on the systems problems of educational administration; a Center of Management Studies, again focusing on the inherent problems of large organizations, public and private.

There is nothing new about this. Other people have been doing it for a long time. We have been doing it in various corners of various departments and schools.

Our effort was perhaps somewhat different because we will try to have it both ways. We will not have the applied sector of social sciences incorporated in a separate faculty, with all the dangers of intellectual obsolescence which that entails; and at the same time we will not have the appointments or the degree-granting programs of the problem-oriented groups subject to the dominant voice of the basic department.

Compromises are inevitable—that is, on the appointments process, although those who do not hold academic appointments by the Institute or their various centers without the concurrence of departments; those who have academic appointments, professional and otherwise, would be appointed jointly by those departments concerned with the relevant disciplines or by the Schools responsible for the relevant professions.

I think this is a reflection of the fact that even a traditional arts and sciences university like ours realizes, as the social sciences have become more scientific and more socially useful, that there is a very important professional demand which must be met by the Ph.D. program. Therefore, we are "joining the party" and trying to take advantage of the mistakes which others have made before us, while trying to borrow from their successes.

I think the Government faces three difficulties in dealing with a university. One is that the university, in order to provide the standards which make for good education as well as good research, must expect that anyone appointed to a significant position bears the warranty of his discipline by the rather stuffy standards of established faculties, even if he is not working primarily in the refinement of that discipline.

You always run the risk of a split-level faculty if you have some people who bear the warranty of the discipline, and others who do not. It is injurious not only to morale but to the productivity and ultimately to the standards of those who live on a lower level of the split-level arrangement.

Secondly, you have to expect that, no matter how problem-oriented the work of a center or an institute may be, there is and must be a high degree of freedom for people to decide what their work is going to be.

Basically, the tradition of faculty self-determination in terms of research is going to be a privilege which should be grudgingly given up even by those working in a problem-oriented center.

Finally, I think that it is clear that the same tradition of faculty self-determination and freedom and security which is a peculiar privilege of the university appointment means that you are not going to get really effective drafts upon this resource unless it is funded with that degree of continuity which allows the institute to honor its commitments to those who hold faculty appointments.

These are inconveniences. Perhaps they are worse than that. Maybe they will undercut the effectiveness of the university as an instrument for work in the kind of field we are talking about.

We are best at work at the fundamental level, if the problem has not yielded to massive systematic attack but still has fundamental puzzles, whether social, scientific, behavioral, organizational, or engineering and natural scientific. If the problem is really just a question of mobilization of existing knowledge for the purpose of bringing about a result, then I do not think a university is particularly good.

A university is best at the advancement of knowledge, and that advancement and emphasis can be directed, as it has been in the biomedical and physics fields, by the availability of Government support.

I have my own preconceptions about the nature of the unsolved problem of population. I think solutions lie in the realm of human values, human behavior, and social organizations, not just biomedical science.

It seems to me that much more fundamental inventiveness, not just the application of existing knowledge, is necessary. And I should hope that the university would be able to put its rather peculiar but unique tradition and talents to work in seeking timely answers to some of those unresolved problems.

Chapter Nineteen

VIEWS OF A NATIONAL LABORATORY DIRECTOR

ALVIN WEINBERG

IN MANY quarters, there is an unstated but implicit assumption that the population problem is susceptible to solution or resolution by the methods of science, and that therefore if some kind of all-out scientific attack is unleashed, the problem will be diminished or even destroyed.

I submit that this is an unproven assumption.

We are assuming that the methods of science, of hard, rational analysis, are indeed relevant to resolving the population problem—and I repeat that this is still a large and unproved assumption. The population problem, just as other great problems (e.g. the three "P's": poverty, peace, pollution), creates an interest among the scientific community for at least one rather crass reason: the not-too-affluent scientists may smell the possibility of money. Though the problem certainly contains technological and scientific components amenable to scientific investigation, one cannot ignore the fact that there are some strong economic inducements attracting many to the issue.

Whereas it was clear at the time of fission that the large laboratory was the proper instrument to deal with the development of bombs and reactors, it is not nearly so clear that a large multidisciplinary institute will have the same impact on the big "P's"—including population.

Let me state, however, what the big national laboratory is good at doing. Scientists in the national laboratories generally are prepared to do what is necessary to get on with the job. The structure is hierarchial to a much greater extent than in a university. A member of a national laboratory is supposed to be prepared to take orders and to concede that someone can tell him what to do.

222

In contrast with the not-for-profits—and there are many similarities between, say, a place like Oak Ridge and Stanford Research Institute—the national laboratories are supposedly more independent in their funding than are the not-for-profits. Therefore, they are supposed to have more flexibility and independence from their sponsors than does an institution whose survival at every instant depends upon negotiating a contract. Even so, the national laboratories have to do an awful lot of scrambling for funds in much the same way as a not-for-profit institution does.

Nevertheless there is a distinctive institutional "ecology" in the national laboratories which suits for specific types of projects. They are most efficient in building things like reactors and accelerators.

Moreover, because of their interactive, multidisciplinary style, the national laboratories—and this I think is a very important point—are often able to reimpose at the working level a reintegration of problems which were once whole, but which were later fragmented by the realities of Washington's bureaucracy.

I think this is perhaps one of the most important functions of these large, interdisciplinary, supercritical institutions—that they can take a cut at a problem that was originally whole, but becomes fragmented as it channels through the different pieces of Washington bureaucracy. When it gets to the working level, if the institution involved has enough breadth of scope, enough expertise, it can impose a certain amount of reintegration at the working level.

A few years ago our laboratory was involved in the problem of desalting sea water. It turns out that in any desalting device there are two separate aspects: the device itself and the energy source. Because of the way Washington bureaucracy works, desalting sea water was the responsibility of the Office of Saline Water. Energy was the responsibility of the Department of the Interior, of the Atomic Energy Commission or of some other agency, depending upon what source of energy was used. There was no place in Washington where energy and desalting were brought together. This was later accomplished, however, when desalting became a part of the Oak Ridge National Laboratory. We had the energy already and were able to put the two things back together, as they were when the problem was originally posed.

Thus, insofar as technological or hard scientific components can be identified in the population problem, I have no doubt that structures like national laboratories can do a good job. They can, for example, mount very large-scale biological experiments with very large protocols. For twenty years we have been doing work on genetics at Oak Ridge which by now has involved many millions of mice. At any given time we have hundreds of thousands of mice available for study. In terms of the low-level side effects of the pill, for instance, researchers will have to operate on a similarly large scale. This sort of thing is commonplace in a big institution like a national laboratory, but not in most other institutions; it takes as a matter of course the interaction of many different disciplines.

Can this pattern of interdisciplinary and multidisciplinary cooperation that has been successful in the development of atomic energy be brought to bear on problems that have much stronger social components, that do not have nearly the same definitiveness as does building a reactor?

I do not really know. All I can say is what our own experience has been. Down at Oak Ridge we have dipped down into three fields that have required social sciences.

We have done some work in civil defense, in the application of desalting water to problems in the Middle East, and the question of urban decentralization. I will not say that all our efforts have been tremendously successful. On the other hand, in one case, a demographic study of factors underlying urbanization in the United States, the social scientists, mostly demographers, were much impressed with their first experience at a big hardware-oriented national laboratory. Professor Everett Lee, from Massachusetts University, who was in charge of the study, told me that if the enormous logistic power of the national laboratories could be really brought to bear on demography, that demography would enter a completely new phase in its development. He felt that these big institutions with their tremendous computers, with people ready, willing, and paid for being helpful to you, can do things that cannot be done in smaller institutions.

Let me close with a remark about the role of information in any major field of research exploration. The problems that we are describing now, like population and pollution, are diffuse and complex. They have little underlying theoretical or conceptual framework. I cannot help but speculate on the possibility that by organizing and controlling information in these fields, one might be able to impose a coherence on the thinking and experimentation that in a better-defined field like physics is done by theory. This is relatively easy to do in a well-defined field like theoretical physics, but in a poorly defined, amorphous field like population, theory development could be enormously aided by the control, collation, and coordination of information on the subject.

What I have in mind is the key role that information centers ought to play in such fields as population. Any discussion of population centers should certainly concern itself with this aspect of the problem. In the Oak Ridge Laboratory alone, we now have about fifteen such information centers that do work mostly in complex fields.

Chapter Twenty

NATIONAL LABORATORIES AS A CENTERS PROTOTYPE

JAMES L. LIVERMAN

THERE is no more important problem facing this nation and the world than the question of ever-increasing population, from which arises problems in pollution of our environment, pollution of the gene pool with inborn errors, depletion of the earth's finite natural resources, and other yet unsuspected things.

I do not believe this or any other group will arrive at the conclusion that there is a single unique organizational setup that can be devised to insure success of a population centers program. What is important in any arrangement is the commitment of the people in the organization to the objective of the program, to understand its nature, to propose and try various solutions, and to insure in some way that the workable solutions are implemented on a broad base.

My seven years with the Atomic Energy Commission before joining one of its laboratories was at the middle-management level. Thus, I will be addressing my topic of the national laboratory as a centers prototype from the view of Government middle-management as well as from the laboratory's top management.

I want to discuss national laboratories, their organization, their manner of operating, both internally and in relation to the parent agency, and in particular to draw contrasts in the manner in which they and universities operate.

The AEC has six national laboratories: The University of California manages the Los Alamos Scientific Laboratory and Lawrence Radiation Laboratory; the University of Chicago and Argonne Universities Associated operate Argonne National Laboratory; Associated Universities, Inc. operate Brookhaven National Laboratory; Batelle operates Batelle Northwest Laboratories (formerly known as Hanford Laboratories); and Union Carbide Corporation manages the Oak Ridge National Laboratory, my own organization. These laboratories are characterized by their broad competence in physical, biological, and engineering sciences which they use not only to do the research but also to carry that research to the proof-of-principle stage, to insure the transfer of technology to the public sector and to institute the broad information programs needed to get the message across to the man in the street.

Each of these laboratories has developed its own personality, its own scientific programs, and its own approach to problem-solving, as well as its own particular attitude toward national problems. The Oak Ridge National Laboratory in large measure reflects Alvin Weinberg's philosophy, "to mobilize around the problem with all the resources necessary to make a major impact." In a sense it is a philosophy of "if anything is worth doing, it is worth doing well." Most of what I say will reflect how Oak Ridge operates rather than how all the AEC laboratories are run. There are similarities and differences between us, but I suspect the general principles of operation will be sufficiently alike that my descriptions may be generalized to include the others.

These laboratories are managed under a cost-plus-fixed-fee prime contract with the Atomic Energy Commission. If these laboratories do work for other government agencies, there is simply the cost of doing the work; no additional fee is involved.

A very important aspect of AEC's stewardship of the laboratories is that it assigns broad missions in the various program areas—life science, reactor development, and similar fields—and then gives to the management of the laboratory wide discretionary powers to accomplish those missions.

The AEC is guided at the policy level by five commissioners appointed by the President with the usual Senate approval. Within the Congress there is a Joint Committee on Atomic Energy that has developed a most unusual working relationship with the AEC, and it is from this fountainhead that some of its troubles spring, but also many of its strengths. The General

Manager of the AEC is the chief operating officer and he is flanked by a group of assistant general managers, who act as co-ordinators of the program divisions operating under them, such as the Division of Biology and Medicine and the Research Division.

These program divisions are the foci for action in the AEC, for it is at this level that programs are conceived, developed, and implemented as a result of budgets defended before the Bureau of the Budget and the Congress. It is with this level in Headquarters of the AEC that the principal interactions with the national laboratories occur.

There is an arm of the AEC staffed by Government civil servants which is located physically near each of the national laboratories, and whose responsibility is the detailed aspects of the contract management: The Oak Ridge Operations Office (ORO) for instance has about five hundred employees and is headed by a manager. The ORO actually manages the contract between the AEC and the prime contractor, in our case Union Carbide, and it also handles the fiscal management of all university-supported programs of AEC which involve the Southeastern United States. The San Francisco Operations Office handles the Lawrence Radiation Laboratory contract, and the Albuquerque area Office handles the Los Alamos contract. While these officials handle the fiscal affairs of contracts, the actual matters related to the conduct of scientific-research business is routed directly between the laboratories and the program divisions in Washington. On these matters, the field offices are simply given informational copies of actions. In this manner it is clear that implementation of research flows around the field-operation offices and there is no interruption of the scientific program by them. This element in the organization is different from that found in the university, and for that matter, in most other agencies of the Government. This close proximity of the contracting officer usually has beneficial effects. The major difference between AEC's method of management and that of other agencies in this regard is the fairly clear separation of the bookkeeping aspects and the scientific aspects of contract management. This is a very positive thing from the standpoint of the laboratory.

Let us now move into the actual laboratory organization and discuss the general relationship with the AEC.

Each of these large multipurpose laboratories is headed by a laboratory director and a group of assistant or associate directors. Management at the laboratory level acts primarily in a coordinative role to keep things moving between the laboratory program workers and the officials in the AEC branches in Washington. This type of management permits the laboratory to be immediately responsive to the needs of the Commission and occasionally to function on a "crash basis" if the Commission has a need for rapid action. Such a need recently arose with regard to having the AEC address the environmental question.

The national laboratory writes its program in $100,000 to $500,000 packages and submits its total collection of proposals to the AEC. The Commission then reviews these and ultimately allocates funds. The Biology Division of the Oak Ridge National Laboratory, for example, received about eight million dollars per year from the Commission. This amount is funded from Washington in a lump sum, without detailed and specific guidelines being given for the expenditure of these monies. This policy permits the management of Oak Ridge a very wide latitude in the employment of its funds for research efforts. Of course, the programs implemented by the Laboratory must be in general agreement with the proposed plan submitted earlier to AEC. The latitude given us, however, allows for a fast response time and wide options for decision-making at the scientific level where the effort of integrating all the staff to the optimal scientific effort must take place. Our attitude, and I believe that of the AEC, is that science can be integrated only at the working level and not on a piece of paper in Washington. Little attempt is made to exert the philosophy that says, "If we control the dollars, we will thereby manage the program." I do not believe a program based on science and technology can effectively be managed by stressing the amount of money spent rather than judging upon the basis of an overall excellence, and its relevance to the issue being researched. In this philosophy of management, I believe, lies the reason for the success of the national laboratories in effectively mobilizing around the AEC's problems.

When you think of a center program in the population-research area, I would urge that you recognize the importance of allowing for this wide latitude in order that freedom of action to pursue the most promising scientific leads may prevail.

Let me talk now about how national laboratories operate within this framework. The Oak Ridge Laboratory is organized, as are most universities, along disciplinary lines—chemists with chemists, physicists with physicists—but the resemblance largely stops there. The Laboratory's major objective is to solve problems. While each individual researcher is allowed a wide degree of freedom in selecting his research area, the program of which he is a part is definitely mission oriented, probably more so than in most universities. If we took on a program of research in the population area, for example, we would try to understand and do something about the problem, not just to continue research for the sake of furthering a given discipline. The discipline is used simply as a tool or an approach to solving a problem. When the time comes to launch a major program, we assign competence from the disciplinary groupings as we think it is needed to attack the problem. The scientists are assigned on an as-needed basis to a project leader who controls his own budget and program. The individual scientist, then, becomes immediately more responsive to the scientific requirements of the mission. Until the task is completed (and there are both short- and long-range tasks), the scientists on the project may be housed within their disciplinary areas, but they are essentially totally attached to the project leader and the respective project or mission until their contributions are finished.

It should be quickly emphasized that the Laboratory also maintains a major activity in fundamental research. This work serves to back up the applied projects. In our Biology Division at the ORNL, while the principal objective of a one-million-dollar-a-year program is to evaluate the genetic hazards of radiation, this applied program is backed up by a 1.5-million-dollar fundamental research program in genetics. The two are designed to interact closely with each other. We find that this blend tends to keep all the staff quite content while it permits the interaction of the pure researcher with the application-oriented professionals.

The national laboratory has another characteristic which differentiates it from the university in a general way. In my career in the university, I often found it difficult to get statisticians or specialists in other fields to talk with me about problems which concerned me and with which I needed their help. They usually were not willing to work with me long enough to understand what I needed, so my needs were given a low priority. In contrast, at Oak Ridge we have been set up by design to assist the scientist in meeting just such needs. There is, therefore, a willingness on the part of the various disciplines to sit together and work with one another to a greater extent than I found to be the case on the campus; that is, we work in an interdisciplinary manner. If I may be permitted one observation in this regard: *National laboratories employ people and mobilize them and its resources to seek a solution to an important national problem. The university more frequently employs individuals who in their research efforts take on programs of their own individual interest.* It is rare that a university professor is mission oriented; he is more often self-oriented. This characteristic is not universal in the university, of course, but it is prevalent enough to permit me to make it a feature which distinguishes the university from the national laboratory as a research institution.

I should make clear, however, that even mission-oriented laboratories such as ours have strong links to universities and are deeply involved in postdoctoral training, as well as some predoctoral training. Of particular interest is an effort jointly conducted between the Laboratory and the University of Tennessee. Three years ago the University established physically on the premises of the Biology Division of the Laboratory, the University of Tennessee-Oak Ridge Graduate School of Biomedical Sciences with the deliberate attempt of seeing if one could embed within the very fabric of a major Federal laboratory a first-rate graduate-education program without distorting the function of either the graduate school or the mission-oriented laboratory. We are successfully competing on a national basis for training grants and for top flight students. Our mission orientation is still intact. Out of this effort should come basic scientists unafraid of mission-oriented work—an attitude which may very well be needed for major efforts in population research, that is, devotion to a major national problem which has both a technological and a social component. Some have characterized this as "problem-focused education."

I realize there is no unique way to set up population research centers. The problems of population growth and their relation to the quality of life, and even survival in some societies, are of such crucial importance, however, that every method showing even good theoretical sense should be given a practical test.

Chapter Twenty-one

THE INDUSTRIAL CENTER

RICHARD W. YOUNG

SUCH a complex technological, scientific, social, moral, and religious problem as exemplified by any attempt to influence population control requires that all kinds of resources be mounted and coordinated if any significant progress is to be made.

While it may be a bit presumptuous for me to propose a role for industry, let me attempt to examine briefly two points: (1) What are the attributes of an industrial center or the so-called industrial approach? (2) What should industry expect in stimuli and support in return for full cooperation?

It may be that industry is the only place left in American society where meaningful and relevant work can be conducted in an atmosphere which involves the entire community of man— from the creative scientist to the production worker. The industrial community, in addition to being socially integrated, has the unique advantage of encompassing the entire action spectrum from conception to implementation.

Thus, the good, modern industrial enterprise begins with the recognition of the need for a product or a service, followed by research and development to meet the need. We use the best available science and technology, and in many cases conduct our own fundamental research to fill in the gaps that may appear in an orderly movement toward meeting the need.

The cycle is one of experimentation, of hypothesis, of re-experimentation, of changing hypothesis, of successes and failures, and this research and development cycle is followed by manufacturing and distribution, usually of a product, coupled with the necessary advertising and promotion to create awareness.

The rewards for successful solutions accrue directly to the

people most involved with achieving the results. This occurs at all levels—in the creation of the ideas and in creation of the products. These rewards may come in the form of prestige, pay, expanded opportunities, or a more rewarding life.

There has been much discussion of the dissemination of research results, of studies of family planning, of training, but not so much about what I call "product." What are the objectives? What is needed? What is the product? Is there any analogy for the population problem to be found in John F. Kennedy's charge to the space scientists: "Man, moon, decade"?

Another important attribute of the industrial approach is the ability of that type of organization to make excellent use of people. Successful modern industrial laboratories have mastered the art of allowing the individual entrepreneur to "do his thing" while at the same time inspiring individuals to work together as groups in a unified way.

High productivity in any kind of activity is a product of individuals working as individuals and individuals working in groups where they subjugate their private motivations for the interests of the total product of the activity. In too many institutions, especially those in which individual results are measured by publications, papers, and attendance at learned symposia, the collaboration of individuals may be inhibited or ineffective.

On the negative side, however, unless imaginatively led, the industrial center may take a conservative approach. It must produce tangible results and therefore may be slow in opening new domains in a way that is possible when only ideas are the product. This problem can be avoided by having a "big payoff"—a really major task. If the end is worth it, boldness is encouraged.

Although it is not my purpose to suggest areas of development, I cannot resist suggesting a couple of areas in which industry might appropriately participate.

I attribute the expansion of our own industry to our ability to make our products more available, less difficult to use, foolproof—and to deliver them to people who need and want them.

It seems to me that research on delivery systems for drugs and contraceptives could profit from the enormous experience of industrial laboratories on diffusion, slow release of reagents, polymers, ion exchange, etc.

Another deserving area is the promotion of awareness of solutions to population problems as they occur. The American advertising industry may have a role to play in this field. These communication skills, which we all agree have influenced the mores and habits of the public, have barely begun to be tapped in meeting social problems.

Finally, let me examine the second point that I raised in the beginning. What does industry need from the Government centers? It is my opinion that the Government centers should consist of small groups whose prime goals are aimed at defining the specific tasks and objectives which need to be met. They should concern themselves with the overall management of the programs in the various centers, thus providing for appropriate balance of competitive approaches with a minimum of duplication.

Perhaps the model of the NASA Program Office for the Apollo program is one that should be studied. If I recall the numbers correctly, at its peak, the Apollo program employed over half a million people throughout the country, but, fewer than ten thousand of them were employed within the Government.

But the most important activity of the Government center, I believe, should be in the social and political arena where it must tackle several key problems. I list these as follows:

1. Provide continuous funding and maintenance of priorities with long-term planning.

2. Provide proper incentives to industry.

3. Protect the proprietary interests of the industrial corporation for work it does in a particular field.

4. Assure an industrial organization an appropriate return for the investment of the talents of its best people, and the use of its most valued resources, on a given project.

5. Guarantee long-range support for a project, so that good scientists and good industrial experts will be willing to make careers of such a project, without fear of being abruptly frustrated by a political decision that ends the project.

6. Devise systems of continuing analysis to make sure a project is on target, as well as making summary judgments somewhere along the line, of whether a project has achieved, or will achieve, its ultimate goals.

These requirements may sound harsh, but they are boundaries that we, in industry, must live with every day. They are standards which force us to ask ourselves over and over: *What problems are we trying to solve?* The Government center should keep this fundamental question in front of the house at all times, persistently but without heckling.

Another important psychological consideration is follow-through. Nothing is more frustrating to research scientists, and nothing is more painful to industrial management, than inventing a cure for a problem that does not exist, or even worse, inventing a cure for a real problem, and not being able to implement that cure because of political difficulties, lack of finances, or a variety of other reasons, most of which might have been anticipated.

Unless these problems can be met, industry will have little motivation to participate in the field. Perhaps this is not necessarily bad; some of the concepts I have outlined, some of the methods industry has worked out, can be applied to nonindustrial centers. But I personally feel the nation, and mankind, would lose if the wisdom of industrial laboratories and the shrewdness of industrial companies is not used to help solve this problem that threatens to reach cataclysmic proportions.

Chapter Twenty-two

THE NOT-FOR-PROFIT RESEARCH INSTITUTE

CHARLES ANDERSON

I MAKE no pretensions whatsoever to being an authority on population problems, but I share with other concerned Americans a feeling of the urgency of the situation and have a sense of the complexities that are involved. When I think out loud, so to speak, about the potentialities of the center as an organizational unit, to handle these urgent complexities, I do so from the point of view of a representative of a private, not-for-profit research institute. Our organization, Stanford Research Institute (SRI), services the Government and industry in the physical and life sciences, urban and social systems, engineering, industrial and development economics, management sciences, and various combinations of disciplines within these broad fields.

Our staff numbers 2,700 people and includes physicists, chemists, economists, engineers, metallurgists, systems analysts, educators, and many from the social sciences. Whereas a university might be described as discipline oriented, SRI is problem oriented. Problem-solving is the essential characteristic of our operations.

At present we have five research centers at SRI supported at levels ranging from about 500,000 dollars to about 3.5 million dollars annually.

We have learned some rather basic lessons from our experiences with centers. One such lesson, and it bears repetition though it seems self-evident, is that the primary challenge in the work of a center deals with the development of software rather than hardware, and with ideas rather than technology. Particularly in the formation of basic, long-range policy, the crucial problems and policy alternatives have to do with values, attitudes, perceptions, stereotyped roles, cultural patterns, and the like.

In terms of our discussions here today, the pill may be thought of as "hardware." The critical problems involved in obtaining its effective use in an undeveloped area such as India may be called "software"—that is, they involve fundamental attitudes and values that must be accommodated in the development of population-research policy.

In general, the not-for-profit research institute, assuming SRI is reasonably representative, sees the center as a valuable and productive organizational unit characterized by unconfined, creative thinking that uses whatever tools, moves in whatever directions, and crosses whatever disciplinary or organizational lines, that the quest for solutions to a problem may make appropriate.

Let me attempt now to deal with the strengths and weaknesses of centers for accomplishing various types of tasks. Within the framework of the not-for-profit research organization, the strengths of a center operation would seem to consist chiefly of the following:

First, it flourishes in an atmosphere in which the basic mission is to solve a problem rather than to expand the horizons of a particular discipline. In broadening its focus to embrace a whole spectrum of disciplines and capabilities, it uncovers new insights; and in doing so, it provides intellectual stimulation to a wide range of specialists who might not otherwise have imagined that they had a useful contribution to make in a field removed from their normal work.

In establishing the SRI Educational Policy Center, we had at first assumed that the staff would consist primarily of social scientists and systems analysts. Not so. It soon became clear that many others had a role to play—humanists, clinical psychologists, neurophysiologists, historians, and computer scientists among them.

A *second* major strength of the center organization is its flexibility, the ease with which it can expand or contract its staff as the current status of the work may suggest, the varying kinds of skills it can absorb on full-time or part-time or consultant bases, and the adjustments it can make in its plan of operation as new findings may indicate that certain paths should be abandoned and new ones pursued.

A *third* strength, growing out of flexibility and particularly applicable to dealing with extremely complex problems, is the ability of the center to build a pyramid of research. The foundation of such a pyramid is specialized basic and applied research, or what we sometimes call "component research." The next layer of the pyramid is composed of systems analysis and operations research, which focus the component research on a particular problem. The capstone is policy research involving a multiplicity of skills and disciplines and holistic, value-oriented analysis.

A *fourth* strength is the center's special adaptability to risk-taking. Since it is not necessarily enshrined in the overall organization, it can venture into relatively unexplored areas and it can risk involving individuals and skills and points of view that defy accepted attitudes or values and that are not bound by tried, traditional methods.

As for the weaknesses of a center, as seen by at least one not-for-profit research organization, I would stress first of all what maybe is not a weakness, really, but a simple fact. This is that the center, particularly a center employing the pyramidal approach I have mentioned, may not be ideal for every kind of research endeavor. There may be very good reasons, for example, not to include component research and policy research in the same organizational unit.

Given that reservation, I am not really aware of any major inherent weaknesses so far as our internal operations are concerned, and in preparation for today's discussion I reviewed this matter rather thoroughly.

There is, of course, the general matter, applying to our overall operations, of funding. As a not-for-profit contract research institute, we operate without hidden subsidies. The organization must be self-sustaining; it must bring in at least as much money as it spends.

In assessing this type of operation, it would seem useful to agree to certain criteria for a population-research organization.

These might then be used as a sort of checklist toward determining what kind of general organization and setting might be most useful. Such criteria might well include the following:

Fostering objectivity: The organization should provide detachment from the day-to-day operations of the government so that long-range thinking is not unduly constrained by such matters as present research emphases, legislative constraints, politics, or organizational limitations.

If predictive research is to be undertaken, objectivity also will be enhanced if the organization is not exclusively Government funded. Someone is sure to be unhappy about some of the conclusions reached in such predictive research, and it is thus handy to have the discontent spread around.

A second criterion is *completeness of approach.* The organization should be one which is likely to promote a complete systems approach—that is, projecting future needs in terms of goals, assessing possible future capabilities, generating alternative means of achieving goals, analyzing uncertainties, and rationally comparing alternatives in terms of costs, gains, risks, and desirable subgoals.

A third criterion I suggest is *some connection to basic research activity.* It is advantageous to have a basic-research capability or a close connection with a strong basic-research activity. The goal is not so much access to research results, which are available in any event, but to provide the stimulation of easy and informal discussion with minds highly trained in basic scientific disciplines. This condition can perhaps most easily be met through affiliation with or proximity to a major research university.

A fourth criterion is *provision for self-renewal.* The structure should be planned in ways that promote continuous rejuvenation. It is essential to have an environment which promotes vigorous and imaginative thinking, and to practice extreme selectivity in adding staff members; there must be suitable ways in which people can leave the active working group, and ways to facilitate the entrance of desirable personnel.

In the permanent staff and in the management segment, there should be ways by which individuals might move toward more specifically applied research, toward more academic and basic research, or toward administrative activities as their interests and their aptitudes change.

The fifth criterion I would suggest is that of *promoting commitment and responsibility*. The organization should stimulate a responsible involvement in the overall population problem and a sense of commitment to it.

Experience suggests that such involvement and commitment are most likely to occur when the structure is associated with a larger social organization having a closely allied function.

A sixth criterion is a *capacity to promote interdisciplinary interaction*. Population research problems involve issues from many different disciplines and professional fields. Communication among these professional people having these diverse interests is difficult and must be assisted by organizational proximity. The availability of experts in these various areas, physically close to each other and organizationally accessible, is a strength furnished through a strong connection with a university, general research institute, or large general industrial laboratory.

A seventh criterion is *stability and long-term orientation*. Stability, achieved through endowment, or diversity of long-term funding, promotes a sense of security. The sense of continuity is impossible in an organization which is never quite sure of where the next dime will come from.

The eighth criterion is *attractiveness to a high-caliber staff*. The structure chosen should be conducive to developing a stimulating, prestigious environment likely to attract staff members of the highest caliber. The opportunity for a faculty connection with a major university is a significant attraction.

The last of the criteria I would propose is *contact with the real world*. The research-planning function, for example, must maintain relevance with evolving world-population developments and deal realistically with the problems of disseminating research results and seeing to it that innovations are carried out and implemented.

In summary, I would suggest that the center form of organizational unit can make a valuable contribution to population research and to identifying and dealing with the complex issues involved. The success of such centers will essentially be determined by the nature and scope of their assignments and by the nature of the larger organizations of which they become a part.

Chapter Twenty-three

REACTIONS

VIEW OF A BIOMEDICAL RESEARCHER

SHELDON SEGAL

M Y WORK in population involves primarily the field of contraceptive development. Although the population problem
will not end with new contraceptives, we do need them. The
question is, How can we use our resources to best advantage and
maximize the reproductive biologists' contribution to solution
of the problem?

As I see it, contraceptive development consists of three phases
of effort; we have expert resources to carry out each phase, if
we use them correctly.

Phase One involves the very fundamental research that universities are set up to do superbly. Of all biological systems, the
reproductive system is probably the least understood. This
means that a great deal of basic information is required in order to turn up leads for further investigation.

Population centers can offer the setting which expedites the
fundamental research process. I would find them most exciting
as centers for either biomedical or social science research. Contact between scientists of both groups is, of course, necessary.
But too close and too sustained a proximity can promote bore-
dom rather than useful exchange.

Phase Two involves following the leads that the initial investigator found interesting and promising. As an example, there
is a relationship between an enzyme in the seminal fluid and an
inhibitor in the cervical mucus of the female. Is there anything
important about that? Could it be applied to contraceptive development?

The man who made the initial observation may shrug his
shoulders and do nothing about it. But someone should take it
to the next research step. This is the kind of project that war-

243

rants the mission-oriented or problem-oriented approach that would make use of a population center's fullest potential.

In Phase Three research ideas are ready for practical, applied product development. Here industry is the expert.

I can list and, I think, defend thirty prospects for new contraceptives beyond the kind we have today. Perhaps only a handful of these are strong enough possibilities to warrant an all-out immediate investment. But the others deserve further study.

Industrial know-how is particularly pertinent in two distinct areas. One is at the very beginning of therapeutic or chemotherapeutic contraceptive development—the process of actually synthesizing compounds, developing structure and activity relationships, and even knowing what kinds of compounds to make. And, at the other end, the final stage of product development, lies the work industry is geared to do. Industrial expertise in this area is unsurpassed; it cannot be matched in a university or research institute.

At the Population Council we have arranged to protect industry's proprietary rights while at the same time protecting our interests in making new contraceptives available to the public at an acceptable price, a price assuring global distribution. I know the Federal Government's goals are similar to ours.

The continued support by Federal and private agencies to all of the research resources I have mentioned will not only advance contraceptive development, but on a broader scale, it will assure that we have made our best effort in contributing to solution of the world's population problem. And that, as you know, is why we are in business.

VIEW OF A UNIVERSITY ADMINISTRATOR

JOSEPH F. KAUFFMAN

My only experience with the Federal Government was in the original staff that developed the Peace Corps, and my memory of the Federal Government is very different from some of the stereotypes I have heard.

With the Peace Corps, I was Director of Training and therefore developed contracts with some seventy-five to one hundred colleges and universities to perform training services for Corps' volunteers. One thing I learned from the Peace Corps experience was that the "fight your way to the public trough" approach with colleges and universities is decidedly inappropriate.

Much of the contract procedure, as of a decade ago, was related to competitive bidding; eager defense contractors and the like were mostly trying to sell things. So the Government approach was, You are lucky if we let you have a contract. We are suspicious of how much you will make. We want constant inspection, and to get everything into writing, and so on, which turns off many people on university faculties who might ordinarily contribute a great deal. Thus, the approach for involving universities has to be different.

We may have trouble persuading those with the highest degree of competence to reorder their priorities and be willing to take on what could be a burden for them.

I also agree that you cannot establish anything of this importance on a year-to-year basis, that there has to be some kind of promise of continuity in order to involve the best people.

Another difficulty has to do with the credibility of the Federal Government these days in the eyes of students and young faculty, and I include young faculty now because this is a fairly new phenomenon.

But I do think that in setting up population centers on university campuses one problem may be the credibility of the Federal Government, which has been badly in need of repair as a result of the last five years, during which students and faculty members, including some gifted research people, have begun rather cynically, to subscribe to a "Government as the enemy" syndrome.

I am heartened by the fact that on my own campus environment and pollution are major issues and one of the hottest books on New England campuses is *The Population Bomb*.[23] So there seems plenty of interest on the part of faculty and students if we can use it effectively.

Then there is the question of public policy on the population issue. The Federal Government would be creating and funding population centers, and yet we are uncertain about public policy on the population issue and whether or not the Government seeks to develop such a policy.

What should that policy be if the Government does wish to develop one? The Government has in the past developed policies in very difficult and tender areas. Manpower policy is certainly analogous. We have had little or no hesitation in developing manpower policy that would move people and change their lives dramatically in order to meet emergencies, including war and the need for conscription.

In the post-Sputnik NDEA* legislation, we rewarded people who entered certain fields such as teaching. We bribed them. We made money available, and made opportunities available in one field but not another in order to direct and control the use of our manpower.

The feasibility of similar methods must be raised about population policy. If it is to be only a kind of information and education approach, than I think that a lot of university people who would be getting involved would become quickly frustrated and disenchanted. It must deal with basic questions. I think the possibilities of contributions by colleges and universities are limited. We in universities have failed to develop effective, ethical strategies of intervention in social problems, as witness our industrialized agriculture, which grew out of research in our land-grant universities, but paid little attention to the problem that would haunt our cities two or three decades later when rural people were forced to leave the land because that industrialization had destroyed their livelihood.

So I think a good deal of attention ought to be paid to the study and development of effective strategies of intervention that have very high ethical concern as well.

Finally, it seems to me university centers ought to be required to demonstrate that the curriculum and the relevant disciplines are stimulated by the presence of a center. Creation of a center, merely for the sake of physical expansion, may please some people, but I doubt its ultimate validity within institutions com-

---

* National Defense Education Act.

mitted to education, a situation we have seen in some of the urban-affairs centers.

Certainly the universities must be involved, but not in the same way as industrial corporations, the national laboratories, or other models. The universities can, under proper circumstances, make their own unique and powerful contribution.

VIEW OF THE NON-PROFIT RESEARCH FOUNDATION ADMINISTRATOR

BRUNO AUGENSTEIN

First of all, I am thoroughly in sympathy with the theory that there is room for all sorts of centers of various designs, and I am assuming that what we are talking about is a pluralistic collection of centers which does not fit any common mold but exploits individual strengths in the best possible ways.

In particular, I think it is clear that there are already in existence a number of centers for population research which are doing good research and which should be strengthened.

It does seem to me that there is room for another kind of center. The idea is perhaps based on the fact that The Rand Corporation, with which I am most familiar, although I do have some university and industrial experience, is close to being an intersection of many often-voiced but seldom-implemented clichés used in discussing such things as population.

The Rand Corporation is a fairly small organization, with a research staff of about five hundred. At the last count we had something like 125 different disciplines on the staff. Some of these are quite standard; some of them are fairly exotic.

We have a specialist on east European folklore. We had a resident artist for a while. We had a producer of a somewhat unsuccessful Broadway musical. So Rand is a pretty catholic enterprise.

We have found at Rand, a degree of freedom which neither universities nor industrial centers have, and while everyone uses the words "interdisciplinary" and "multidisciplinary," these are very difficult concepts to implement. We do have successful interdisciplinary projects, but they are successful at the expense of pretty hard work.

We differ from a university in a sense that we try to make an interdisciplinary project pretty hard-nosed. I do not think there are too many universities in which the research paper of an economist can be greatly influenced by, or perhaps even stopped from publication by, the criticisms of a mathematician, a physicist, or a demographer.

This is one of the things that we do at Rand, so in a sense we have put teeth into the concept of "interdisciplinary."

Also, we are policy oriented. What we are trying to do is influence policy decisions. We are trying to implement programs and not simply research them. We have had a number of successes of some magnitude, along with a number of significant errors.

Against this background, I think it is highly important in a field which is as complex as the field of population research, to keep your eye on an objective goal, on what it is you want to do. You want to influence societal actions. You want to influence them to some quantitative extent. Your problem is to try to figure out ways of doing this.

One thing that we have learned at Rand by hard experience is that it is fruitless to search for the perfect policies or the perfect solutions before you take any action. You will just never make it by that route. You can get acceptable solutions which you know will steer you in the right direction even though you find out later they may not be the best solutions.

The kind of experience we have had at Rand is based on a variety of work now in progress:

We are in a major program with New York City. Even though this program numbers only about sixty-five people, it is to my knowledge one of the largest urban programs in the country.

The program is committed in a very clear way to reporting to the administrators of the several administrative organs in New York City.

It is not a program which researches urban problems, writes reports, and then goes away in the expectation that these pearls will be picked up and properly used. We have a responsibility which is written into our charter with New York City that says we are supposed to stick around and make sure that whatever we recommend can be implemented. It is a very chastening experience.

We work with a number of city organizations: the police department, the fire department, the health department, and three or four others. It is one thing to write very learned research papers on a particular problem, and quite another to face the fire commissioner and tell him that he has been deploying his fire resources entirely incorrectly and that you have a much better solution. Indeed, it is very difficult to have to face his fishy eye and really make your point.

I think that is the kind of experience that is needed in the population research field.

I think there must be a program that has as its objective a policy influence on those in position to make policy.

I think this is one of the ways in which the not-for-profit centers, more or less by historical accident, are stronger than the universities, simply because the guild system and perhaps even the caste system in the universities do not really permit such strong policy influence.

Another important point is the role information plays in a program of this sort. Any program which aims at understanding how society behaves, and tries to influence that behavior—and we might as well admit that is exactly what we are trying to do—relies to an enormous extent on having a statistical repository and a very good information base.

It was surprising to us, particularly with our experience in New York City, how sparse this information base really is when you come to grips with it.

In New York City there are some thirty thousand different organizations, more or less autonomous, which influence the lives of the city residents. One of the rudimentary things that the Rand program did when it first went into New York City was something so elementary that a number of our senior researchers felt demeaned by having to do it. It was an inventory of offices and agencies, for example, an inventory of all the agencies that influenced housing decisions in New York City.

We put together a report with a statistical compilation of

who did what to whom and how and who had money and who did not have money and who had policy guidance and who instituted policy guidance. This, it seems, had never been done in New York City before.

I suspect in the population research area there can be found a thousand and one instances of this very elementary thing which one would expect to find but which simply does not exist.

I am struck by the fact that the attention being given to influencing the end objective of the population research program (namely, the determinants and consequences of population change) is by far the least funded. There appears to me to be great emphasis on problems of reproductive biology, for example, and almost no emphasis on problems of behavioral sciences.

Yet it is clear that, in spite of the fact that we say that the problems of family planning are very critical, it is also a fact that a great many families have exactly the number of children that they wish to have. There is an important and powerful set of factors which are completely independent of foolproof and reliable contraceptive device. What these determinants are is a very important research factor that ultimately may have a great deal to do with the success or nonsuccess of the population-control program.

I am also struck by the fact that there is a considerable amount of support being funneled through the Bureau of the Census. One of the things that probably could have been done two or three years ago, and hopefully might yet be done in the future, is for Federal agencies, including the Bureau of Census, which are charged with gathering statistics and various other groups to undertake the important research job of reviewing and redefining information received from census and other data. There is already an enormous repository of useful data that remains to be tapped, which can and should be strengthened even more in the future.

I would hope the whole question of designing the information needs and then generating the kind of information gathering sources that you have in mind be given a great deal of attention.

It is always tempting, of course, to say you should really define your information needs and then do your research. In the real world it does not operate that way, and clearly you will be doing research with incomplete information, and you will be getting information which is perhaps not useful or perhaps even in the wrong areas. Only by having the research and the information-gathering resources working side by side will you make much headway.

Now, as I said, I am writing mostly from the point of view of the not-for-profit agencies, because this is where most of my experience is. But there is a great deal to be done with all sorts of laboratories. I do not think we need to make a commitment to some master mold which will be the panacea, because it is clear that such a mold does not exist.

The greatest contribution that the Government could make at this stage is, first of all, to back intelligently the existing research centers, and, secondly, initiate discreetly and appropriately additional kinds of research and research institutions, mainly interdisciplinary research centers which have a problem-policy-orientation and a mission-objective-orientation. I think this is where an expansion of the present population research can most profitably be made.

VIEW OF A POPULATION CENTER DIRECTOR
ROGER REVELLE

I should like to discuss the problems of population centers in universities.

We people who direct these centers tend to believe—and we say perhaps even more than we believe—that if we just had enough money, success would be assured and that the population problem might soon be solved.

There are some other very serious constraints in universities. One of them is their function. What universities are good at is research and teaching, particularly when research and teaching can be combined. They are not very good at action programs except as these primarily concern research and teaching.

The other difficulty in universities is their organization. Universities in this country have been for quite some time, and for all anybody can see will continue to be, primarily organized around disciplines rather than around problems. The disciplines are represented in departments.

Any of us who have had much to do with the organization of universities have been forced to realize the overwhelming strength of departments, even in a new university, one that is just starting. The departments very quickly become dominating.

This means that it is difficult to have an orthogonal organization in the university which is organized around problems or oriented toward problems rather than disciplines.

I once heard somebody say that it is as difficult to change a university as it is a graveyard, and there is a good deal to this statement. There is nobody more conservative about his own business than a professor.

The third difficulty is that universities tend to seek permanence. They have had a long history, and they are fascinated by this history, and they tend to be concerned with things that they think will last forever. The nature of the real problems of society, or at least many such problems, is that after a while they go away, and universities are therefore sometimes frightened at the idea of getting involved with things that they think may be ephemeral.

Nevertheless, I would claim that if university population centers did not exist, they would have to be invented. The reason is the very great pressure on the part of the new generation of students to learn about and to work on the real problems of the real world.

Even so, university population centers must recognize that the university is primarily good at research and teaching, and not at action programs. The question then becomes, What are the functions of a university center, and what can it do well?

Clearly, one thing is to foster, stimulate, and organize teaching at all levels, including undergraduate teaching. I must confess that I was most pleased when a young woman taking a course which I called "Human Populations and Natural Resources" told me she was quitting college. This may seem a strange reason for considering my course a success, but she was leaving school to go to Africa to work in a family-planning program, so inspired was she by the prospect of action to help solve the problems I had been describing in my lectures. Even with all the modesty I could muster, I still saw this episode as an example of meaningful teaching which inspired the student to action.

In addition to undergraduate teaching, teaching of population-related problems should be fostered by the center at all levels and in many different departments of the university—economics, sociology, government, anthropology. In our case, we have involved several of the schools of the university, such as the faculty of arts and sciences, the schools of government, of public health, medicine and education, and the divinity school.

Another function of the center, which experience suggests makes sense, is that its very presence in a university can make it easier for departments to attract and recruit faculty members who have a deep concern with population; they will find appealing an atmosphere that will encourage their interest in the problem, and allow them to concentrate on research in this field.

The center can also, by pushing hard enough, influence the appointment of new faculty members who are interested in population problems, in a wide variety of areas where such an interest might not previously have coincided with the department head's interest, and where such an interest might not previously have been considered important. I am thinking of fields such as economics, reproductive biology, and public health.

A center can be an enormously effective means of recruiting and guiding students, students at all levels, even high school students, as well as undergraduates and graduate students and postdoctoral people, many of whom are looking for a change of career or change of purpose in their lives, and people even beyond the stage of being postdoctoral students.

It can also give some kind of coherence and unity to an attack on these problems within the university by developing a special library, by a series of reprints and publications, by holding conferences, and particularly by organizing seminars and workshops, and by continually bringing the results of research right into the teaching programs within the course of the semester.

It can provide jobs for people in research because of its multiple sources of funding; it can offer multiple possibilities for supporting research projects with a lot more stability; in many ways it can help get better people into this business.

It can also influence not only the design of individual courses but entire curriculum design, the design of courses throughout the university, which together will lead to definite kinds of concentration and specialization.

Finally, and perhaps most important, it can be a center for sophistication, a center for focusing the ideas and the attitudes and the concerns of many members of the university on population problems. It can get people throughout the university to think about population problems in a more sophisticated and more meaningful way.

I should like to emphasize as strongly as I can that we are dealing with an enormous problem, a problem just beginning to be revealed in its full dimensions, one in which we have so far seen only the tip of the iceberg. My belief, after having been involved with this business for several years, is that our number one job is to define and enrich our understanding of the nature of population problems.

We Americans tend to be instrumentalists. We tend to be fascinated by gimmicks and gadgets. We tend to be what we call problem solvers rather than problem definers.

The population problem of our time has two aspects which we have not talked about very much today: One is human ecology. How do people live in the spaceship Earth? How do they live with each other? And how do they live on the planet?

The other, perhaps even more fundamental, is that the population problem is primarily a moral problem.

The real question we should concern ourselves with is, How do we increase the level of individual freedom and the quality of justice that all men deserve and should have, not only the living generation but individual human beings to come and generations to come?

The human dilemma is that people have to act regardless of whether they have understanding or not; this is particularly true of the Government as the agency of action. The Government frequently has to act on the basis of insufficient knowledge and understanding and do the best it can with what it knows and whatever is available.

But the Government needs more understanding, and the people need more understanding, so they can modify policy and improve the effectiveness of action.

It seems to me that the modern American university is the best device ever invented for gaining understanding, and particularly for achieving that interaction between people of different generations, the new generation and the old, which leads to an organization and a continuity of understanding.

The conclusion I would arrive at is that university population centers are a good thing and that, in fact, they can and should play an important role in any Government approach to this enormous, profound, and little-understood problem.

SECTION FIVE

REACTIONS OF TENANTS AND LANDLORDS: CENTERS AND HOST MANAGEMENT

Section Five includes the remarks of three directors from organizations other than population centers. In their respective chapters the commonality of problems each faces is made apparent to the reader. The final chapter of this section is written by four administrators expressing the viewpoint of the researcher, the dean, the department head, and the center director.

Chapter Twenty-four

THE MENTAL RETARDATION CENTER

GEORGE TARJAN

A S YOU may know, following legislation passed nearly seven years ago, twelve research centers in mental retardation and related aspects of human development were established. One is at UCLA.

Also eighteen university-affiliated facilities primarily for clinical teaching were established, again with one at UCLA.

It is my privilege to be a director of a program that combines the two fully.

I shall discuss the aims of the UCLA Center, its organizational arrangements, and its relationship to other units within and outside the University. I shall focus on positive as well as negative experiences based on some four and a half years of work and six months of existence of the Center, and also comment on some strategies and tactics that my co-director and I used in the problem resolutions.

The general aims of the Mental Retardation Research Center —and I shall not speak about the university-affiliated center— are the acquisition of new knowledge and training of research personnel in the field of retardation.

The specific aims include equal opportunity for the biomedical and behavioral sciences, with equal emphasis on basic research toward prevention and applied or clinical research relating to treatment, care, and management.

Since the Center is within the health sciences complex, the program must fit into this milieu and involve a number of departments, including some outside of the health sciences complex.

The traditional strength of UCLA obviously has to be made use of, and gaps in the field of mental retardation research particularly as these refer to UCLA must be filled.

Research must be interdisciplinary, or at least multidiscipli-

259

nary, with encouragement of interaction particularly between the biomedical and the behavioral components.

I suppose I was selected to represent these centers because everything at UCLA is so complicated that this center was given little chance of excellence or even survival; but some people think we have been and will continue to be successful, largely because of our organizational pattern.

The pattern reflects the construction and operational funding composition which includes the Federal Government, the State Department of Mental Hygiene, and the University.

The State Department of Mental Hygiene is a general funding operation of the state.

The mental retardation program is a part of the Neuropsychiatric Institute, which has been a joint venture of the State Department of Mental Hygiene and the University for over a decade. My associate director and I were jointly selected by these two agencies.

To make my life simple, I have three lines of authority and responsibility. Within the Department of Mental Hygiene I am an associate medical director of the Neuropsychiatric Institute. Academically I am a member of the Department of Psychiatry. And as Center Director I am responsible directly to the Dean.

All scientists within the Center have regular appointments within the department of their academic discipline, assuring full academic screening. This situation is not true at some other centers.

Because of the magnitude of the operation, some grouping of the scientists has already occurred. The development of Center-wide cohesiveness and the resolution of competition among investigators posed some problems. Four factors aided in the solution of these problems:

1. Strong emphasis on the primary target—namely, mental retardation. In this respect, we developed close proximity to the University-affiliated operation, that is, to the patients themselves.

2. The availability of implementation and, later on, a grant from the National Institute of Child Health and Hu-

man Development. These grants are dependent on demonstrated cohesiveness and demonstrated center-wide quality. These were of tremendous help to the personnel in developing the center.

3. Center-wide research-training grants, which again focused on cohesiveness.

4. The use of the program-project approach rather than the individual-project approach in the support of research; the program-project approach also emphasizes interdisciplinary cohesiveness.

I can safely say that by this time the loyalties of most senior investigators lie more within the Center than elsewhere.

Now, let me speak about the relationship to other campus units and units outside of the campus.

The relationship to other campus units went through two chronological phases. In the early days, when we had no laboratories and when research funding in general was not too difficult to obtain, few scientists outside the Center were willing to submit to any restrictions inherent in a categorical program. Recruitment was therefore a challenge.

Later the availability of our laboratories and the unfortunate retrenchment in Federal funding completely changed the situation. Previously uninterested scientists became instant devotees of retardation. Some administrators and department heads began to view the Center as a territory for colonization. It is even possible that a few could see the new laboratories as repositories for less-talented tenured faculty.

Defensive maneuvers on our part were necessary to maintain quality and focus on mental retardation. Recruitment became a secondary item, at least within the campus.

Support by NICHD, the Dean, the Director of the Neuropsychiatric Institute, the Director of the State Department of Mental Hygiene were significant advantages. But, more importantly, unless we have continued support of this nature, we will not be able to maintain either quality or a focus on our target.

I want to mention an unusual affiliation of extreme importance—affiliation with a typical field operation. In our case it is

Pacific State Hospital, a large, traditional institution for the mentally retarded, located some fifty miles away. This affiliation has provided us parochial UCLA people with open channels of communication to other universities throughout the southern California area, with which the Pacific State Hospital maintains a strong liaison.

In closing, let me simply say that, in my judgment, complex problems, whether in the field of retardation or population research, can at least in part be resolved through this type of center operation.

Chapter Twenty-five

THE INTERNATIONAL DEVELOPMENT
RESEARCH CENTER

GEORGE J. STOLNITZ

A S THE name International Development Research Center implies, we are a population-related and not a population-oriented research undertaking. We deal with a number of development issues into which population feeds, sometimes directly, but quite often indirectly. Essentially, we operate in the area of international research; the United States, when part of our focus, tends to be taken up in comparative contexts.

We operate with Ford Foundation funds, which raises a number of problems about continuity and duration. Basically a research institution, our objective is to house and support a group of research scholars engaged in major-length, book-type investigations. We operate as a community of interacting scholars representing a variety of disciplines. One of our major—and perhaps unique—targets is a Center series of monographs concerning interactional development subjects. In addition, various series of papers are forthcoming from staff to insure not only the preservation of the detailed information and by-product studies we deal with, but their widest possible dissemination to specialized audience groups.

The theory behind our high-quality, high-cost undertaking is that the university, we believe, has tended to become an increasingly difficult, even an unfavorable, place for undertaking long-range, major scholarly investigations of career-type dimensions.

Our procedure is to carry out a careful and systematic review of a study project when our research scholars first present a proposal to us.

One is Human Resources and Development, where for example we have been dealing with family-planning-evaluation problems; migration and settlement patterns in the United States,

263

Venezuela, and elsewhere; case studies of human-resource-development problems, as in Venezuela; and a number of other topics. The disciplines represented in this group of projects, incidentally, have been geography, economics, political science, and demography.

A second umbrella area is the Theory and Practice of Development Planning, in which we have a number of theoretical studies on techniques of planning, along with a number of partially theoretical or semiempirical works on how planning experiences have actually worked out in individual regions or countries.

A third category is Rural Modernization Processes, in which a political-science study of change in the Egyptian village, and an economic study of market power in the agricultural and retail-trade sectors are included.

A fourth umbrella area, which we call Development and Planning Transitions in East Europe, features a large-scale series of investigations, so far by economists, of actual or attempted changeovers of eastern European economies from Stalinist or command-type systems to more market-oriented systems.

Originally we arrived at our umbrella-area selections inductively. That is, we did not preplan the selections, but started to operate where we found we had a series of projects that looked good plus the people to do the projects. The projects and people determined our subject-matter selections rather than vice versa.

About half of our research scholars come from our own campus at Indiana University. The other half are either visiting personnel or working outside under special research arrangements with us. We try to plan their objectives and research designs from beginning to end, from the formulation of the design through its scheduling, the resources and help needed, the contents, and eventually the publication possibilities. Support can cover any or all derivative phases of research undertaking, including field surveys, graduate assistance, outside consultations, and publication support.

As part of our procedure we check with individual departments to see whether and when they can give up the men we need, and under what financial and related arrangements. Sometimes, when we try to corral certain personnel, we run into complaints from their departments: "Where are the bodies we must have for classroom presentations?" This is something we are very aware of; it is an ever-present consideration, and justifiably so.

I want to emphasize that until now we have not been involved in direct training. We do, however, indirectly encourage training by fostering Ph.D. studies, and an occasional M.A., and by engaging a number of graduates and even especially promising undergraduates to work with us as research assistants.

We run conferences on topics of special interest to us. We have had one on world population which has appeared as a conference volume. We recently had a conference which will appear as a volume on rural politics and social change in the Middle East, which in significant ways was perhaps the first of its kind in this country.

In terms of coverage or subject matter, we do not handle anything or everything in the development line. We focus on what I call "umbrella areas." These are four sets of subject categories under which are subsumed most or nearly all of our individual projects.

As to population and its role at the Center, it is varied. It can be direct, as in a number of undertakings under our human-resources umbrella area. Or it can be indirect but pertinent because of the nature of the problem. For example, in eastern Europe we found we needed to do something about investigating population and labor-force aspects of the recent overall economic transitions there. We feel a distinct lack of information on the problem, perhaps because available economists have not compiled it, have not wanted to compile it, or have lacked special competence to compile it.

One major problem in our mode of operation has been the limited duration of our basic backing grant. Long-range programming is difficult, and sometimes made impossible, because of the uncertainty of continuity of funding.

It would be very useful if we could obtain at least but a minimum level of endowment for a certain period, in order to permit an institution of our type to have at least a minimum continuing program. Such support would help us pursue our own "seed corn" kind of research without having to get prior funding commitments.

Another point I should emphasize is the true long-run burden of involvement on the part of a university administration as it approaches any center-supporting venture, whether in population, international study, or other areas. There can be misleading "halo" effects. There is a honeymoon period, though even then there are problems. Substantial overhead and administrative costs must be borne by the university from the very start; the needs and limitations of space can be another major concern. Later comes the longer pull, and typically much more burdensome, when one needs the renewed assurance of fiscal support for all purposes. If this is no longer forthcoming from outside sources, the university may be left holding the bag and not being allowed, whether morally or by explicit prior agreement, to drop it. The necessity for a university to pick up a center's program when its outside funding ends can hit a state university such as ours very hard. For this reason it is important to have minimal program support for longer periods of time; we should at least have a flexible arrangement for meeting the vagaries of state legislatures and budgetary stringencies.

Another point of special relevance to intrauniversity aspects concerns potential confrontations with departmental needs. Our attempt to work harmoniously with departments includes special scheduling of released time for faculty, timing the duration of the projects, and going heavily into summertime involvements. This way we hope we can offer an opportunity for longer-run undertakings, often involving overseas travel, and at the same time help to keep the people involved on campus as much as possible, or at least at the best possible times.

Chapter Twenty-six

THE EDUCATIONAL POLICY RESEARCH CENTER

WILLIS HARMAN

A T THE risk of perhaps repeating myself on some points, I would now like to express some ideas strictly from the standpoint of a center director.

I think there has been a fair amount of agreement expressed here on the need for diversity in kinds of research, some basic, some applied, some in the biomedical sciences, some in the social sciences, and some at the policy-analysis level.

A somewhat similar situation in the field of education existed about three years ago when a decision was made to put a small fraction of the total research effort, less than 1 percent, into the area of policy research. The Office of Education set up two policy-research centers. I shall give you a thumbnail history of how one of these has evolved in these two years and then conclude with a couple of remarks about what I think we might learn from that.

As you go from basic research to policy analysis, you are going in the direction of increasing multidimensional complexity, of increasing involvement with political processes, and with policy decisions and alternative choices with extensive implications, and of requiring a broader and broader view of the problem and a richer resource base from which to draw. There is nothing incompatible between requiring a precise problem definition in basic research, while insisting in policy research on a broad look at the problem and all of its intersections with other aspects of the society. In fact we need to do both.

Our charge from the Office of Education was to look at the next thirty years, because in dealing with education, as with population, things happen slowly and have enough momentum so that looking several decades ahead is essential. Because the future is a function of human will and hence inherently unpredictable, it was necessary to examine *alternative* futures.

But how do you look several decades ahead? We started out asking what I think are fairly obvious and appropriate questions relating to such things as early childhood education, urban education problems, what we know about change processes in other than the strictly cognitive domains, and what are the alternative futures for the educational system. As we began to push these questions down to deeper and deeper levels, we found repeatedly that our original formulations of the questions simply were not the right ones.

As we looked at some of the specific areas, we kept getting pushed back to very, very basic premises in the general culture or in the scientific subculture. Some of the issues which emerged are ultimately resolvable by research findings. Others, however, have to do with which research activities get done and which ones do not, and with which research findings are likely to come up and which ones are not. That is to say, they are resolved—if at all—on some basis prior to research findings.

As we looked at alternative futures for the educational systems, we began getting pushed into wider and wider domains. What are the alternative futures for technology? For the whole society? For the whole world?

We ended up after a year and a half of this kind of floundering around by saying, "Brash as it seems, we really have to see the range of possible alternative future histories for the whole society between now and the year 2000."

One could very legitimately raise the question as to whether you can do this or not. If it could be done, it would have many uses. For one thing, a proposed policy could be tested against these different future histories, to see where it looks good and where it looks as though it might be headed for trouble.

Such a projection of history also could help in avoiding undesirable future developments and trying to edge toward the more desirable ones. The word "desirable" does not necessarily betray a doctrinaire value commitment here. Some alternatives are clearly and unequivocally desirable or undesirable, while others fall into an in-between category.

In considering how we might evolve such a historical perspective, we decided that we needed some kind of skeletal description of the society, so we did the following:

We chose six aspects of the society that were essential even to the minimum description, including science and technology, economic pattern, political pattern, and so on.

For each of these we chose a range of five or six alternative one-sentence pattern descriptions which covered the feasible range fairly well.

As I have said before in this book, we came out with over twenty thousand possible combinations. By logical examinations, we ended up with approximately forty alternative future histories between now and the year 2000.

Out of this emerged some very important observations. Obviously, the forty are not equally probable, and one has to impose another set of variables relating to values and attitudes and cultural beliefs, and so on, to say something about the relative probabilities. But about half of the forty end up by the year 2000 with much more highly authoritarian states than we like to contemplate.

All but one or two either ran into some very serious difficulty before the year 2000 or involved such a fragile world ecology, that it seemed they might precipitate catastrophe within the next half-century.

One, for example, involved a successful green revolution, feeding the people around the world until about 2000; but the whole system would be so fragile that if anything went wrong, it could, and probably would, fall apart.

One point was inescapable. Society had to deal in one way or another with what we came to call the world macroproblem, by which I mean the composite of all of those problems which result from the combination of high population level and high technology and industrialization levels.

It consists of at least three important components, one of which is population, and related environmental and ecological problems.

The second is the increasing gap between have and have-not groups within the nation and between nations.

The third component is what you might call new technological threats: The most obvious is nuclear and biological weapons, but the component also includes man's ability to control the human body, the human mind, the human fetus, human evolution.

Adding these factors together we felt justified talking about a single macroproblem and in feeling that we could not properly deal with policy issues about any part of the problem without considering the whole problem. One reason was that its many aspects all stemmed from the same two driving forces, namely population level and industrialization. Population pressures, in turn, came from certain technological developments. The second reason was that the whole macroproblem, with all of its aspects, seems to be related to certain premises in the culture of the developed world, which raises the question whether it is not essentially unsolvable in the context of the present cultural values and premises of the industrialized world.

This is not an assertion; it is a question which we found ourselves obliged to face.

What makes the future different from the past is that a great number of choices which we have left to nature in the past—that is, what species of animals and plants will be allowed to live where, what the future of human evolution is going to be, what the quality of the environment is going to be, and so on—these choices suddenly, almost instantaneously in an historical sense, have become human choices. We have not yet developed the ability to make choices of such importance.

This is the kind of basic question that population policy research inevitably runs into, so somewhere in the network of research centers there must be the capability to deal with such profound questions.

I think population policy research centers must have characteristics a little different from other kinds of research centers. We found extremely useful the capacity for flexibility, the ability to reach out and borrow temporarily different types of personnel, and the ability to shift direction completely within a period of a few months. A long-term commitment from the funding agency was most valuable. Besides this we have been helped by a cooperative auditing procedure with the auditors considering not whether a project should be stopped but rather how the job can better be done.

Chapter Twenty-seven

REACTIONS

VIEWPOINT OF A RESEARCHER

ANSLEY COALE

I WHOLLY subscribe to Dr. Freedman's view that we should consider what is going on before talking about what the center program should be in the future.

I should like to say something more about our own work and see what lessons might be drawn from it.

First of all, in talking about research organizations in a wide spectrum from pure research to applied research, the Princeton tradition is on the purely scientific side. As has been said, we are more in the puzzle-solving area than in the policy problem-solving area. But, as at Michigan, our research program is shaped by the interests and curiosities of our professional staff which on occasion have led to problems that are most intimately and importantly connected with policy.

One example: about a dozen years ago a colleague and I made a study of the relationship between population growth and economic development in certain low-income countries. We decided that perhaps the best way of looking at that relationship was not by trying to forecast whether there would be famine or disaster as a result of continued population growth, but rather by trying to estimate how much difference it would make in economic development if fertility were reduced and population growth slowed down.

We were able to conclude that a country that reduced its fertility would probably attain a higher absolute national income in a generation than one that did not reduce its fertility, before one even began to divide by the smaller population.

A more recent example: Professor Westoff, Associate Director of the Office of Population Research at Princeton and a sociologist, has collaborated in a project[60] funded by the National Institutes of Health to make the very interesting finding that roughly 20 percent of the births that occur in the United States are unwanted.

If this finding is correct, and I think it very persuasive, we see that, if there were no unwanted births, the current American fertility would be only very slightly above replacement, a scientific finding with interesting policy implications.

Turning now to the relationship between a population research center and the other activities in a university: From the outset, in our own organization there has been a connection with both economics and sociology, and graduate training for students in both disciplines, also graduate training in population.

My impression is that in demography, success in research comes from using the skills of any discipline that help solve the puzzle. Rather than making conscious efforts toward interdisciplinary measures, the nature of the puzzle suggests the kind of technique that should be applied, when and if necessary.

In connection with the relationship between demography and other fields within the university setting, I should like to emphasize the importance in our experience of offering demography as a field of study to social science students. In the thirty-three years that there have been population studies at Princeton, there has been a graduate course in population offered to students of economics and sociology; population is one of the fields a student can choose for general examination for a Ph.D. in those two disciplines. Every year a small number of students have written dissertations on population.

As a result of the population courses offered at Princeton, the university can, in the field of demography, claim among its distinguished alumni, John Durand, formerly director of population work at the United Nations, and now professor and associate director of population studies at the University of Pennsylvania, Professor George Stolnitz at Indiana, Professor Norman Ryder at Wisconsin, Alvaro Lopez at the University of Los Andes, Bogota, Colombia, Harvey Liebenstein at Harvard, Melvin Zelnik at Johns Hopkins, and Paul Demeny, Director of the East-West Center of

Population Studies in Hawaii. I speak from personal experience, since I am among those who entered the study of population (in 1939 as a graduate student at Princeton) largely because the course was available.

Let me finish by seconding Dr. Freedman's proposals—that there should be a reasonable balance between alternative strategies of strengthening existing centers and of creating new ones. In looking forward to an expanding activity in this field through new centers or expanded work at the existing centers, there is indeed a shortage of trained persons and there is the risk of robbing Peter to pay Paul. But a hopeful aspect is the very rapid increase in enrollments in the graduate courses and the very rapid increase in Ph.D. dissertations being completed.

There is a rapidly expanding cadre of very able young men that will make the manpower shortage a little less acute in a few years than it is today.

VIEWPOINT OF A DEAN

SANFORD ELBERG

The Center in Berkeley's tranquil campus in the Far West is normally set up for the definite purpose of seeking interaction where it seemed to have been lacking or where someone felt it to have been lacking.

A requirement we impose upon all research activities, whether they be unorganized in the form of faculty or organized in the form of groups, is that they must also serve the purposes of graduate-student training and education.

Strange as it may seem, we do listen to students, and we find that students in the training centers are one of our best means for insuring interaction between centers and departments, and between various centers. The students are often in my office complaining about the lack of interaction between departments or between centers or even within centers. They help to rectify this felt deficiency by setting up seminars, conferences, journals, et cetera. They likewise stimulate the formation of group or interdisciplinary degree programs, which often tone up lagging departmental programs.

The role of the Center and its impact upon the basic department of instruction may be difficult and troublesome, but in some cases may be absolutely necessary.

The center may be in an institute which is a collection of centers, or the center may be simply a fund which revolves in some high administrative office, such as the president's. This fund is available on request to centers wherever they may be set up on the various campuses of the university. Such a fund may also reside in the office of the chancellor for the various schools and colleges.

A center may also be designated in terms of a grant for training purposes, for research purposes, or to provide services.

The centers which appear too mission oriented sometimes attract the hostility of powerful faculty influences, and this can mean a reduction in the ability of these particular centers to communicate with others.

But if the present trend of reducing research appropriations to unorganized faculty researchers continues, it seems inevitable that it will compel new alignments of faculty interest, student support, and possibly a less academized viewpoint of research toward a given purpose.

The "sacred cows" of research often dry up. When this happens, the efforts and sometimes the interests of the faculty change in order to accommodate to the reduction of support, and in order that the faculty can continue to maintain currency in their university life. This kind of accommodation can be accomplished in the political and social climate of a state university only when that climate has broad acceptance by the public.

The problem is not simple. Much effective communication is called for. The university has the task of balancing the value of research centers and of providing broad support to the entire educational process. In this, university administrators share a burden with Federal administrators who must keep two special things in mind as they administer their programs: (1) they must capitalize upon public support to insure continuation of funding and (2) they must keep the operational aspects of the programs in the hands of specialists who are best equipped to understand the needs of the researcher and the academician. In short, the Federal administrator must be mindful of the voter and the scientist, the public and the teacher, national policy and efficient educational procedures. So must the university administrator. The dean and faculty together have to examine the value of the research center—in which a specialized scientific activity is taking place—and compare that with the need to provide for general support of the entire educational process. The aim is to maintain balance in the organization.

It is in the latter aspects of balancing the research and educational function that we find the greatest success in the communication between centers, and between centers and departments, and even to a reversal in the flight from the department to what seems a small movement back to departments.

Our population efforts are at the moment formally centralized in the Department of Demography and in an allied Institute of Population Studies. The Demography Department in the College of Letters and Science does offer the higher degrees, and the growth of the graduate-student applicants and acceptances in that department is from one point of view gratifying, but from the point of view of trying to support students it is a horrendous problem.

At the same time, on a campus which has fixed limits on graduate-student population through 1973, it means that every admission has to be very carefully watched, almost as carefully as in smaller private schools.

Thus a growing unit such as population studies acting with the related departments of sociology, political science, public policy, et cetera must be balanced by denying growth to some other unit on the campus—not a matter to promote general tranquility. It does promote communication between departments and centers, but the communication is not always pleasant.

VIEWPOINT OF A CENTER DIRECTOR

MOYE W. FREYMANN

The complexity and importance of population problems demand a concerted mobilization of scientific and professional talent through the device of the university population center. The Carolina Population Center exemplifies this approach. It aims to (1) strengthen the development of general theory in the population field, in order to increase the meaning of present knowledge and clarify further research priorities, (2) mobilize the best possible scientific and professional talent to attack population questions and develop optimal conditions and working strategies for this purpose, (3) facilitate "horizontal" interactions between specialists from different disciplines, so as to reduce unnecessary assumptions and gain reinforcing effects through joint approaches to a particular aspect of the population system, (4) foster "vertical" interactions between those working at fundamental research levels, at applied research levels and those in action programs and policy situations, so that new research findings are more rapidly carried over into application, and so that clues from field experience can be fed back to researchers, and (5) build and maintain interaction between workers in different geographic areas, for more rapid transfer of new experience and testing of observations under different human situations.

Achievement of such goals by a university-based population center will depend, in turn, on a variety of key organizational relationships. Brief comments are offered here on five categories of relationships: with the university administration, with university departments, with related centers at the same university, with collaborating institutions in other areas, and with population-related agencies.

University Administration

The administrator can find in the population-studies center a force toward building a broader universe of basic knowledge and away from the fragmentation of university life. It also represents the social relevance expected increasingly by the public and students. The center's effectiveness, however, depends on strong administrative support from the university administration in dealing with the complexities of cross-disciplinary work. A population center also derives important economic advantages from its location in a university setting. The relatively scarce funds available can best be used to attract new talent to the field and a university situation, and can also challenge the university to mobilize matching support from other sources for such work.

University Departments

Departmental relationships are obviously crucial for university centers which aim to mobilize the intensity and variety of scientific and professional talents now required in the population field. Traditional departments may be viewed as means for promoting particular types of analysis to approach truth, or particular types of methods to minister to human affairs. The area-oriented center, on the other hand, aims to involve all relevant research methods to approach broader truth about that problem area, and to muster all related professional skills to minister to it. Where the warp of departmental, methodological interests intersects with the woof of center problem-area interests, new stimulation and gain can accrue for all concerned. Strong and balanced representation of both of these approaches, though still rare, will characterize the great university of the future.

The optimal pattern of flexible interaction with a variety of departments is discouraged by forces which push university population centers either to "go it alone" or to be dominated by a particular department or discipline-area emphasis. Development of links with relevant departments often invokes tensions and requires continuous nurturing, in ways different from each department. Optimally for such relationships, each new faculty appointment for population-related work should be made jointly between the center and a department representing the relevant basic discipline, but the center should have the power to make its own appointments if necessary. Strong joint relationships help to advance departmental as well as center interests, and tend to attract more and better faculty members and students to the population field than in the case of the "isolated" center.

Other Centers in the University

Other centers dealing with such broad problem areas as urban planning, environmental studies, or child development may have many common points of concern with a university population center. Seeking out such points and building strategies for mutual reinforcement can be very productive. In the Carolina situation, we have joint interests now with the Institute for Research in Social Sciences, the Ecology Training Program, the Health Services Research Center, the Center for Urban and Regional Studies, as well as with a university-associated research center, the Research Triangle Institute.

Institutions in Other Areas

The university center can gain, and give, much through collaborative work with institutions in other geographic areas, which facilitate sharing experiences and testing ideas in different human situations. Such relationships are best focused in a few other locations, to maximize the continuity of contact and cumulation of joint experience. Their success will depend on person-to-person identification of common interests in specific problems, and on shared institutional concerns for basic staff development.

Population-Related Agencies

Outside agencies can find the university population center an effective "middleman," able to link their needs for help in research and manpower development with relevant internal university resources. The center facilitates communication between such agencies and the university community, helping to clarify scientific questions, to interpret requests and responses, and to match needs and capacities. University-based population centers in the United States are especially able to help private agencies, other governments, and United Nations agencies in ways impossible for a U.S. Governmental group. Tasks requested of the Carolina Population Center by U.N. agencies, for example, range from specific research, training, or consultation work to a review of global needs for further population research. Such activities are quite compatible with the goals of a university center, if approached with a broad frame of reference; they can provide clues for new fundamental studies and can enrich teaching, as well as provide practical service.

VIEWPOINT OF A DEPARTMENT HEAD

WILLIAM K. LINVILL

As I have written in a previous chapter, I am a department head of "an experiment" to see what a department might and should be. In connection with my colleagues here, I shall be speaking as the department head of the departments I know and also of the type of department I think will be needed if centers are to flourish and to be efficient.

Why do this experiment in what a department might be?

We are really interested in technological transition. We think that the world is faced with an increasing rate of change, and are concerned with how a university and a department in a university should respond to this change. In my earlier chapter, I indicated that two kinds of activities are involved here, and that they are very different. The first is an exploratory activity, and the second is an implementation activity.

An exploratory activity is necessarily a term activity. It is hopefully one of discovery and illumination. The implementation activity which follows is productive and is not flexible.

Our problem as a society is to move from the exploration, where we already get adequate illumination of the new problems, to implementation, where we are able to reap the rewards of our exploration.

This operation, as has been pointed out, must build on the strength that we have. We obviously do not exploit the future by throwing away the past. We simply help the institutions of the past to accommodate to the future.

In that sense, the function in which we are all involved is basically that of broker. We are advocates only of the problem, not of an institution. For me, a center is a home away from home. It is the place where the exploration can be done; and when the exploration is finished and implementation follows, the center must necessarily disappear.

What interests me particularly is the place of the university in this process. I was at M.I.T. at the beginning of World War II, and noticed what happened to engineering at that time. The applied physicists had basic understanding of foundations, and they had the flexibility to meet the new challenges of technology in World War II, while the conventional engineers held the coats.

We need persons to work on the population problem who are professionals with the flexibility that comes from foundation disciplines available only at the university. Any center which is not associated with a strong university, with a strong-foundation discipline base, is doomed to failure because the people will not have adequate flexibility to move.

At the same time, a center or a program which does not have the focus of a specific problem is in a hopeless situation. So the flexibility of the broad-foundation discipline of the university and the focus of a specific problem are both needed.

Centers can provide the real-world coupling. They can provide a place where the foundation disciplines in a strong university program can build a new professional discipline that will ultimately provide the brokerage function which adapts exploratory work to implementation.

The comparison of the population centers to the Space Program or the Atomic Energy Program is valid only to a limited degree. The problem for each of those programs is well focused, the client is very identified and the objectives are clear.

This is not so for the population problem. The population problem on a larger scale is more akin to that faced by regional development programs such as that of the Appalachian Regional Commission. It is a much harder institutional problem than those of AEC and NASA. The institutional organization required to cope with this enormous nonuniform, sponsorless job must be innovative, flexible, and varied. In its development, it must mount an effective communications system which will be able to gain the attention of the billions of people in the world who are its independent clients and who are not nearly as well organized as the buyers of nuclear products and Apollo missions.

SECTION SIX

EVALUATIONS

In February 1970, approximately seventy thoughtful and eminent leaders in science, industry, academia, and government met to discuss the issues related to creating population centers. During the two day conference many of the authors of these chapters spoke on the topics of their particular competence. Certain participants of the conference were charged with listening and evaluating. Three panels were formed for this express purpose, and a fourth panel was formed to derive a summary and any possible conclusions which might have emerged.

Leora Wood Wells has recorded the remarks of the speakers and representatives of these panels in the two chapters of this section. In presenting the commentary Mrs. Wells digresses from the style of previous chapters, reporting the material with attribution to the authors.

Chapter Twenty-eight

REVIEWS OF COMMENTARIES OF THREE PANELS

LEORA WOOD WELLS

D URING the course of examining the concept of institution building to meet the population problem, the reviews of many were sought. The author of this chapter and Chapter Twenty-nine, upon listening to remarks made by several experts at a conference* held on the subject in February 1970, has summarized the thinking of three panels asked to evaluate the proceedings, and a fourth panel which reviewed all the issues raised and offered some conclusions.

A major purpose of the conference was to consider whether centers are a practical tool to use on the population problem. With material presented earlier as a base, three panels examined the center concept.

PANEL I

Panel I consisted of CHARLES LLOYD, J. M. STYCOS, JAMES LIVERMAN, and WILLIAM LIU.†

In listening to the comments about the millions that may be invested in the support of population research, construction, training, and information systems within the next few years, said DR. CHARLES LLOYD, Senior Scientist, Worcester Foundation of Experimental Biology, he could not imagine where all the bright young people are going to come from who will be needed to spend this money well.

Training must be stressed. The Worcester Foundation has programs supported by the Ford Foundation and NICHD for

---

* Conference sponsored by the Center for Population Research of the NICHD on Management of Consolidated Research Institutions for Population Research, Pan American Health Organization Building, Washington, D.C.

† Dr. Liu's remarks are omitted here since they have been presented earlier as Chapter Eleven.

the training of postdoctoral M.D.'s and Ph.D.'s in reproductive biology with particular emphasis on contraception. Some of these trainees will become scientists contributing new knowledge to the field; others will spread the word through teaching.

A third and essential group has received little attention. Someone should be training people to go back into the communities and train the "activists"—the people who can reach and influence the population.

Training faces a serious problem in erratic Federal Budget policies; with periodic and unpredictable cuts in funds, it is hardly worth training people because when they complete their training there may be nothing for them to do. Well-trained young people are unable to get grants. The number and quality of applicants for grants tend to be lower than they should. This may be due to the fact that many young scientists feel it is not worth the trouble to apply, simply because they will not get the money. It is not enough to have funds available to train people for basic research in the population field. Something must also be done to assure that qualified people receive research support after they complete their training.

There seemed to be an assumption at the conference that more centers are desirable and required, said DR. J. MAYONE STYCOS, Director of the International Population Program at Cornell University. This is a questionable assumption.

Perhaps his most helpful contribution, DR. STYCOS said, would be to relate some of his recent experiences as head of a center in trying to raise money, since this has considerable relevance to the question of whether there should be new or expanded centers.

The first thing a center usually does is to go to the private foundations. They are nice to deal with, and you have private dollars rather than Federal dollars. But there is a new cast that seems to be coming over the foundation eye: the "how come you are talking to us instead of the people in Washington" cast.

So you hide your tin cup, slink out of the room, and get on the next plane to Washington.

In Washington, if you are interested in major support for a center, AID and NICHD are two likely places. Without criticizing either, it should be pointed out that the process of getting money is tantamount to a month or more of intensive shock therapy.

At the present time, the International Population Program has a training grant from NICHD which it has had for three years, at about $75,000 per year. Every year in Ithaca in the springtime when the crocuses begin to push their heads through the snow, around May, DR. STYCOS said, he begins to think expansionist. He thinks, "Wouldn't it be great to get this out of the department of sociology and have a true multidisciplinary program?" There are mass-communications people who are dying to do something. There are extension people who have run out of a cause, and animal husbands who are tired of dealing with animals. Why not really put a multidisciplinary program together?

As he is about to reach for the telephone, DR. STYCOS said, a message comes from NICHD. It goes something like this: "Although we have generally appropriated $75,000 for your program each year, this year, if we wish to increase the number of centers at all, we are, unfortunately, going to have to take the money from existing centers. Do you suppose it would be possible to reduce the size of your budget this year?

Here we are, all talking about marvelous plans for new centers while the existing centers are being asked to cut back on the modest programs they now have.

You get nowhere if you start talking about going multidisciplinary and point out that what we need is not more demographers but people in other disciplines with competence in the population area. Cornell has a flexible enough graduate system to handle this. But NICHD says, "You mean give fellowships for somebody that is not in the profession of population? We do not give that kind of support."

This is the kind of atmosphere in which we operate, yet we talk and dream of tremendous breakthroughs in kinds and sizes of centers.

We should look at what has been achieved and what should be done. The centers have systematically neglected the undergraduate aspect of education, and that is where much of the steam is. Among the undergraduates there are young people who are raring to go on the population problem, but they are offered no opportunities. This is where some of the training emphasis needs to go. But there are other considerations in approaching the problem, personal and economic.

If he were black, DR. STYCOS continued, he would say, "Our women are definitely more and more interested in family planning, but the idea of spending 800 million dollars and turning loose 21,000 workers on us gives us pause. We would like in your center a little more consideration given to some of the broad economic questions that confront us along with the population question. For example, what would it save if abortion laws were liberalized and some of the remaining money were used to improve economic circumstances?"

If he came from an underdeveloped area, DR. STYCOS went on, he would say, "You are trying to convince us that there are too many of us. But we have news for you. We think there are too many of you. We are worried about these centers, because we feel that in a short time they will be turning out masses of population experts. You are going to turn them loose on us, and we have too many of you guys already. What we would most like to see is more consideration given to the employment situation, and how we can improve the training of our own people. You have plenty of problems already connected with your centers. Why do you not take a look at the questions there?"

We have a tremendous analytical job ahead of us, DR. STYCOS said. Before we get involved in the creation of new centers, we first need to find out what the experience has been, both good and bad, in the centers that already exist, and how we can correct their problems.

In at least a few centers, said DR. JAMES LIVERMAN, Associate Director for Biomedical and Environmental Sciences, Oak Ridge National Laboratory, we need to approach the population problem as a whole instead of in isolated parts. In practice we take the problem, which is well integrated in nature, and disjoint it so that we can research it in pieces that we can understand and can handle in the laboratory. This sort of research is important, but if the population problem is as large, complex, and urgent as everyone thinks it is, we need to be sure our thinking and our actions have the scale and comprehensiveness that is required.

There must be created at least a few centers which bring together in close proximity a conglomerate of social scientists, behavioral scientists, natural scientists, and professionals in law, public administration, politics, and other fields. They must be made to interact in a truly interdisciplinary manner so as to insure by continued vigilance that all of the impacts of proposed changes are considered. Before either technological solutions or social modifications are kicked out into the marketplace and the stream of human endeavor, we need to be sure their full impact is understood.

We seem at this Conference generally to agree that population centers should have strong ties with an educational institution. What we also must stress is that the education offered there must be directly relevant to the problems of society. I make specific reference to the recent report of the Office of Science and Technology on "The Universities and Environmental Quality Commitment to Problem Focused Education."[35] Students are demanding a qualitatively different kind of training from what they have been getting in the past. Many have left the university after the B.S. degree, worked in their chosen fields, and then have returned to the university for further training in problem-focused programs. They are not satisfied with a test-tube world; they want to relate their studies to the real world as they have found it to be. These youths are insisting, as has the Chairman of a House Appropriations Subcommittee, "We must make science the workhorse of man, not our own private hobbyhorse." We must make sure that we are not developing solutions to non-existent problems and which have no real relevance and no possibility of implementation.

Part of this tie with reality centers in the communication of scientific knowledge, not only to our scientific colleagues but to Federal, state, and local officials, our Congressmen and others in positions of policy-making or power. We need also to communicate this knowledge to the people everywhere who need to know about the choices that are open to them.

At this stage we need to ask, "Can we do what we are trying to do? Are we doing the right kinds of research?" Our objective at the present time should perhaps not be aimed so much at the solution of specific narrow population problems as at understanding the broad range of underlying issues—social as well as technological. Only with this broad-based understanding, which I maintain can come only from a consideration of all the issues in a simultaneous manner, shall we be able to achieve a stable population with a decent quality of life.

PANEL II

Panel II consisted of CALVIN TAYLOR, PAGE PROCTOR, PAUL HENSHAW, and ANTHONY WIENER.

Any new population research centers that are created should be fresh, different types, said DR. CALVIN TAYLOR, Professor of Psychology at the University of Utah. Most of the conference participants represent people who are successful in the present establishments. This introduces a certain bias which may obscure our vision of recreative possibilities. If the centers continue to operate in certain predetermined limited ways, they may not fulfill all their potential. If the workers become too "locked in" to their assumptions, on their theories, or to current trends, they may miss important opportunities and possibilities. Overcrystallization or premature crystallization can deter the unlocking of complex problems. Instead, more of a spirit of challenge is needed. We need to discover which current approaches are fruitful and why and what new approaches need to be taken. We should create climates for creativity and develop leadership to facilitate creativity.

One area of his own particular interest, DR. TAYLOR said, is research on creativity and research. One finding that has emerged from studies of research and development centers is that it is often difficult to predict or foresee what research will produce significant outcomes. A project may be focused on something the investigators think will be fruitful, but its greatest value may come out of its unexpected new insights which then lead them to unanticipated directions in perhaps even an informal or unofficial project which produces important results.

The greatest force for upsetting long-range forecasts is creativity. The more creativity you can unleash, the more capability you create in people that was not there when the forecast was made. And the more new capability that is created, the more you can upset the forecast.

In the population problem, we should try to upset the forecasts not to fulfill them. We need to open up positive approaches that will allow creativity to take over. Yet the research findings to date indicate that practically no existing research centers have anything even closely approaching an ideal climate for creativity. Before existing population research centers are expanded or used as organizational models for new ones, their working climate should be assessed to determine what conditions are stifling the productivity and creativity of the scientists working there. Such features should be eliminated there and also not repeated elsewhere in the expansions.

The surprising and revolutionary ideas of creative people tend to be a lot of trouble in highly organized establishments, so that administrators are often inclined to stifle rather than encourage the creatives. We really have not improved working conditions for creatively productive scientists in our scientific laboratories much since the early days of the Sputniks.

Establishing optimum working climates and placing the centers under the guidance of leaders who know how to foster creativity in others can increase the output of an organization many times over. In effect, the return on each budget dollar would be much greater, because there would be little or no increase in overhead costs. This does not mean just adding more layers of people and activities in the existing organization. The effectiveness and fruitfulness of the organization needs to be checked at every step of the program, and positive rewards for creativity need to be built into the system.

The recent report by Steinhart and Cherniak, *The Universities and Environmental Quality—Commitment to Problem-Fo-*

cused Education,[35] takes a look at some of the problems of inter-disciplinary work in a university setting which create conflicts because of the established departmental structures. Such problem-oriented approaches almost invariably run against the tide of the typical organizational structure and functioning. The members of different professions are often much more ready to work together, DR. TAYLOR said, than their departments are ready to have them do so. This creates a vacuum between research and its effects on society. Although this interprofessional approach is sorely needed to tackle successfully some of our most troublesome, unsolved problems, problem-focused education is still a comparatively rare occurrence. We need to encourage all kinds of new ways that the disciplines can be coupled so that their joint efforts, in turn, can help to couple the fruits of research with the problems it is designed to solve.

If we are willing to involve youth of all ages (from the elementary school level on) in the solution of population problems, DR. TAYLOR said, we shall have a sure winner. There is a multiplicity of creative talent among members of the younger generation which our educational system leaves largely dormant, but this can be made functional. The potential total mindpower of all our youth in our schools and colleges is unbelievably large and ready to function effectively as soon as we provide the opportunities. Young people coming up through twelve or sixteen years of our educational system should not have the feeling that research and problem-solving actions are things that happen somewhere else and have nothing to do with their educational experiences.

In some ways, high school students are more ready to do research than are graduate students, and this may be even more true of elementary students. If we would give the youth problems like the population one to solve instead of keeping education within narrow bands of tradition and "learning" well-established knowledge, we could develop a more enlightened and capable citizenry who would be glad to be included in tackling the problems of society. This is better than depriving young people of the opportunity to be concerned and involved until a much later time when these problems that they have inherited are suddenly thrust upon them as their own—and when they no longer think as children, but are in the patterned thinking of adults. Yet it may take the less traditionally patterned thinking in our youngsters to solve these as-yet-unsolved problems.

When he asked his own students what they thought solutions to the population problem might be, they came up with some fresh new insights, DR. TAYLOR said. They said that if we would eliminate poverty, we might find the population explosion less of a problem. They said if we would reduce frustrations and provide productive and creative ways for people to release their tensions and use their energies, this might help. They pointed out that we are dealing with values and attitudes which tend to honor motherhood and big families. They expressed concern that there may be too much manipulation of human beings for the good of mankind.

As a follow-up, a group of teachers in Utah has asked its students to think up all the problems that would arise if the population should continue to increase in our nation. From this collective list of problems, each group of students can select one problem area and work on possible ways to cope with it both preventively and after it arises. Even first grade students have worked on the population explosion problem and the results have been fascinating. The teacher said she had never had a livelier session with these young *thinkers* than when she gave them the challenge to think and discuss this topic. The kids immediately abandoned the main approach and assumptions that the adults are using in their research. Then they went after other approaches, which in certain ways, are better for solving these problems than those used by adults who are already locked in on the "way to go about it," and sometimes even locked in on what the outcoming answer must be. But the youth go at it in some new ways that adults are not trying, and they thereby supplement the adult approaches, which is very fortunate. The students thought of it as a great adventure rather than a set of problems full of headaches. Furthermore, they fought through all the objections raised by the teacher to each of their ideas as they gave them. In other words, they were young and lively enough in ideas that they would not yet allow themselves to be squelched by the killers of ideas used by their teacher. We also learned not to let adults interfere or they might stop this good work of the youth—this was discovered when one turned-on class was asked to talk it over that night with their parents. The next day it was found that the children had been turned off very effectively at home. They had been told authoritatively by at least one parent that either there was no problem (in our state) or that it was *not yet their problem.*

There may be no limit to the creative solutions we might devise. We know that we have the capability to increase agricultural productivity in some parts of the world fifteen to twenty fold. We have the potential for designing new environments much better than those in which the bulk of the people of the world now live—not just physically but also psychologically better environments.

Why do we not combine all these capabilities to reduce some of the population pinch? We need to select a critical problem locale and bring every technique now available to bear on it to see whether changes in the desired direction can be brought about. Radically different action programs and incentives for society should be tried first in spots along an overcrowded population strip such as the east coast and then in open areas where overpopulation is not a problem. With our potential scientific capabilities, new towns and cities could be better designed for people than have ever before occurred in the history of the world.

Approximately 75 percent of our population in the United States lives in something like 2 to 4 percent of our space. The suburban areas around the cities are continuing to expand, while the small towns of the country are getting smaller. Vast healthy sunshine areas are available in many states in the West which lack nothing but an adequate water supply to make them capable of absorbing a considerable part of the present population explosion without stress, and the water problem could be solved. All of the population-research centers are located in places where population stresses exist. Should not some of the population-research effort be directed toward exploring redistribution of population as one possible alternating solution? Perhaps we need another Moses to lead the people out of the wilderness of our critically crowded cities into the open spaces where they would have time and freedom to be creative and fruitful in designing new futures.

Advertising is an action-oriented business that faces some of the same problems as population research, said MR. PAGE PROCTOR, Senior Vice President of the J. Walter Thompson Agency. It works against inexorable deadliness; it formulates action programs based on research; it must persuade the public, and it must study the effects of what it does and modify its approaches on the basis of this feedback.

As the Center for Population Research seeks to establish its role on the national scene, it might consider these possibilities suggested by the experience of advertising:

1. That even at this formative stage a center should view itself as an action-oriented, decision-making system whose purpose is not only study of the United States population level but improvement of the quality of American life.

2. That it should take as one of its provinces synthesizing knowledge that already exists in the field of population control, and that it should do this with a sense of wartime urgency to establish whether a viable basis for action exists in terms of goals and guidelines for population control.

3. That it should call upon many disciplines, making sure that sufficient emphasis is given to understanding American mores as a base for changing patterns of propagation.

4. That it should recognize the need for public communication if population-control efforts are to succeed.

Through its market research and motivational research, the advertising field has learned a good deal about what makes human beings act or not act. Thousands of advertising practitioners in New York are waiting to be of service, free of charge, on the population problem. The sooner some of them can be cranked into the population-research effort, the more they will be able to contribute when the time for public communication efforts arrives.

DR. PAUL HENSHAW, Visiting Professor, Department of Government, University of Arizona, underscored the need for a sense of urgency and a time goal for solution of the population problem. At the close of the conference DR. HENSHAW supplemented his earlier remarks with additional comments which he wished to share with the conference group.

As MR. CATER pointed out in his remarks on institution building, some institutions fail while others succeed, depending especially upon goals, design, and timeliness. Institutional models used successfully in the past may prove totally inadequate in dealing with the problem of numbers of people. The question is how to set appropriate goals and datelines and how to proceed effectively without evoking backlash. This should be kept in mind when evaluating existing programs and developing recommendations concerning NICHD's work in the population field.

MR. CAMPBELL had indicated that NICHD's Center for Population Research hopes to become a major source for institutional and project support of population research. DR. HENSHAW expressed concern that the population program described for review and evaluation by the conference group seemed to center heavily around substantial enlargements of existing programs of voluntary research in reproduction, fertility, and demography carried forward mainly by centers in academic institutions.

The population problem has similarities to the radiation-protection problem faced a few years ago by the Atomic Energy Commission. In the public interest it became necessary—if such were possible—to set a permissible level of exposure, one which was safe and achievable within reasonable means. At that time, few guides or models were available. Unsolicited or academic research provided some useful information but in itself did not constitute a move to provide the protection that was needed. Explanatory and provisional steps were undertaken; and, over a period of time and in the face of much controversy, a reasonably good program was hammered out. Now an effective system is in use without restrictive legislation.

A program of academic research, no matter how elaborate, will, by itself, exert no influence on population growth rates. Stated but modifiable goals are required, together with a specific but broad-scope action program to achieve these goals by a designated time. The comments made during the conference seemed to express more concern for the academic institutions as they are now participating or might participate in an enlarged program than for the importance of the program itself.

The population problem does not stand by itself. It is not an island. Needed at the earliest possible time is a means of knowing from moment to moment the influence of all key determinants of standards and levels of living, including population. Needed also is a commitment to deal straightforwardly with the whole problem; a population approach alone is apt to be futile for reasons other than those of motivation and techniques. After adequate information and reasonable commitments, there must be a Federal-level action agency with powers sufficient to insure consistency of the program and to carry out guidance and regulative steps as required. Primarily such work should apply in the United States, but to be realistic, it should correlate with related work in other countries.

Education and motivation efforts based on real data will, without a doubt, be the major steps required. Beyond this, Federal guidance and assistance in achieving compliance will be required.

In order to determine whether new population centers should be established, we need to know a great deal about the distribution of work in the existing centers, said DR. ANTHONY WIENER, Chairman, Research Management Council, Hudson Institute. If we had unlimited resources, each of the existing centers should be strengthened and all activities should be reinforced. But, given scarce resources, what are the strategic gaps that most need to be filled? It appears that what is in shortest supply is analysis of policy.

It is clear that some of the things that need to be done can best be done in academic settings or centers within academic settings. Such work does not necessarily need to be either interdisciplinary or problem oriented, nor must it necessarily include training researchers as one of its functions. All of these approaches are important, but not every center needs to do them all. Much biomedical, demographic, and sociological work can be pursued perfectly well outside of an interdisciplinary context and outside of a problem-oriented purpose, because the goal of such work is to answer questions about particular issues. Academic research should ask such questions as how well do we really know the things we think we know? Can we learn them better? Can we generate more powerful theories? Can we produce better data?

At the other end of the scale are the government agencies where policy is being formulated. Here, the tendency is to think in terms of marginal changes in existing policies, because we do not know much about the consequences of policy, and fear that if we depart very much from an existing policy, we may be in a great deal of trouble.

In between these two areas, the one of academic research to define theories and data and the one of direct formulation of policy, is a vast empty area. In this area, people should be utilizing the results of academic research to answer such questions as what difference does all this make? And what should we do about it? The job of these people should be to interpret, organize, and integrate the findings of academic research to provide perspective and make recommendations on which policy changes can be based. This may be the point on which a new center should be focused. Such a center should also have some capacity to fund research elsewhere when it has identified gaps in the attention being given to various aspects of the population problem.

When one focuses on a particular aspect of a problem, there is always danger of forgetting to ask what the more general problem is. Almost every academic discipline sharpens the mind by narrowing the focus. This is unavoidable. Every professional orientation builds in a set of blinders which forces people to neglect concerns that lie outside the questions of greatest interest to their own professions.

In the population area, people neglect to ask what the problem is. There is an assumption that we know the problem, so people work in particular aspects of it which they think will contribute to the solution. But we do not, in fact, understand the total problem in the kind of detail that would be desirable for development of effective policies.

Certainly the problem is not mere numbers. The birth of most babies is an occasion for joy, even if they are the third or fourth babies in the family. Most deaths are occasions of grief. So the problem is more complicated than numerical totals of births and deaths.

Nor is the problem one of food supply in the United States. We have agricultural surpluses. It is not a problem of population density. Much of the most expensive real estate and many of the most desirable living areas are densely populated. A great many people go to the cities where population density is high, because that is where the action is and that is where they want to be.

Is the problem ecology? Economic growth? These are familiar complexities, but no one seems to be devoting serious full-time work to analyzing this range of problems.

Once the problems are clear, objectives must be analyzed. In money terms, this is relatively cheap. It would probably require less than 1 percent of the total research budget. It does not require laboratories or equipment or a great many people. What it does require is a few people who will confront each other and think hard and over a long period about what we are trying to do.

Take, for example, the question of zero population growth. Few would argue with the proposition that ultimately we must achieve zero population growth. But the more important questions are how do we reach zero population growth? At what rate?

Then we begin to ask, what are the effects of alternative population policies? How do they change reproductive rates differentially? Who needs to do what for whom to bring this about? What sorts of inducements or pressures should be used? And what is going to happen to society in the meantime?

When we begin to ask about the objectives of a population

policy and what the priorities for allocation of research funds should be, we have to ask additional questions. Where does population growth really pinch the most? For what kinds of reasons? What kinds of policies will affect this growth most appropriately? What is most needed—better contraceptives, a public education campaign, liberalized abortion laws, or some other approach to the problem? What are the relationships among the gross national product, individual productivity, and the consumption of energy; and how do these relate to the population problem?

We often use the term "research" in too narrow a context. In relation to population, at least, we need to cover a whole range of analyses and studies. In order to find answers to questions like those just cited, population research has to be conceived as taking in projections of resources, ecological issues, economic issues, and many other factors. At least a few people need to address themselves explicitly to this broad range of problems. It is for such a purpose that a new population research center might usefully be created.

Such a center probably should not be located either within a university or within Government. In the university setting, the center would face the problem of the dominance of the goals of the academic professions. The orientation of the academic researcher is primarily toward his advancement within his own profession. This means he wants to make a publishable contribution to knowledge, but publishable contributions may not be what is needed most. It may be more important to decide how to make use of the knowledge in doing what needs to be done about the problem. But this does not result in publication of scientific papers, and the closer people are to a university, the harder it is to get them to do this kind of work.

Within Government, also, there are difficulties in trying to ask what we shall do about the problem; because there is a limit to how freely people can speculate about policy changes that are more than incremental changes from existing policies. Furthermore, when a policy-analysis group is attached to an action agency, the agency is apt to decide the research group "isn't doing anything" and should be put to work at something "useful." If the research people are put to work that way, they will lose the capacity to do far-reaching speculative analyses with an orientation toward future action rather than current policy. If they refuse to be drawn into the action level, they will find themselves treated as irrelevant and will cease to have any influence.

The best solution may be a "halfway house"—a center in which people are in close communication both with the university researchers and with the Government agencies and foundations engaged in policy-making and action programs. These people need to learn, on the one hand, what the researchers are finding out and what assumptions need to be modified on the basis of these findings. They need to know also what are the policies and the actions being carried out by various government agencies and foundations, what decisions are coming up, which ones can be influenced, and which ones are beyond influence for the time being.

They obviously cannot study everything in the hope of discovering significant new truths, but they can do a sufficiently comprehensive analysis to determine what additional research is needed and what changes in policies and action programs would be desirable.

PANEL III

Panel III consisted of LILLIAN HARVEY, FORREST LINDER, JOHN CUTLER and LYNTON CALDWELL. DR. LILLIAN HARVEY, Dean of the Tuskegee Institute School of Nursing, summarized the viewpoints of the panel. DR. LINDER supplemented her remarks later in the conference, and DR. CUTLER and DR. CALDWELL* forwarded additional comments after the close of the conference.

Reporting for the panel, DR. HARVEY said that the country needs a firmer policy on population than it has had in the past. We do, she said, appear to be approaching development and enunciation of such a statement.

This coming decade must be viewed as a period of crisis, and

---

* Dr. Caldwell's remarks are presented as Chapter Nine.

our responses must reflect the gravity of the situation. We do not yet have all the answers, and additional research is needed; but we must not delay sounding the alarm, telling the people what we know about the crucial nature of the problem and where we stand in relation to solutions.

A non-Governmental institution adequately financed through non-Governmental sources is needed to keep the total problem in view. Its function should be to identify unmet needs and monitor progress across a broad spectrum of interrelated problems including population. It would assist communication and multifaceted cooperation among sociologists, economists, political scientists, historians, religious leaders, biomedical experts, and others who are working individually or collectively to cope with these problems.

The people who are most concerned in this problem should be involved in practically every aspect of the planning and delivery of whatever solutions we are able to develop. This is not an "ivory tower" situation. It is a situation which must reach from the ivory tower down to the grass roots where the people are and where those responsible for implementation of programs are.

We must recognize the pervasiveness of our domestic problems in relation to the demands of the human organism on his environment, the impact of technological advances, and all the problems surrounding proliferation of the species within our complex and affluent society. We need to face the fact that the proliferation of human life in America is not confined to minority groups or the poor; it may also move into the upper and middle classes, and the problem must be viewed in this total context.

There must also be a reevaluation of basic American values. Our society places great emphasis on producing and selling more and more of bigger and bigger products. At some point we are going to have to shift gears and do something about changing over to an emphasis on quality rather than quantity.

New centers for population research need to be developed on as broad a base as is feasible, taking into account the need for diversity of size, organization, and management; scope in relation to the program goals of the individual centers; flexibility of operation within universities and other institutions; and availability of personnel in the necessary disciplines.

These centers should be strategically located. They should be generously funded on a stable, long-range basis which takes into consideration the need for growth, development and continuity of program, for training of personnel, and for ways of meeting the special needs and requirements of both basic and mission-oriented research.

DR. FORREST E. LINDER, Professor of Biostatistics at the University of North Carolina School of Public Health, supplemented DR. HARVEY'S description of panel III's concept of the new type of center that is needed. What we really need to consider, he said, is how we proceed to invent a kind of center that does not now exist, because there is an essential role for a different sort of institution.

There are a number of important differences between the population problem and other problems. For example, our current view of the population problem runs counter to long-established aspirations in our society. One never hears an American chamber of commerce boast about its city's pollution or poverty, but every chamber of commerce boasts about the growth of its community. This aspiration for growth is an individual thing, a family thing, a community thing, and a society thing; yet when we talk about population control, we are talking about the opposite value.

There are other intrinsic differences. Some of the most successful public health programs have been ones in which the public health organization has done things to the environment like putting in a water supply or sewage facilities or vaccinating all preschool-age children. The less successful programs have been those in which people have to do something for themselves. With the present stage of contraceptive development, population control falls in the category of a *more* difficult rather than a *less* difficult problem in terms of control through a public health program.

Another difference is that the population problem is diffuse. Many social problems are concentrated in finite numbers of geographical locations or cities or factories. The population problem spreads over millions of households and involves people in every part of the country and the world.

We could identify many other ways in which the population problem differs from other problems. We need to give this a lot of thought and exploration and then try to think what are the implications of those differences in terms of the way centers should be organized.

The population problem is multifaceted, but it does not necessarily follow that all the institutions that work on it must be multifaceted or interdisciplinary. It is possible to dissect a problem into its different elements and have institutions that specialize in each. The question is not whether we need more population centers or fewer but whether we need any different kinds than we have now. Or does our present mix provide a proper balance that corresponds with the problem?

His own concept of what we need as a new kind of population center, DR. LINDER said, is one that would analyze the total problem, study the programs of the other centers, and separate the many facets into pieces that can be studied separately. This center would make a continuous systems analysis of what ought to be done, who is doing it, and how to proceed so that all aspects of the problem are dealt with in the proper proportions.

Although he is interested in international work, DR. LINDER said, he feels that such a center should be heavily focused on American population problems. Some participants have said that the population problem in the United States is not acute because we have adequate food, space, and so on. This is not entirely true because the demands Americans place on their environment are very different from those found in other countries. It is said that each American, in terms of what he demands of the environment, what he consumes, and the trash he produces, is the equivalent of about six citizens in other parts of the world. If this is true, we need to view the problem as if the population of the United States were not 200 million but more than a billion.

Whatever the exact comparisons may be, the point is that we have a much bigger problem in the United States than is indicated simply by looking at our population in numerical terms of 200 million people, and we need to create a new type of center that can cope with the problem in this broader context.

In considering how we can best cope with the population problem, we need to look at what has been accomplished in relation to other problems through interdisciplinary research and public health programs and how these relate to population research opportunities, said DR. JOHN CUTLER, Director of the Population Division, University of Pittsburgh. This nation has had major experience in developing research and service programs involving large groups of people and we should draw on this historical experience.

Whatever the character of the center engaged in population research, certain types of studies require access to well-defined groups of people for longer or shorter periods of time. For some types of studies, the group required may even be of community size. One source of study populations of the desired size may be found within existing Federal, state, and local public-health programs dealing with certain diseases or the maintenance of community health. Specific population research projects could well be added as an accompaniment of services already offered. These projects must be planned in such a way as to be perceived by the patients, the community, and the administrators of the service program as contributing to the welfare of the group and adding to, rather than detracting from, the service itself. Adding research components to existing programs has the advantage of avoiding repetition of the institution building and administrative complexities and problems involved in setting up large-scale, long-term studies of the type required by certain of the unknowns in population.

There are three major programs of the United States official health agencies at Federal, state, and local levels in which opportunities might be explored to combine population research with delivery of services: the venereal disease program, the tuberculosis-control program, and the programs for individuals with rheumatic fever or rheumatic heart disease.

The venereal disease program got under way some thirty years ago. A tremendous amount of research was involved in which Federal agencies, foundations, international and voluntary organizations, universities, and industries participated as well as individual researchers. The success of the program was due in part to the fact that action at the Federal level was reflected at the state and local levels, both in the conduct of operational research and in application of the results. The diversity of approach and the plurality of funding also contributed heavily to the success of the effort. Basic and applied investigation in all aspects of the problem—ranging from socioeconomic factors through treatment, from patient and community-management measures of the manufacture and distribution of drugs—contributed to the success of the program to control the disease.

Unfortunately, the very success of the program caused a drop in scientific and public interest so that venereal infection has once again become a serious problem. Utilization of existing knowledge has been neglected, so that it is again necessary to step up the entire machinery of research, treatment, and education for prevention and for administration of the program.

In the fiscal year 1969, nearly 600,000 cases of venereal disease were reported in the United States. More than 400,000 positive diagnostic tests and sexual contacts were investigated, and over 800,000 positive blood tests were reported to health departments. The health departments were the chief source of service for these patients and suspects.

The opportunities for research on both the biological and social aspects of reproductive behavior in this group are self evident. What is perhaps not yet appreciated is that there may also be opportunities for investigations of ways to add the dimension of prevention or unwanted pregnancy to the efforts to avert transmission of venereal infection. This would involve fundamental research of a social as well as biologic nature.

The second public health program with which population research and control efforts might be combined is the highly successful program for detection, prevention, and cure of tuberculosis. For some categories of patients, pregnancy while the mother or father is under treatment is undesirable. The total number of new active cases of tuberculosis reported for the United States for 1967 was 45,647. When related to the question of prevention of untimely pregnancy, the size of the group and the socioeconomic problems which have been studied suggest another possible field of population research.

The third public health program deals with individuals who have rheumatic fever or rheumatic heart disease. A large and effective program of prophylaxis exists for this group. A conservative estimate of the potential size of the national register is 665,000. Approximately half of these individuals are in the fifteen to twenty-four-year age bracket. The problems of case management in pregnancy, both in relation to the disease itself and in relation to the impact of unplanned, untimely pregnancy on the patient are subjects for investigation in these large, well-defined population groups.

Groups of centers concerned with population research might well consider public-health programs at national, state, and local levels as sources of populations for research in association with the delivery of services, DR. CUTLER said. Experience shows that such research can be successful.

Finally, the introduction of family-planning components into public-health and medical-care programs can help to improve the quality of medical care. This must be one element of a successful national population program.

Chapter Twenty-nine

AN OVERVIEW PANEL SUMMARIZES AND RECOMMENDS

LEORA WOOD WELLS

A N OVERVIEW panel summarized some of the major points that arose in most of the preceding chapters. While their observations were based on the conference* proceedings of February 1970, the summary is most relevant to the questions raised throughout this book. The panel consisted of five members, all eminent in the population field: BERNARD BERELSON, OSCAR HARKAVY, SAMUEL WISHIK, HUDSON HOAGLAND, and REUBEN HILL. DR. BERELSON served as principal spokesman for the overview panel, and the other members added points they felt particularly needed to be stressed.

The summary, DR. BERELSON said, is based on seven assumptions.

1. *Population problems are important.* Everyone seems to agree on this, although the problems are defined differently by different people. The problems include not only undue population growth in developing countries like India and advanced countries like the United States, but food supplies, educational opportunities, ecological issues, and many other problems all the way to moral issues.

2. *Time matters.* The population problem is urgent, and whatever is done later is going to be more expensive and harder to do than what might be done now. We need to telescope the problem as much as possible, speeding our efforts to solve it rather than letting it stretch out over decades.

3. *Science matters.* There are specific contributions that science can make that will bring us closer to solutions.

---

* The conference sponsored by NICHD on Management of Consolidated Research Institutes for Population Research; Pan American Health Organization Building, Washington, D.C.

4. *The focus of this summary is on research and training.* Undergraduate education, action programs, and other components of the total effort have been mentioned repeatedly in this book, but the principal target here has been to identify the most effective ways to produce knowledge through population research and to train knowledgeable people.

5. *We are concerned about population problems both in the United States and in other parts of the world.* Although it has been stressed that priority should be given to development of U.S. population policies, we are concerned with other areas as well.

6. *Whether we like it or not, we are concerned about human intervention into "natural" processes.* Deep moral issues are involved in this kind of intervention. Once man has taken the road of intervening in "natural" processes of life and death, implications for other types of control are difficult to escape. What makes the population question distinctive is its central and delicate nature. It is central because it concerns life and death. It is delicate because it is deeply imbedded in the cultural, religious, economic, and political institutions of a society.

7. *Every effort in the population field faces serious limitations.* Manpower is limited. Money is limited. Opportunities are limited. The only things that are not limited are the problems and the urgencies.

These assumptions, DR. BERELSON said, bring us to five questions that lead to conclusions and recommendations.

First, What is the definition of the population field? The population field consists of three rings of activity: biomedical, programmatic, and human sciences. The biomedical ring consists of work in reproductive physiology and contraceptive development. The programmatic ring consists of public health administration and education. The human-sciences ring consists of demorgraphy, the social and behavioral sciences, and some humanistic concerns.

These rings overlap at the edges. There are some areas in which all three are directly involved, some in which different pairs of rings are involved, and some parts of each that belong solely to these fields themselves.

As for whether the concern of population workers should include such problems as food supply and ecology, these matters belong in the field only when they touch the edges of one of these rings of population considerations. For example, the ecological costs of continuing population growth in the United States are an appropriate area of concern; general ecological considerations are not.

Questions have been raised about whether the population field differs from other fields of concern. This, in itself, is not important. The important question is, Does it differ in any way that affects how research should be handled?

The second question is, What resources do we now have for work in the population field? We have a number of major centers in which activities of some moment are going on. There are some twelve to eighteen major biomedical centers; five to eight public health centers, all of them of fairly recent origin; and about ten demographic and social science centers, most of them of some duration. We have also a few broader-scope enterprises such as the North Carolina Center which covers all of these fields and more. We have all three rings represented at the University of Michigan. We have a committee in Chicago which encompasses two of them. We have one at Harvard and a number of other more general ones elsewhere. Most of these centers are university centers.

In addition, we have other sorts of enterprises: laboratories; nonprofit organizations and institutes; organizations like the Population Council which cut across the whole range of population concerns; and in the United States Government, the Center for Population Research.

Third, What additional resources are needed? The commentary in the preceding chapters indicates that we definitely need to build up three types of resources, and it has given a number of reasons why we need more emphasis on a fourth. We need more trained people. We need more knowledge. We need more money. And the question has been, Do we need more centers?

At least three reasons have been given why centers, as against simply activities in university departments, are needed. One is that a center makes a close, integrated focus on population problems possible. The second is that the complexity and range of the interrelating problems require the impact of many disciplines. The third is that the size of the problem requires massive effort if appropriate impact is to be made on the problem.

Fourth, What sort of mix is needed to provide the pluralism *and diversity of effort the problem requires?* This has been a major theme emerging throughout this text. The authors have stressed that there is no single best way to approach the population problem. Some have suggested that a crash program is needed. A crash program is needed when one knows where the solution to a problem is to be found. If the site of the solution is not known, one must look everywhere.

In the population field, do we know roughly where some solutions might be found; and can we, therefore, initiate a crash program of research to find the solutions? Or must we look in a variety of places?

The answer is "both." We have some of each in this field. There are numerous specific leads we know we need to pursue. For example, DR. SEGAL mentioned that some ten to fifteen new contraceptive leads have been developed to a point that indicates they should be investigated intensively; and of these, three to five may ultimately turn out to be useful.

On the other hand, in relation to population policy, we do not really quite know where to look for solutions. We do not yet understand all the moral, ethical, personal, political, and humanitarian ramifications of various types of action. We can set a goal of zero population growth by the year 2000 without X amount of loss of personal freedom, but achieving this goal is extremely difficult. During the preceding pages, discussion has been addressed to three factors in diversity of approach to the population problem: disciplinary roles, purposes, and organization.

Great stress has been laid on the importance of interdisciplinary and multidisciplinary work, but it is important not to make a fetish of these approaches. There is, of course, work that needs to cross these boundaries. At the same time, each discipline also has important individual contributions to make.

In regard to purposes, many authors have spoken of the need

for both basic and applied research. They have talked of discipline or puzzle-oriented versus mission-oriented approaches. In general, the purpose of the academic approach is to contribute to the theory and methodology of the discipline, while the professional approach is to solve an individual problem or keep it from getting worse. In this sense, physiologists are academicians and physicians are professionals.

All of this relates to the question of what sort of action is needed. The need to tie research to action has been referred to many times even though the principal focus of this particular book has not been action on the development of research institutions. However, an important part of population research needs to be experimentation and demonstration to find out what sorts of action should be taken. This should be a major role of the population-research centers.

A third element of diversity that has been discussed is organization, which has fallen into three major categories: universities, Government, and other organizational units such as non-profit institutions, foundations, and corporations.

Each mode of organization has advantages and disadvantages which have been discussed in some detail. In regard to the role of Government, two particular problems need to be mentioned. One is the hazard of concentrating work on population policy solely within a Governmental or quasi-governmental agency where it may be vulnerable to political considerations. The second is the question of how much control over the work of population centers is inherent in Government support.

If these are the elements of pluralism and diversity, the first order of conclusion is that we require a mix of approaches across the whole range of possibilities to overcome the handicaps of each and close the gaps that have been identified. There are ethical and legal gaps, gaps in our understanding of the relationship between population and ecology, gaps in contraceptive technology, gaps in geographical coverage of population research and policy.

In looking across this mix of approaches to see what can be done to close the gaps, we need to take a long-range as well as a short-range view. We need to look at the problems of the future. For example, by the 1980's we may be facing questions of how economic growth can be sustained without population growth; or how spirit and creativity can be maintained in an aging society, which ours will increasingly become as we move toward zero population growth.

It appears that we need both to strengthen the present population research system and to fill the gaps in it. It is appropriate to strengthen it because it is economical to do so and because we can get further faster by strengthening what already exists. It is appropriate to fill the gaps in the present system in two ways: by adding layers to the present system and by developing whatever new types of institutions are needed. What the nature of these new institutions should be has not to this point been clearly defined.

Part of this strengthening and expansion should be a statement to the American people that will help them understand why the population problem is so important that it deserves to be an extensive, highly visible enterprise. We need to be able to explain to them what the centers are and what they do; how they differ from other enterprises and what their significance is.

Finally, the fifth question the conference explored is, What about the money? It has been generally agreed that the present budget for population research is off by a major magnitude in relation to the total needs of the field. It is off by a major magnitude even in relation to protecting its good investment in the existing centers.

Two points were particularly stressed in relation to funding needs: that funding should be on a long term basis and that it should cover not only core support and research-project support but support for construction. The problems are long term. The needs for personnel and other types of support are long term. The foundations have been carrying a major load in financing population research, but long-range, broad-scope Government support is essential.

The center for Population Research has a budget of 15.6 million dollars for this fiscal year and expects to have about 28.4

million dollars next year. If this is the magnitude of financing that is going to be available, it will be impossible to grapple with the population problem in an effective way. All of this money is either already committed or will have to be committed to continuing programs. There will be very little out of a budget of that size to deal with the kinds of issues that have been raised in this book.

What would be required to deal with the problem adequately? In order to give twenty-five major centers already in existence assurance of core support and layering, something like three quarters of a million dollars would have to be set aside for each. That comes to 20 million dollars per year to support twenty-five major centers.

Assuming that another twenty-five minor centers would need a quarter of a million dollars apiece, we need to add another 8 to 10 million dollars.

Then there needs to be project money on the order of about 25 million dollars per year. This brings the total to 50 or 55 million dollars per year.

There was some feeling among members of the overview panel, DR. BERELSON said, that brand-new centers should not be developed unless funding for this type of organization gets to be above 50 million dollars per year. A new center would probably require about 10 million dollars per year. With funds as scarce as they are, priority should be given to financing the existing major and minor centers, research projects, and the work of the Center for Population Research at the NICHD itself.

In closing, DR. BERELSON said, he would like to stress his own conviction that the proper stance of the Government is to provide support but not control or even guidance of the centers. It can control and guide by determining what the mix of approaches will be, but once it supports the centers, it should leave them alone. The centers should be managed by the people who run them. They should be free to make maximum use of the diverse intellectual inputs available to them rather than having to attend to activities parcelled out by the funding sources.

We need all sorts of windows opened on this problem. It is

that big and that consequential. Nothing is going to solve the total problem, but every approach will make some difference. Some people feel the answer lies in better contraceptives; others feel that technology offers no solution. Some feel the key lies in ethical and behavioral research, or in more efforts directed toward motivation of families to take greater responsibility for planning.

All of these approaches are needed, DR. BERELSON said. We need to try any rational mixture and arrangement of resources in a systematic effort to cover the whole variety of possible solutions. The central question is, Given scarce resources of personnel and money, what system of research support is most apt to lead us toward our goals?

The other members of the overview panel added brief comments. Decreases in the NIH budget for construction are causing serious problems for some of the population centers, said DR. OSCAR HARKAVY, Director of the Office of Population for the Ford Foundation. If the Government is serious about wanting to do something important about the population problem, it must find out what sorts of facilities and resources are needed to make the best attack upon the problem. The Government should decide what mix of center types it feels will be most effective and then provide them with whatever they need to do the job.

It is apparent that there are many ways to develop centers for population research, said DR. SAMUEL WISHIK, Director of the Division of Program Development and Evaluation at the International Institute for the Study of Human Reproduction. Several different types have been discussed, and each has its unique contribution to make. Each has certain desirable features, and each encounters certain difficulties. We need to capitalize on these comparative merits and work to counteract the deficiencies so that all types are strengthened and each can move postively toward the desirable end results.

One aspect of center responsibility has been underemphasized, DR. WISHIK said. We cannot separate their responsibility for research from their responsibility for training. Any center that attains excellence in research becomes a mecca to which people come for training. This kind of responsibility is associated with excellence. The more unusual or unique a center is, the more responsibility it should have to be a place for training. We must develop the next generation of researchers to carry on what the present generation begins.

Great emphasis has been given to the concepts of population research being carried on in centers which are parts of universities, said DR. HUDSON HOAGLAND, President Emeritus of the Worcester Foundation of Experimental Biology. It is perhaps significant to remember that the pill was developed by an independent research institution that had no university connections. It is equally important to recognize that one of the most important contributions of this product has been to catalyze a lot of thinking about the whole question of population problems. Better contraceptives will undoubtedly be developed. The important thing is that development of this first oral contraceptive opened many new lines of thinking and inquiry.

Much more information is needed about the basic processes in reproductive physiology. Over the years we have known a great deal more about kidneys and blood and heart and other organs than we have about the reproductive process. Intensive study of reproductive physiology is relatively recent, and much basic research is needed on the biomedical aspects of the problem.

There is also a tremendous need for education about population control. A participant indicated that some 20 percent of births in the United States are of unwanted children. If this is so, it suggests that more and better contraceptives, widely distributed, might sharply lower the population growth rate if women are educated in their proper use.

Greater emphasis in the quality of life is also needed. The impact of rapid population growth on the quality of life differs from place to place and from culture to culture and depends upon a great many variables. These need to be studied more intensively than they have been by behavioral and social scientists.

Crowding is one such factor. Many studies of animals in their natural habitats, in zoos, and in laboratories have shown that crowding disrupts and destroys the quality of life and social organization, and pathology develops. We need to do comparable research on the effects of crowding in human societies. How much crime and delinquency, how much psychosis, how many riots are results of crowding in city slums? How much of the instability of our international relationships with highly populated countries is due to the stresses of overcrowding? The ability of crowding to induce stress and illness in animals has been clearly demonstrated, and there is no reason to suppose that this does not also apply to man. The stress physiology of responses of mammals in general are similar.

Crowding, pollution, the wasteful exploitation of resources are making our world less stable to live in and are reducing the quality of life. The industrialized countries are by far the greatest offenders. They place tremendous emphasis on growth. We are beginning to realize that growth must be controlled and that the public must be educated away from its cultural belief in growth as a great desideratum.

The critical population issues that need to be attacked are not biomedical but social and behavioral, said DR. REUBEN L. HILL, Professor of Sociology and Research Professor in Family Studies, University of Minnesota. The current budget setup in all funding agencies is pitifully small. If we continue to strengthen the present system, we shall give to those who have and not give to those who have not, and crucial areas of research will continue to be neglected.

The dearth of papers on the population problem being presented at anthropological, sociological, and psychological meetings around the world indicates that precious little basic research in population is under way in these disciplines. Unless there is a change in systems of funding there will be precious little in the future.

Many of the biological scientists seem to feel that the final solution is to bring out better hardware. The issue is much too complex for hardware to settle anything. For nearly twenty years, family-planning services have been available within walking distance of practically every family in Puerto Rico, but only a small minority of Puerto Ricans can be called effective family planners.

Simply bringing good hardware to five million families is not going to solve the problem. What we overlook is that families are not passive accommodators to whatever is put before them. They are reactive. As they are pressured toward zero population reproductive levels, they will defeat this aim.

What we fail to recognize is that there is a yearning for child-bearing in the majority of people. No one pays attention to this. Instead, we look at the numbers of unwanted children and assume that if the hardware were available it would be used and the consequences would be zero population growth.

Decisions about when to marry, when to start childbearing, what the spacing shall be, and when the family should be closed are not made in Government circles or universities or family-planning clinics. They are made in the homes by young people who understand little about the long-term consequences of their decisions for national population growth.

In this country, childbearing takes place over a relatively short time span of about ten years. This passage of time brings a certain amount of wisdom, but by the time it is achieved, it is too late to act upon it. If the decisions about when to have children and how many to have were made by the parents of young married couples, the desired changes might come about; but this is not the way the decisions are made. We need to develop the same sense of urgency about studies of decision-making and problem-solving at the family level that industry and service agencies now have about the development of contraceptives. A long-range, statesmanlike view of research needs is important, but we must also focus realistically on immediate, short-range issues and needs.

INSIGHTS AND AFTERTHOUGHTS

This section is more a "windup" than a summary. In the early chapters we looked at institutions vis-à-vis the population problem. Norman Hilmar opens this section by discussing the information system in the population field and suggesting ways to improve it. Robert McCormick, as a professional journalist, challenges the scientific community to accept the indispensability of the news media in delivering the "Message." Anthony Wiener suggests that there is a strong need to increase the emphasis placed on policy research, as he follows the theme that "research plus action is not necessarily policy." Sylvan Kaplan, in the final chapter, examines the means we have at hand and how these means may best be used in developing an all-out attack through an ecological systems approach to the population problem.

Chapter Thirty

BABEL OR BONANZA? SCIENTIFIC AND TECHNICAL INFORMATION IN THE POPULATION FIELD

NORMAN A. HILMAR

K NOWLEDGE that remains in the head of the most creative scientist or languishes in a report gathering dust on a library shelf beyond the ken of those whose actions might be enlightened by such knowledge serves no useful purpose. Our increasing specialization and division of labor make it even more essential that knowledge be imparted in comprehensible form to those responsible for acting rationally as clinicians, engineers, educators, scientists, policy-makers, administrators, or simply as individuals trying to influence their own personal futures. Let us then examine the process by which scientific and technical information in the population field must be identified, collected, stored, retrieved, translated, and disseminated as the world draws upon yesterday to lay a more rational groundwork today for a more promising future tomorrow.

Consider first the users of scientific and technical information or, if you will, the varied audiences to which our growing knowledge must be communicated. The nature of the potential user ideally determines not only the kind of information he needs, but the form of the "packaging" of such information that will be most helpful to him in carrying out his responsibilities. Examining the information user in his natural habitat permits us to ask a series of questions, the answers to which may in many cases challenge our existing ways of doing business and perhaps help us speed the transformation of knowledge and ideas into innovative, constructive actions.

For example, scientists quickly think of other scientists, especially those of their own disciplines, as the audiences to which they wish to deliver the results of their studies. Timely reports

of planned or ongoing research obviously facilitate early corre-
spondence and exchange of ideas among members of the research fraternity who make up the so-called "invisible colleges"
so important to the rapid exploitation of promising avenues for
scientific inquiry. Once the research has been completed, the
findings, including negative results of experiments, must be rapidly disseminated to other scientists if they are to benefit from
new knowledge painfully obtained. However, if science is to
serve man most conscientiously, there are several other users or
audiences for the researcher's findings whose needs or responsibilities may be such as to require "decoding" scientific reports
into a form which these other users will find comprehensible
and relevant to their needs.

Just as Egyptian hieroglyphics were incomprehensible to modern man before the Rosetta Stone was discovered, epidemiolog-
ical reports on the incidence of untoward side effects from a
particular type of intrauterine device or a particular oral contraceptive may be meaningless to the gynecologist or to the mid-
wife until they are translated into what would amount to a
primer of recommended practice including contraindications
for initial or continued use, advice and warnings to be given the
patient, and so on. Administrators of family-planning programs
may need their own unique equivalent of the Rosetta Stone to
help them assess the significance of their new findings for the
level and type of training needed by their clinical personnel and
for the types of educational materials required to enhance effective cooperation by the woman in her own birth-control regi-
men. Policy-makers such as Congressmen and agency heads need
yet a different translation of the same research results to help
them appraise potential public reaction and political consequences from continuing or modifying policies regarding any
particular contraceptive. Science writers, journalists, and television commentators often need the very same research results in
still a different form in order to help place them in perspective
and assess their importance in the eyes of the wider publics to
which they address themselves.

The predicament of the scientist in attempting to share the

fruits of his intellectual labors with such disparate audiences is identical to the predicament of the practicing gynecologist, the nurse-midwife, the medical school dean, the high school teacher, or the demographic or economic consultant to underdeveloped countries, whose experience relevant to the population problem he would like to share with others. Each of us tends to be cut off from communication with audiences outside our own particular specialty and activity. Since population phenomena are so complex, the required multidisciplinary attacks on our problems are badly handicapped if communications are restricted to parochial or even incestuous channels.

As we think about getting timely, relevant, comprehensible scientific and technical information into the hands of those needing the information, let us not forget that communications should ideally be a two-way street. Serving the user effectively requires that we listen carefully to his need for certain kinds of information. If the kind of knowledge he needs literally does not exist, we have identified a topic requiring further research of either a fundamental or a directly applied nature to be taken into account in the determination of future research emphases and priorities. The more effective the process of two-way communications between researchers and information users, the greater the likelihood that scientific undertakings will be relevant to the human condition and that action programs as well as policy decisions will be enlightened, intelligent, and salutary.

Since it seems unreasonable to burden the researcher with packaging his conclusions to satisfy the unique information needs of all these different audiences, one can readily see why there has been such a proliferation of scientific and technical information "middlemen" valiantly trying with varying degrees of success to bridge the communication gaps between the researcher and numerous, diverse audiences. Now let us consider the plight of these middlemen who seek to move scientific and technical information from the producer to the user. Time and space do not permit a complete enumeration of organizations now actively engaged in the acquisition, storage, retrieval, translation, and dissemination of information in the population field, but I would like to mention a few so that you may comprehend better why I call my paper "Babel or Bonanza."

Planned Parenthood World-Population publishes a quarterly journal, *Perspectives*, which disseminates practical "how to do it" material concerning the design and development of family-planning programs to approximately 25,000 individuals, hospitals, and health departments concerned in one way or another with family-planning programs in the United States.

The Population Council in collaboration with the International Institute for the Study of Human Reproduction at Columbia University produces a variety of regular and occasional publications including *Studies in Family Planning*, distributed monthly to approximately seven thousand recipients in the United States and abroad; *Current Publications in Population Family Planning*, which is a four-page bibliography with abstracts of selected articles considered particularly noteworthy for administrators and scholars; *Reports on Population-Family Planning*, which will cover twenty-five or so central topics setting out the latest knowledge and practice; *Country Profiles*, which covers the nature, scope, and accomplishments of population activities in each country, and is based on a uniform outline designed to be useful to administrators; and a quarterly, *Population Chronicle*, designed to provide a reliable source of sound information on development in the population field to cabinet ministers, industrial and medical leaders, journalists, members of planning boards, civic leaders, etc.

The Population Reference Bureau produces, as educational tools for laymen, a number of publications dealing with the interaction of demographic, economic, and social factors. The Bureau's *Population Bulletin* explores major issues in depth; *Population Profiles* covers similar topics but in more concentrated form; *Readings in Population* is an annotated bibliography of books; *PRB Selections* makes available to its audience statements or articles of unusual merit which have not been previously published or have appeared in journals with specialized circulation; and the *World Population Data Sheet* gives basic demographic information on over one hundred countries and provides a source of information on current population trends.

The Department of Interior publishes monthly *Population Trends and Environmental Policy*, containing abstracts of current interest on these topics.

The World Bank Group publishes articles and information in their several house organs about population and family planning as they relate to economic development.

The Agency for International Development disseminates selected population information in the *Development Digest* as well as in their annual reports entitled *Food for Peace* and *Population Program Assistance*.

Dr. Donn Casey in Cambridge, England, produces a monthly *Bibliography of Reproduction* and also periodic bibliographies on special topics as primary efforts of the *Reproduction Research Information Service Limited*.

In addition to the plethora of printed materials they distribute, these and many other organizations usually attempt to answer specific requests for information within the limits imposed by their funds and the efficiency of their retrieval systems.

From this cursory summary, we can readily see that even at present a great number of organizations and institutions, Governmental and private, national and international, collect and disseminate data, reprints, abstracts, and bibliographies of published literature and descriptions of ongoing research bearing on population and family planning concerns. As population becomes increasingly an "in" thing to worry and talk about, scientific and technical information activities will multiply. Existing or future population centers will have to increase their efforts to disseminate the results of their multidisciplinary thinking and research to the various audiences for whom such information might be useful. Linkages between such population centers will quite probably require greater formalization and coherence so that each population center may promptly benefit from the efforts of all such centers. In turn we may envision the growing need, which we are already experiencing, for linking a network of population centers with other kinds of multidisciplinary centers, such as those devoted to ecology, environment, urbanization, economic development, and nutrition, to facilitate exchanges of relevant information about phenomena which constitute the interfaces between population concerns and these other broad concerns. Although philosophically all knowledge constitutes a seamless web, we must, for purposes of meaningful problem-solving, concentrate on the kinds of information that constitute the central core of population knowledge and at the same time find efficient ways to tap into the various other bodies of related knowledge to enhance both research and action on selected facets of the population problem.

The existing information activities concerned specifically with family planning and population matters have grown up for the most part independently of one another. Not surprisingly, they vary greatly in quality, scope and subject matter and in the nature of the audiences they serve. We have been reviewing our information explosion in the population field; and as a result, a number of us have come to the conclusion that both research and action efforts will be advanced by developing a coherent international network of population libraries, scientific and technical information centers, data banks, and similar organizations, which will operate on a voluntary, cooperative basis with the Center for Population Research serving as an executive secretariat until such time as some international agency can muster the will and the resources to serve efficiently as a center for the network.

We need common understandings of what we mean by population and family planning and what phenomena or problems may usefully be subsumed under the rubric. We must strive for a more uniform and logical way of classifying and storing information so that it may be retrieved with relative ease, arrayed and disseminated in a manner to facilitate the preparation of a variety of products and services such as research inventories for scientific use, state-of-the-art reports and advice for program operators on a variety of subjects, status reports and suggestions about policy alternatives for policy-makers, and general reviews or our population problems and choices for the enlightenment of the lay public whose wisdom and concern are crucial to problem-solving in a democratic society. For these common purposes we need an increasingly common vocabulary, and increasingly compatible hardware and software systems to facilitate exchanges of information and divisions of labor among the various Governmental and private information centers and libraries now concerned with population matters around the world. We fully realize that such coherence of our rapidly growing knowledge relevant to population will not be simple or painless; but unless many organizations and individuals can subordinate jurisdictional prerogatives to the common cause of structuring, rationalizing, and sharing what we now know and hope to learn, one can only predict an incomprehensible "Babel" of intellectual anarchy in the population field.

Several concrete steps have been identified as essential if we are to speed and amplify the impact of knowledge in solving the many population problems we face in the real world. For openers, the Agency for International Development has asked the Carolina Population Center to prepare an *International Directory of Information Sources in the Population Field* as a sort of population information "Yellow Pages" characterizing each group's subject matter specialties, its holdings, its services, its audiences, its recurring publications and other products, availability and means of access to its information, and names of its key personnel. As this information is collected we propose to analyze and evaluate their total activities including redundancies in functions, in products, and in audiences.

Closely related to the proposed "Yellow Pages" is the design and conduct of an international sample survey of information users and intermediaries through whom information flows in order to determine user needs and practices. We intend to develop a classification and analysis of subaudiences, to identify potential users who are now overlooked, to assess existing constraints on effective information exchange and to recommend improvements and initiate pilot efforts toward solving the problems identified.

We propose a concerted effort toward the improvement of population library collection and reference methods around the world through the development of international classification schemes to meet the needs of researchers and administrators concerned with population problems and policies. We plan to introduce domestic and foreign population reference personnel to better methods and technology for the handling of information through consultation services to libraries and information centers both at home and abroad, and through training for operational skills.

We propose a concerted effort toward the improvement of models for automated information services to enhance current indexing of publications related to population and the production of bibliographic journals for speedy broad coverage which can augment scientific and technical information activities and publications now underway in the population field.

We hope to take these steps through one or more contracts funded by the Agency for International Development or by the Center for Population Research, NICHD. For guidance we plan to use a board of advisors consisting of the major players in the population information game to assure that what we discover and what we build will be solid contributions to our common purposes.

We will meet periodically to exchange views, to pinpoint problems and opportunities in the scientific and technical information field, and to foster mutual support for one another's efforts to solve the problems encountered and to exploit the opportunities identified. We intend that the Center for Population Research will serve for the time being as the nerve center and switching point for communications among scientific and technical information activities and to help each of us steer inquiries from the outside to the source best able to provide the information needed. In short, we are embarking on a long and arduous undertaking which we think is as urgent as our population problems themselves.

Fortunately, we are not entirely pioneers. Various efforts in other fields can serve us well as models to consider and adapt according to our own needs as "population-niks." The Educational Resources Information Centers System (ERIC), the Air Pollution Technical Information Center (APTIC), and the Committee on Scientific and Technical Information (COSATI) are several examples of what can be done in the science information field. Many other groups, agencies, and individuals are currently struggling to enhance the efficient flow of relevant information concerning sciences to their varied audiences. From these efforts, we can learn much.

As the population centers grow in number, strength, creativity, and commitment they themselves will be in the information game more and more; and, of course, they will be major participants in and contributors to mankind's efforts to address its greatest intellects and most relevant knowledge to the humane solution of one of its most grievous sets of problems.

Chapter Thirty-one

POPULATION AND THE MEDIA

ROBERT K. McCORMICK

THE self-anointed scholar, the intellectually narrow scientist whose interests and thoughts are confined to his own laboratory or "discipline," to use the academic cliche, has for years considered scorn for "the press" essential to his social standing. The words "the press"—or, since the growth of television, "the media"—have usually been used by scientific social climbers in a manner that would suggest they are dripping with stalactites of scorn. Yet, as Dr. Hilmar said in a glancing way, science has no more potent friend than the ignoble "media."

Confining this diatribe only to population: If the mass media had not broken down formidable barriers of prudery, the public in general, in this country and many foreign countries, would never have known there is a population problem.

The thesis is documentable. Way back in 1939, I was Washington correspondent for *Collier's Magazine;* at my suggestion, Robert Cook of the Population Reference Bureau collaborated with the incomparable writer Walter Davenport on an article[61] on the population problem with the daring title of "Bootleg Birth Control."

This was the first time, so far as we could learn, that a publication of mass distribution had openly talked about the dangers of overpopulation, the possibility of massive birth-control efforts, and other subjects now considered routine, or even dull. The response was, predictably, overwhelming, and in large part abusive.

A few years later, on NBC, I was foolish enough, or brave enough, depending upon your viewpoint, to discuss the population problem on a widely publicized television program; again I had gotten my information from Robert Cook. The audience reaction this time was voluminous but somewhat less critical.

330

I cite these incidents to show that even twenty or thirty years ago, a newspaper, magazine, or broadcasting station that talked openly of overpopulation and birth control was considered foolhardy. Now such subjects are discussed with a depth and frankness that would have sent our puritanical ancestors into a state of catatonic shock.

Experts in the population field must realize that "the media" are primarily interested in dramatizing, emphasizing, and popularizing basic problems, whether they involve poverty, racial difficulties, crime, health, population, or combinations of all of them. But to interest the voter—the average citizen who will determine whether adequate funds are available for such things as population centers—"the media" must express the problems in language that the now-famous Kansas City milkman can understand. They cannot confine themselves to the obscure language of the specialist, who sometimes seems to make a deliberate effort to manufacture his own vocabulary so no one outside of his own "discipline" can possibly understand what he is talking about. Yet when the press tries to translate scientific slang— such as "multidisciplinary"—into lay language, it is often criticized for inaccuracy and lack of penetration.

That the press does penetrate is evidenced by the fact that only a few years ago—ten, perhaps—the open use of such words as "abortion" and "homosexual" was forbidden by most big newspapers and broadcasting organizations. Yet today, we have front page stories and elaborate radio and television discussions of legislation to liberalize abortion laws and to permit homosexualism between consenting adults. The blushing modesty of the press and broadcasting industries also, until fairly recently, would not allow the use of the word "rape." It had to be expressed in some such euphemistic phrase as "bodily assault" or "carnal knowledge."

If the press—and that includes radio, television, and news magazines—had not pushed through these walls of linguistic misrepresentation, who would have known about the pill? Who would have known about the IUD? Who would ever have heard of a population center and what it might be expected to accomplish? These are not rhetorical questions. Turned around, they are statements of fact; if the press had not had the courage, the wisdom and the skill to popularize these subjects, this book would probably not have been written.

The press also must be given credit for letting the world know of the tie between ecology and population. Laymen now know what ecology and pollution mean, not only to the country as a whole but to them personally.

Some of my more sedentary friends, even in my own business, would probably be surprised to know that I have heard them, by radio, in the thatched-roof "castle" of the polio-stricken "King" of the island of Fasarai, in the Ulithi atoll in the Pacific; I have heard them in the bars of two leading hotels in what once was Leopoldville, in the former Belgian Congo. I have heard them in the most remote bush areas of Portuguese-controlled Angola in western Africa, while riding in a jeep that had been amateurishly converted into a personnel carrier, by bolting slabs of cast iron onto its sides, for protection against the spears of rebels—spears that came out of the six-foot-high elephant grass with admirable accuracy but with frightening surprise.

All this windy reminiscing is only to testify to the effectiveness of the cummunications system we have that is of proven scope and efficiency. Today we have much more far-reaching communications systems—and they will advance even more, in a technical sense—as we are well aware from the superb coverage of our space efforts in the past few years. The time is close, in fact, when a worldwide symposium on population centers can be conjured up, after a few routine mechanical arrangements, within minutes.

The point is simply this: The population zealot, and I am one, should use the press, in the generic sense, and all of its astounding mechanical achievements. The scientists in the population field, rather than being disdainful, should realize that competent journalists are as skilled in their fields as the scientists are in theirs. If the scientist, the researcher, wants to get action in the area he considers important, he can do so only by communicating his concern to the taxpayers—the voters—the people in general. The press has large numbers of dedicated people willing to help, highly trained in their own discipline, and even in the multidisciplinary approach.

I should like, for a moment, to try to conceive the perfect population center; it would be interdisciplinary and multidisciplinary; it would have barrels of money available in perpetuity; it would be dedicated to both research and action, with great students from all over the world waiting to join its staff. The Federal Government, or all governments, would be flushed with an almost obscene desire to do anything it could to help. And suppose, just for fun, that it came up with all the answers.

There it is—this paragon of political planning, this magnificent representation of human wisdom. But if the press never mentions it, how do the greatest brains the world has communicate with the world that conceived them? Suppose they have the answers—what good is that, if they can talk only to themselves?

If these eminent people, these committed and unselfish people, can communicate with the outside world, if they can unplug their thinking from their own pursuits, they will discover that they have at their disposal not only reasonable, erudite representatives of newspapers, magazines, radio, and television but also such far-out devices as satellites, which can bring into every home, anywhere in the world, the graphic horror of starvation in India, of filth and famine in Southeast Asia, of unrestrained tribal cruelty in Africa. If these everyday communications devices can be appreciated and utilized by our benevolent scholars, the scholars can influence the world. If these instruments of communications, including the people themselves, cannot be utilized, we will probably have a crop of frustrated blossoms hidden under bushel baskets that will make the Good Lord Himself wonder why He wasted six days creating this mess.

Chapter Thirty-two

RESEARCH PLUS ACTION IS NOT NECESSARILY POLICY

ANTHONY J. WIENER

THERE is an old story about a drunk who was wandering around under a street light. He appeared to be looking for something he had dropped. A passerby stopped and offered help.

"What did you lose?" he asked.

"I dropped my wallet," the drunk replied.

After a few minutes the helpful stranger said, "I'm sorry, I don't see it around here anywhere. Are you sure you dropped it here?"

"Of course not," the drunk said scornfully. "I dropped it back there in the dark alley."

"They why are you looking here?" the man asked.

The drunk turned toward his questioner, his besotted face full of triumph and contempt. "You don't catch me looking back there," he exclaimed. "It's too dark to find anything."

We all have a tendency to search where the light is, rather than where we lost something. We try to solve the problems we know how to solve, rather than those which most need solving. When it comes to a difficult and complex social problem, such as the formulation of policy with respect to population growth, the consequences of this trait are very clear. We tend to do the research we know how to do. We work on biomedical studies of reproduction and of contraceptive technology, and we do demographic and sociological studies of the determinants of birth and death rates. At the same time we carry out various birth-control programs. These studies and these programs are, of course, necessary, even invaluable, but they are not sufficient. The questions about which we are most in the dark are those of policy. Since we are better at doing research and carrying out programs than we are at analyzing alternative policies, we tend to neglect this small but essential part of the overall task.

It is quite clear that current rates of population growth cannot continue forever, and perhaps not for very long. In one way or another these growth rates are likely to go to zero and even to become negative in many places. These changes in growth rates may take place as a result of social policies, as a result of voluntary action, or as a result of wars, famines, pestilences, or ecological limitations or catastrophes. These changes may take place over a long period of time or over a short period; abruptly or gradually. They are very likely to take place in different countries, regions, urban and rural settings, at very different rates and with very different results. Alternative policies, too, will produce different results.

As to these policies, there are some basic issues which we have difficulty in facing squarely. They have to do with who is going to be asked to do what, by whom, for whose sake, by means of what kinds of inducements or threats, and with what kinds of results. In the meantime, however, there is academic research, both medical and demographic, and there are many action programs which aim in various ways at persuasion, at dissemination of techniques and information, and at calling attention to the importance of the control of population. People doing the research or carrying out the action tend to be committed to the overall goal of population control. They do not trouble to analyze, on the whole, the alternative policies by which this goal may be achieved or what difference the choice of alternatives may make. This is as it should be. It would probably create even more confusion and ineffectiveness than we now suffer, if everyone were to worry constantly about policy formulation. Fortunately, most of the people taking part in the total social response to the population problem feel, quite correctly, that they ought to be throwing their energies into getting on with their jobs, rather than raising doubts and questions about whether it might not be better to be working on something else entirely.

The point is that there must be a division of labor, and that somewhere in this total social response there should be some qualified people working seriously on the analysis of priorities, trade-offs, resources, comparative benefits, projections, second-order consequences, and scenarios for the political and social conflicts that can occur en route to any "solution" to the population problem. In other words, a small but significant minority of workers in the field ought to be asking, "What is (or are) the population problem(s)? And what are the advantages and disadvantages of alternative policies with respect to this set of problems?"

Analyzing policy alternatives is much like research in that it requires the marshaling of information and the application of intensive thought. However, it is quite different from research in that the emphasis must be on breadth rather than on depth of information. The emphasis is not on describing the present, or accounting for the past; these are but steps toward anticipating the future. One does not ask of the information he gathers, "How well do I know this?" although this question is not irrelevant. The important questions are, "If this is true, what difference does it make? What should I do about it?" In its pragmatism policy analysis is also like an action program. It differs from the action program, however, in that the action program must ask, "How well have we done? Are we doing what we said we would do?" Whereas policy analysis asks always, "Are they doing the best thing? Is there something different that would be better?"

It may surprise those who have been doing research on population, or who are committed to action to try to do something about the problem, that it is not altogether clear what the problem is, and that therefore there is some doubt about the best solution. To say this is not to say that there is no problem, or that partial solutions are not worth pursuing. It is to say that social actions often have unforeseen and undesirable consequences and a failure to think through priorities systematically and to evaluate alternative programs carefully can easily result in wasted or counterproductive acts.

Precisely because the population problem is urgent, it is important that our energies not be wasted or turned against ourselves. One need consider only the consequences of the optimistic public-health programs of the first half of the century in bringing about reduced death rates and the current population explosion, to see how easily well-intentioned efforts can lead to results which are, to say the least, disappointing once they are understood.

Let us sketch, very briefly, some of the considerations any such analysis might start with. First, we must recognize that we presumably do not want to go back to the situation, in any society, in which most babies die. It is ordinarily assumed that we would like to lower death rates at every age up to the point where senility or other extreme disability has taken its toll. Only at that point is the extension of life for its own sake no longer of dominant value to us. It follows that we are not necessarily in favor of reducing all death rates, always and everywhere. But it seems clear that we must focus, in conscience, on lowering birth rates, once we have lowered death rates.

But we must also recognize some ambivalence about birth rates. In most cases the birth of a baby is an occasion for rejoicing in the family and local community. To a great extent in most societies we are dealing with what Garrett Hardin calls "The Tragedy of the Commons,"[62] in which it is to the advantage of each individual (or family) to make an additional demand upon the resources held in common by the community, although it is to the disadvantage of the community as a whole that he does so. One may doubt whether there are many situations in which perfect availability of sterilization, contraception, and abortion would deal completely or finally with the problem of population growth. This is not to say that contraception or abortion or other partial solutions are without value —only to say that ultimately they must be weighed along with other, even more controversial and questionable measures. If we cannot quickly reduce high birth rates everywhere, we must then ask which birth rates are most important to reduce—how far, and how soon? What *is* the population problem?

One may argue that in the short run the problem is not one of food supply. The high-yield grains, vast areas of unused agricultural land in countries such as the United States in which agricultural land has actually been retired even as production has increased, development of better methods of intensive fertilization, prospects for utilization of resources in the sea, etc., all make it plausible that we could double, triple, quadruple the world food supply in time to feed the next generation and perhaps several more generations. The limitations here do not seem to be the familiar Malthusian deficiencies of agriculture, but the less familiar Malthusian fact that if population continues to expand so as to keep pace with food supply, we seem likely to run into worldwide ecological limitations, having to do with nitrogen, oxygen, carbon dioxide, and photosynthesis. If this is *the* population problem, it might be argued that it would be better even in the short run not to increase food supply, since to do so will only increase the ecological problem which lies ahead. But, better for whom?

It seems more clear—though all these issues need further investigation and clarification—that the problem is not primarily one of density, calculations of "standing room only" to the contrary nonwithstanding. High-density living, under some conditions, as in the penthouses on Fifth Avenue and Park Avenue in New York City, is obviously desirable. High-density accommodations command high prices on the open market, provided that the necessary investment has been made to support a high standard of living at that density. Cities have always been extremely attractive to elites, as well as to most people who can afford to go to them. In many Latin American cities, for example, the well-to-do are generally living at much greater density than the very poor who are living in "bidonvilles" on the outskirts of the city. The difference between Park Avenue and Calcutta is one of economics, not of population density.

Is the issue then simply one of poverty? If so, one need hardly be concerned about population growth in the affluent countries unless that growth occurs in sectors of the population which are not able to provide wealth for their children. One would then wish to concentrate, instead, on undeveloped countries, where it is abundantly clear that high birth rates create high dependency ratios for the labor force, and make it very difficult to achieve reasonable rates of economic growth per capita.

But there are also doubts about this formulation of *the* population problem. It is sometimes argued that the average citizen of the developed country consumes more energy and more of the world's resources, and creates more waste, than the average citizen in the less-developed country. The conclusion drawn from these facts is that each individual citizen of the developed country is a greater threat to the world than each additional citizen of the less-developed world. Is this a non sequitur, since it does not take into account the potential contribution of the citizen of the developed country to the solution of these problems, in terms of his greater economic productivity? Is the principal threat then poverty, or is it, alternatively, industrial development? Or is it perhaps the impending conversion of less-developed countries to industrialization? Was that not the goal of foreign-aid programs?

On the other hand, perhaps priorities should go to aesthetic issues, such as crowding and "quality" of life. Again one must ask, quality of whose life, on what terms? Who is going to ask whom to accept what deprivation or even coercion on behalf of whose quality of life as defined by whom? Is that any element of rationality in the complaint of some American black militants that attempts to limit population in poverty areas amount to genocide or at least racism? Domestic as well as international confrontations can be anticipated. There are conflicts of interest about population policies. The issues are political, not merely technical. One cannot expect an easy consensus. Population control, ecological and conservation movements can also have an elitest aspect. Is there never an attempt to preserve the unspoiled character of the environment for the benefit of the few who can already afford it, against the threat of intrusion by ominously proliferating masses?

Obviously, this is not the place to try to resolve any of these issues. The systematic and comprehensive analyses of population policies which could clarify these questions have, as far as I know, not yet been carried out, although many polemics have been written on one or more sides of the question. Someone ought to be asking quite objectively what price growth, what price whose growth, what price to whom, at what rate, and under what circumstances. What happens, for example, if current programs continue, and if population programs are accepted by relatively responsible, better-educated, more-affluent members of the society much more than by those who are less so? Those who are concerned about the quality of life or who believe that the most urgent population problem has to do with poverty would scarcely welcome a result in which the poor multiply while the well-off and better-qualified tend to disappear. If, on the other hand, analysis should indicate that ecological issues and especially the consumption of energy and resources should be dominant in shaping priorities, one might conclude that the earth could support a much larger population of poor people than of rich, and that human life might be better in the former case. On the other hand, it seems plausible that continued technological and economic development could make available the technological and economical means for dealing with environmental issues, such as those aspects of pollution that can be solved by "cleaning up." In that case even ecological problems might be better dealt with by a selective approach to population growth which concentrates on reducing first, to the extent feasible, high growth rates among technologically and economically poor populations wherever they may be in the world. Such a policy might even encourage the growth of well-educated, productive, and well-to-do populations.

Whatever the population problem turns out to be, one must deal, of course, with the political, religious, philosophical, and moral issue raised by asking what would be required to cause reductions of birth rates to take place. There are differences in value-preferences, of course; but we cannot hope for any clarity on the value-issues until we improve our understanding of the facts, and of how the system works in which we are attempting to intervene. Disputes about the relative importance of starvation, coercion, pollution, authoritarianism, impoverishment, ignorance, crowding, etc., are not merely *de gustibus,* to be debated in the abstract; we need to understand much better than we do how much of each of these evils we are facing; what are some of the trade-offs among them; what are we likely t achieve, by various criteria, as a result of alternative strategies and alternative assessments of what is the population problem and its component priorities.

What sort of "center" would work well on a problem like analysis of population policy? A university or a foundation clearly is an appropriate setting for academic research on biomedical or demographic issues relevant to the population problem, and a local, national, or international governmental agency, or again a foundation, is clearly appropriate for the carrying out of the action program. Policy analysis carried on within a university, however, often falls prey to the demands of the academic disciplines, which are appropriate for scientific research, but which when applied to policy analysis often fragment work, drive it into undesirable specializations, and distort interdisciplinary research priorities by focusing on prestige within specific academic disciplines. On the other hand, it is difficult to carry on policy analysis in a Government agency because of the political sensitivities in a situation where planning may be confused with official policy formulation. Again, these sensitivities are functional in a bureaucracy entrusted with political programs, but are destructive of freedom to raise policy alternatives or to criticize current programs.

These disadvantages of existing institutions for policy analysis have been dealt with more or less successfully in many analogous cases by creating a kind of halfway house, which may be funded by Government or by other sources, but which must neither speak for Government nor be dominated by the criteria of the academic professions.

Such an institute may be located at a university or attached to a Government agency or foundation, or elsewhere, but it is important that policy analysts not think of themselves primarily as carrying out programs or as members of (or returning to) university departments. It is important to have professional and intellectual access to members of departments and to be in close communication with them, so as to be able to learn easily what is being produced in academic research in the many different relevant fields. At the same time, it is extremely valuable to be in close communication with decision-makers and program implementors, so as to be able to get relevant feedback of insights gained only in practice. The policy analyst needs to learn both from the researcher and the program manager, and at the same time he must be close enough to provide both these people with the analyst's perspective, interpretation, integration, and recommendations, if his work is to be of any use. The tasks of policy analysis, which include analyzing priorities for research, analyzing objectives for programs, and assessing available resources for both research and programs, probably should receive only on the order of one percent of the total research budget in the field. It is to be hoped that as understanding and research advance, the growth rate of the research budget will be greatly exceeded by the growth rate of funds which will be judiciously allocated to action programs. If such programs are to be effective, they must be based on comprehensive analysis of the many different population problems and of alternative policies addressed to these problems in terms of an informed assessment of priorities and resources.

It may be objected that what I am proposing here requires the policy analyst to study "everything." The answer is that there should be people thinking about "everything," at least to the extent that each "thing" is relevant and important to the problem for which we must devise better grounded and more thoughtful solutions. There is very little light on such comprehensive issues, but that is where we lost our wallet.

Chapter Thirty-three

RESOURCES, REFLECTIONS, AND REACTIONS

SYLVAN J. KAPLAN

IN LOOKING over this book, I wonder whether the scientific community is not deceiving itself by its determination neither to seem dogmatic nor to move to conclusions that cannot be proved beyond a shadow of a doubt. In population problems, we are dealing with arithmetical fact, and perhaps we, as scientists, should simply say so—as Robert Zoerheide[1] did—in order to rouse the population to do something to save itself.

The summary provided in Chapter Twenty-nine calls attention to the fact that agreement exists, that the problem is important, and that time must not be wasted while attempts are made to find solutions.

The question of what is needed to resolve the problem has not been answered; but it has been agreed that population centers can provide a means of mobilizing resources in an all-out effort. It is important to examine the resources available, to review some of our strengths and weaknesses, and to examine a means for increasing research and research training to deal with population problems.

Institutions in the Population Research Field

I have identified and studied ninety-five university groups in the United States doing research and training investigators in the population field as of January 1, 1970. Most of these groups called themselves "centers" and were subunits of departments in large institutions. There were approximately twenty industrial centers addressing population problems. Of these, most were involved in contraceptive development, although several have become interested in policy pertaining to population change. There are undoubtedly a large number of all types of

343

Figure 33-1. Distribution of population research and training centers in the United States.

"population centers" now, for many organizations have formed since this study began in 1969. The map shown in Figure 33-1 roughly plots their geographic distribution.

Approximately 60 percent of the centers were unidisciplinary. Slightly more than half of these were biomedical groups, and slightly less than half were social-science centers. Forty percent of the groups were multidisciplinary, with approximately half in the social sciences and half in biomedical areas. For the most part, the disciplines appeared to be working side by side, yet independently.

The author randomly selected several centers for closer examination. Of twenty-two social sciences centers selected, all had programs in demography; twelve dealt with human ecology and included work in the biomedical fields (family planning, reproductive biology, or mental health), eight with urban sociology, five with problems indigenous to the state in which they were geographically located, and nine included international activities.

The eighteen biomedical organizations selected were working principally on basic research in reproductive biology, with emphasis on physiology, endocrinology, biochemistry, and contraceptive development. Far less attention was given by the bio-medical groups to social problems than was given by the social science groups to biomedical questions. Interest in crossing disciplines for informational purposes only, particularly in the unidisciplinary groups, did not seem to be pronounced.

The sizes of the staffs of twelve biomedical centers studied ranged between six and seventy-five, with a mean professional staff of eighteen. Of twenty-nine arbitrarily selected social science centers, staff size ranged from three to twelve, with a mean of seven professionals. Only three centers heavily involved in the population field had as many as one hundred professionals on their staffs. These groups were all multidisciplinary. Unidisciplinary staffs, in general, were much smaller. Comparing these staff sizes with those of the large mission-oriented national laboratories, which number in the hundreds, indicates the relatively small investment of manpower in the population field as compared, for example, to the manpower concentrated on atomic energy or astronautics.

The author tried to establish annual core-support needs of ten arbitrarily selected centers included in the study. Estimates provided by the center directors ranged between 400,000 and one million dollars annually. At least twenty administrators agreed that the cost per scientist and his support staff should be priced at 40,000 to 50,000 dollars for junior level professionals with an upward range of 100,000 dollars for senior professionals.

Manpower in the Population Field

A major question exists regarding the manpower available for staffing population centers. There could be a real threat of a "brain drain" from other important fields were a centers program to develop without regard for the availability of skilled manpower. An assessment of the manpower question is, therefore, mandatory. A report by Bean, Anderson, and Tatum[63] and the results of investigations by the Center for Population Research in 1969-70 provide some indications of possible answers to this problem.

A study of the availability of demographers and population-program specialists gives a discouraging picture. There seem to be shortages in both quality and quantity for these skills, with large numbers of demographers trained in only two areas—sociology and economics.[64] Moreover, at the doctoral level, the supply appears at least 30 percent short.[65] The report by Bean *et al.* has estimated there are at present in the United States between 800 and 1,000 demographers and 300 to 500 population-program specialists to fill growing requirements from agencies, foundations, and universities, not to mention the operational needs in the family-planning areas at home and abroad. This report further states that "although the numbers of centers appear to be sufficient [to do research and to train professionals], the number of high-level graduates being produced is not."

Speaking specifically about centers, the report goes on to say "the number of graduates in population remains small [and] many of the institutions [in which they are trained] are fragile, and many lack financial support." The implication here of weakness applies to both limited funds and insufficient skilled faculty.

Another study has shown[66] that "while graduate programs in universities have increased 28 percent in the past four years, the programs in population have increased 80 percent." Such growth does increase the training resources, but it also increases the demand placed on institutions for staff. This further increases the danger of institutional weakness due to lack of money and skilled staff.

Time has not permitted a comprehensive study of the availability of skills for research and training in the reproductive-biology field. Some experts have concluded that no shortage exists in this area of the population manpower field, assuming some shift of research and training direction among those already in the field. Others disagree.

The case of availability of medical scientists for the population field does, however, represent a problem, particularly in the operational areas of family planning. As summarized in the report by Bean *et al.*:[63]

The development and expansion of training-research service programs in family planning represent one aspect of proliferating demand for comprehensive health services. This demand clearly intensifies three major and existing problems:

1. The persistent and probably permanent problem of a manpower shortage in the health and medical fields.
2. The problem of motivating medical personnel to become involved in the delivery and improvement of health services in the ghettoes and rural areas.
3. The problem of reconciling the insatiable public demand for increasing medical services with the medical school goal of meeting this demand without detracting from the primary objective of turning out an increasing number of qualified physicians.

In general, because of a manpower problem in all scientific areas, conditions are not optimal for instituting a centers program. But there are many optimistic signs for the years ahead. There is a growing interest among many other disciplines—law, education, engineering, philosophy, psychology, geography, just to mention a few—which insures the population manpower resource will increase rapidly. The curricula of the schools of medicine, public health, and nursing all reflect a strong interest in improving expertise in the field, through increases in numbers of courses being offered on population-related subjects. And possibly no greater assurance of such a positive sign can be found than those noted in the Brim[67] and Hilgard-Riecken[68] reports, in which an awareness on the part of the social-science profession of its obligation to meet national and world social issues head on is strongly recognized. In those reports, which have received public and White House attention, are strong recommendations for greater institutional support, for development of better communication systems, and above all for improving the breed of skilled manpower needed to cope with multifaceted social issues.

Activities Related to the Population Field

The large number of government agencies interested in the population problem is evidenced in the report entitled *The Federal Program in Population Research*,[69] published by the Office of Science and Technology in 1969. That document contains contributions from representatives of fifteen Federal agencies. It is expected that more government agencies will pool their knowledge on their activities in population research.

Already there is evidence of the vast interest in ecology and environmental health taking hold in the nation. This ground swell has been preceded by the presence of at least 123 centers of ecology and 115 centers of urban and regional studies, as listed in the third edition of the *Research Centers Directory*.[70]

The average staff size for the former group of centers is approximately forty, and for the latter about ten or twelve, closer to the staff size of most population centers. There is also much activity in education centers and international centers, and all of these have elements which are addressing the population problem in some form. The great national laboratories of AEC and NASA have entered the environmental field with real concern for man's relationship to his environment.

The field of information has been discussed at length by both Hilmar (Chapter Thirty) and McCormick (Chapter Thirty-one), so I will only mention this vital element in passing. At least 10 percent of the existing centers have some form of publication medium and 30 percent have extensive reference libraries. There are a great number of agencies in the population field now producing materials which afford an ever-increasing data bank to a variety of users, whether these be scientists, institutions, or laymen.

It is important that we not ignore the significance of population-related institutions to any consideration of population centers. The report by Bean *et al.*[63] has reflected this view in the following statement: ". . . it is argued that an ecological approach to population offers a range of alternative approaches to population problems. . . ." It further supports the view in adding that "new approaches should be taken . . . with effort being made to involve more effectively geographers and ecologists in the study of population."

*Funds for Center Programs**

Monies for institutional support can be divided into those

---

* The data accumulated in this section on funds were prepared in 1970 from various documents released by the government or by private foundations. They reflect the views of the author, rather than the position of the CPR.

for core support,* construction, research training, information system and program development. Berelson *et al.* (Chapter Twenty-nine) have already indicated that no extensive centers program should be undertaken unless a minimum of fifty million dollars per year is available for the project. It would be my guess that even more money will be required annually to do the job effectively.

Annual support from all American agencies, Federal, state, and private, might be somewhat as follows: (1) for core support of approximately two hundred institutions: 90 to 100 million dollars, (2) for construction: 60 to 100 million dollars, (3) for research training: 120 million dollars, (4) for information systems: 50 to 100 million dollars.

Thus, for clearly population related activities on an institutional level, excluding grants, contracts and fellowships and such noninstitutional subsidies, one can envision an annual expenditure of between 300 and 400 million dollars. Even with the construction figure as a nonrecurring budget item, this would represent an enormous jump in dollars per year, if compared only with the 23 million dollars spent on institutional support by the Federal Government in 1969. Yet if we project the institutional monies which have been and will continue to be invested by states and municipalities, private institutions, and industry, it seems safe to speculate that this projected requirement for an annual institutional investment is not as exorbitant as it first would seem.

These monies, it is emphasized again, do not include the funds earmarked for environmental health and the problems of ecology, which certainly will have population-related components and thus should indirectly give some relief to the funding burden ascribable to institutional population-research support.

Summary

Resources for population centers are many things. An extensive population-research program exists already in terms of

---

* "Core" support refers to a general fund of money provided to institutions, which may be used at the discretion of the respective administrators.

many players on the field. The authors of previous chapters have endorsed existing centers, called for some new types of centers, and have urged that linkages be established (1) to provide some strength to existing special interest groups, (2) to provide a clearinghouse for collating purposes, and (3) to serve to catalyze new and innovative activities.

CONSIDERATIONS

There is much to consider. There seems to be basic agreement that pluralism is sound as an approach. Cater (Chapter One), Linder (Chapter Twenty-eight), Hitch (Chapter Seven), and Linvill (Chapter Fourteen) have supported it and the summarizers have endorsed it (Section Six).

Yet pluralism without cohesiveness or coordination can be viewed as wheel-spinning by critics who demand action. Hilmar (Chapter Thirty), McCormick (Chapter Thirty-one), and others have spoken strongly of the need for networks and linkages. The field is not organized sufficiently; the attack upon the problem appears to be piecemeal.

Can the university meet the requirement of searching for answers to the population problem?

It would appear that the university is the great repository of manpower and facilities to do the research job needed in resolving the population problem. But as so often has been shown in the preceding sections, universities today are faced with limitations. They are best at basic research, poorest at applied research among the institutions in the research business. They are more inclined toward furthering knowledge than taking on explicit missions.

It is clear from the thoughts of the professor (Nash, Chapter Fifteen) and the student (Pepper, Chapter Sixteen) that professors want freedom of action; students are asking for greater opportunity for expression.

And from the university administrators, it is clear that collaboration and linkage is not an easy action to effect. In the university this comes either naturally or not at all.

A center in the university has problems. Yet such centers have been remarkably successful in answering many questions raised by population problems. Their survival as integral components of the institutions in which they work attests to their effectiveness in educating trained researchers and providing knowledge as well as expertise to the field.

Linvill (Chapter Fourteen) has suggested that the university must become both an evaluative and an operational entity (that it must have, concurrently, capability for contemplation and action) if it is to have relevance in this world of change. He has pointed to the importance of linking various elements of socioty (industry, academia, and government) into a holistic force, so that the university might catalyze a rapid response when such is needed, and be a sanctuary when contemplation is called for.

Harman has amplified this view (Chapter Seven), in asking that we look at the "world macroproblem." He urges that we see "the big picture" so that we can better understand the alternatives which we will face in the future. He and his colleagues give an example in Chapter Thirteen of an institutional form by which this might be done. His asking for policy research is reiterated by Wiener (Chapters Twenty-eight and Thirty-two), Linder (Chapter Twenty-eight), and others. All are in agreement that options and available choices can be determined only if the assimilated facts are based on policy considerations.

Hilmar (Chapter Thirty), McCormick (Chapter Thirty-one), and Henshaw (Chapter Twenty-eight) have strongly urged that holism be promoted. They have urged that research, training, service, and usage be achieved through linkages. All agree that effective communication will improve such linkages. We have been enjoined to reduce our stiff-necked biases as scientists (Nash, in Chapter Fifteen, has acknowledged this characteristic in the academician), as businessmen, as laymen, and to join the human race. If we do not, "man the magicians' apprentice," as Cook so aptly calls him (Chapter Two), will produce the final artifact to bury himself. And we will need no population centers.

Just as the university has been reviewed for what it can and cannot do well, so the representatives of the private research organizations, the national laboratories, and industry have shown the strong and weak points in their respective institutions for contributing to population research. It is clear that these institutions have greater operational capability, to use the Linvill terminology (Chapter Fourteen), and can take on missions and "targets of opportunity" with greater flexibility than can universities.

Industry, in addition to being eminently equipped to do mission-oriented research, has demonstrated another particularly unique characteristic relevant to centers program development. It has highlighted the property of "synergistic motivation," which inspires a researcher to work for personal gain, while at the same time his bosses encourage him to work for the good of the annual stockholder's report (Young, Chapter Twenty-one). This sector feels that it has been tapped by society for less than its capacity to serve. It has many kinds of expertise available to help work on population problems and is standing ready to be invited by the scientific community to join the action (Procter, Chapter Twenty-eight). McCormick (Chapter Thirty-one), while making this same offer in behalf of his profession, has reminded us of the human frailty of prejudice and bias which continues to separate the representatives of the industrial and scientific sectors and thus weakens the total effort.

AN ECOSYSTEMS APPROACH

Is it possible that we can become sufficiently aware, sufficiently motivated, and sufficiently enlightened that we can develop an ecological systems approach to the population problem?

A population research center can serve a useful purpose in creating a mass of expertise in a defined area. If we have many such centers, devoted to many aspects of the problem, working on a unidisciplinary or a multidisciplinary basis, much research and research training can be achieved. But the necessary linkages, alluded to throughout this book, must be part of center structures. A population center, or two hundred centers working independently and publishing independently, will move too slowly to provide the impact needed to bring about resolution of this complex problem.

Rather than talk of a centers program and support of centers *per se*, let us talk of a centers system.[68] As Daniel P. Moynihan says in the preamble to the July 4, 1970, National Goals Research Staff Report to the President,[71] it is important these days to think in terms of processes and systems rather than in terms of programs. The centers operation must be a dynamic system. This is why I call for an ecological systems approach for resolving the population problem. By this term I am referring to man *and his institutions and* their interactions with the environment in which they flourish.

I propose that all the actors in this drama of the population problem mobilize and coordinate their efforts. Let each grantor know the others' policies, and let them actively coordinate their respective activities. Let the recipients of grants for research do likewise. Let the media translate research findings to the user, and let the user have a means for providing rapid "feedback" to the researcher.

Let this ecosystems approach be one in which findings are weighed for relevance. Let there be a locus in the system to evaluate what and how the work of other centers applies to the problem. Let there be a communication center wherein a feedback loop can be created to supply all users—science and laity. Let the applied (operational) and the basic (exploratory) workers maintain close and continuous functional relationships.

Finally, although the thrust of this book for the most part has been directed toward the activities devoted to population problems in the United States, let us not delude ourselves into thinking of a centers system in terms less than that of a world problem. The system must encourage participation by centers and related organizations throughout the world.

REFERENCES

1. Zoerheide, R.: "Population: Trial of the Soul" (A Sermon). Cedar Lane Unitarian Church, Bethesda, Md., 1970.
2. Malthus, T. R.: *An Essay on Population.* Everyman's Library Edition (1st ed. 1798), Dutton & Co., New York.
3. Lazarsfeld, P. F.: "Observation on Organized Social Research in the United States." *Information,* International Social Science Council, December, 1961.
4. Hallack, T., and Turner, C. E.: *Edward Jenner.* Heath Co., Boston, 1928.
5. Linton, R.: *Tree of Culture.* Knopf, New York, 1955.
6. Cook, R. C.: "How Many People Have Ever Lived on Earth?" *Population Bulletin,* Population Reference Bureau, Inc., February, 1962.
7. Braidwood, R. J.: "Near Eastern Pre-History." *Science,* June, 1968.
8. *World Population Prospects as Assessed in 1963.* United Nations Sales No. 66X111-2, 1966.
9. *Growth of the World's Urban and Rural Population, 1920-2000.* United Nations Sales No. E 69X111-3, 1969.
10. *Determinants and Consequences of Population Trends.* Population Studies #17, United Nations Sales No. 53X111-130, 1953.
11. Cook, R. C.: *Human Fertility, the Modern Dilemma.* Wm. Sloane Associates, New York, 1951.
12. Cook, R. C.: *Playing God in World Population.* Farmer, Long, and Stolnitz (Eds.). Indiana University Press, Bloomington, 1968.
13. Taeuber, I. B.: *The Population of Japan.* Princeton University Press, Princeton, 1958.
14. Himes, N. E.: *Medical History of Contraception.* Gamut Press, New York, 1964.
15. Ellis, A.: *The Folklore of Sex.* Grove Press, New York, 1961.
16. Flugel, J. C.: *Population, Psychology and Peace.* Watts and Co., London, 1847.
17. Carleson, A.: *Machinery of the Body,* 5th ed. University of Chicago Press, Chicago, 1961.
18. Brown, H.: Address to Seminar. Center for Population Research, National Institute of Child Health and Human Development, 1970.
19a. Calhoun, J. B.: "A Glance into the Garden." *Mills College Assembly Series,* Mills College, 1965-66.
19b. Calhoun, J. B.: "Space and the Strategy of Life." Address to AAAS, 135th annual meeting, Washington, 1968.

20. Errington, P.: *Muskrat Populations.* Iowa State Press, Ames, Iowa, 1963.

21. McNamara, R. S.: Address to the University of Notre Dame. Notre Dame, Indiana, 1969.

22. Kahn, H., and Wiener, A. J.: *The Year 2000: A Framework for Speculation.* Macmillan, New York, 1967.

23. Ehrlich, P.: *The Population Bomb.* Ballantine Books, Inc., New York, 1968.

24. Udall, M.: "Standing Room Only on Spaceship Earth." *Reader's Digest,* December, 1969.

25. Keynes, J. M.: *A Treatise on Probability.* Macmillan, London, 1952.

26. Blumenfeld, H.: "The Modern Metropolis." *Scientific American,* September, 1965.

27. Kerner, O.: "Commission Statement on Violent Crime." National Commission on the Causes and Prevention of Violence. GPO, November, 1969.

28. Rhyne, R.: *Contingent United States Patterns 1970 to 2000.* Johnson Research Associates, Santa Barbara, California, December, 1969.

29. Ferkiss, V. C.: *Technological Man: The Myth and the Reality.* George Braziller, New York, 1969.

30. Mendel, A. O.: "Robots and Rebels." *The New Republic,* January 11, 1969.

31. Roszak, T.: *The Making of a Counter Culture.* Doubleday, New York, 1969.

32. Maslow, A. H.: *Toward a Psychology of Being.* Charles Tuttle Co., Tokyo, 1962.

33. Rogers, C. R.: *Client-Centered Therapy: Its Current Practice, Implications, and Theory.* Houghton, Boston, 1951.

34. Huxley, A.: *The Perennial Philosophy.* Harper and Brothers, New York, 1945.

35. Steinhart, J. S., and Cherniak, S.: *The Universities and Environmental Quality.* Office of Science and Technology, Washington, 1969.

36. "Environmental Science Centers at Institutions of Higher Education." Legislative Reference Service, Library of Congress, GPO, Washington, December, 1969.

37. Berelson, B.: *Graduate Education in the United States.* McGraw-Hill, New York, 1960.

38. Caldwell, L. K.: "The Universities and International Technical Assistance: The Uses of Government Contracts." *The Journal of Higher Education,* May, 1965.

39. Caldwell, L. K.: "Centers of Excellence for the Study of Human Ecology." *Proceedings of a Symposium on Human Ecology, Warrenton, Virginia, November 24-27, 1968.* Department of Health, Education, and Welfare, Washington, 1968.

40. Freedman, R., and Takeshita, J. Y.: *Family Planning in Taiwan: An Experiment in Social Change*. Princeton University Press, Princeton, 1969.
41. Blau, P. M., and Duncan, O. D.: *The American Occupational Structure*. John Wiley, Inc., New York, 1967.
42. Berelson, B.: "Beyond Family Planning." *Science*, Vol. 163, No. 3867, 1969.
43. Westoff, C. F., and Potvin, R. H.: *College Women and Fertility Values*. Princeton University Press, Princeton, 1967.
44. Coale, A. J., and Demeny, P.: *Regional Model Life Tables and Stable Populations*. Princeton University Press, Princeton, 1966.
45. Coale, A. J., and Demeny, P.: *Methods of Estimating Basic Demographic Measures from Incomplete Data*. Manual IV, Manuals on Methods of Estimating Populations, United Nations, New York.
46. Hacke, J. E., Jr.: "The Feasibility of Anticipating Economic and Social Consequences of a Major Technical Innovation." Final Report to the National Science Foundation, Project 6013, Stanford Research Institute, Menlo Park, California, October, 1967.
47. Howard, R. A.: "Decision Analysis: Applied Decision Theory." In *Proceedings of the Fourth International Conference on Operational Research*. John Wiley and Sons, Inc., New York, 1966.
48. Howard, R. A. (Ed.): "Special Issue on Decision Analysis." *IEEE Trans. Systems Science and Cybernetics*. Vol. SSC-4, No. 3, September, 1968.
49. Harman, W. W.: "Alternative Futures and Educational Policy." Research Memorandum 6747-6, Contract OEC-1-7-071013-4274, SRI Project 6747, Educational Policy Research Center, Stanford Research Institute, Menlo Park, California, February, 1970.
50. "Managing the Environment." Report of the Subcommittee on Science, Research, and Development, U.S. House of Representatives, Emilio Daddario, Chairman, June, 1968.
51. Snow, C. P.: Address at the University of Liverpool, 1965.
52. Bundy, McGeorge: Annual Report, Ford Foundation, 1969.
53. Tydings, J.: "Stabilizing Population Growth: A Political Strategy." Address to U.S. Senate, May 4, 1970.
54. Smith, W. C.: Personal letter to Arnold Nash.
55. Myrdal, G.: *Asian Drama*. Pantheon, New York, 1968.
56. Hill, R., Driver, E. D., and Way, M.: *Needed Social Science Research in Population and Family Planning*. The Ford Foundation, New Delhi, August, 1968.
57. Statement issued in 1968 by the National Council on the Humanities.
58. Freyre, G.: *The Masters and the Slaves: A Study in the Development of Brazilian Civilization*. Translated by Samuel Putnam. Alfred Knopf, New York, 1956.

59. Wolfe, T.: *The Electric Kool-Aid Acid Test.* Bantam Books, New York, 1969.
60. Rider, N. B., and Westoff, C. F.: "Oral Contraceptives and the American Birth Rate." *Family and Fertility.* University of Notre Dame Press, South Bend, Indiana, 1967.
61. Cook, R., and Davenport, W.: "Bootleg Birth Control." *Collier's Magazine,* July, 1939.
62. Hardin, G.: "The Tragedy of the Commons." *Science,* 162:1243, 1968.
63. Bean, L. L., Anderson, R. K., and Tatum, H. J.: *Population and Family Planning in the United States: Manpower Development and Training.* The Population Council, New York.
64. Schmid, C. F.: "Some Remarks Concerning Contemporary American Demographers and Demography." *Population Index,* 32, 1966.
65. Stycos, J. M.: "Preliminary Report to HEW on the Status of Demography Training in the United States." *Population Index,* 33, 1967.
66. Leo, E., and Mehta, S. K.: Unpublished manuscript. Department of Sociology, University of Massachusetts, 1969.
67. Brim, O. G.: *Knowledge into Action: Improving the Nation's Use of the Social Sciences.* National Science Foundation, U.S. Government Printing Office, Washington, 1969.
68. Hilgard, E. R., and Riecken, H. (Eds.): *The Behavioral and Social Sciences: Outlook and Needs.* Prentice-Hall, New York, 1969.
69. Hilmar, N. A. (Chairman, *Ad Hoc* Group on Population Research): *The Federal Program in Population Research.* Office of Science and Technology, U.S. Government Printing Office, Washington, 1969.
70. Palmer, A. M. (Ed.): *Research Centers Directory, 3rd ed.* Gale Research Company, Detroit, 1968.
71. *Toward Balanced Growth: Quantity and Quality.* Report of the National Goals Staff. U.S. Government Printing Office, Washington, 1970.

CONTRIBUTORS

CHARLES A. ANDERSON is President and Chief Executive Officer of Stanford Research Institute and a member of its Board of Directors. He received his A.B. degree from the University of California at Berkeley and his M.B.A. degree from Harvard. After the war he joined the faculty of the Harvard Graduate School of Business, serving until 1948. He has held executive positions in industry and in universities and was elected President of Stanford Research Institute in 1968. Mr. Anderson has been extremely active in civic affairs and has occupied many positions of public trust.

BRUNO AUGENSTEIN is currently Vice President of The Rand Corporation, with which he has been associated off and on since 1949. Working in both the university and industry, he has done major work in astronautics, weapon systems, operations and systems analysis, and in strategic policies. His memberships include AAAS, Physics Society, Nuclear Society, Philosophy of Science Association, and The Institute of Aeronautics and Astronautics.

BERNARD BERELSON came to the Population Council in 1962 and succeeded to its Presidency in 1968. As a sociologist, he has specialized in the areas of communication, public opinion, and population. Since 1964 he has served on the population committee of the National Academy of Science. His publications include books and papers on education, public opinion research, population, and human behavior.

KINGMAN BREWSTER, JR. has served in his present capacity as President of Yale University since 1963. The many positions he has held include faculty posts in M.I.T. Department of Economics, the Harvard and Yale schools of law, and the President's Commission on Law Enforcement and Administration of Justice 1965. Dr. Brewster is a member of the Massachusetts Bar Association, the American Academy of Arts and Sciences, and the Council of Foreign Relations. He has many publications to his credit including *Anti-Trust and American Business Abroad* and *Law of International Transactions and Relations*.

LYNTON K. CALDWELL has been Professor of Government at Indiana University since 1956. With degrees from Harvard and the University of Chicago, he has been active in political science and public administration in many areas of the world from the Middle East to the Philippines. His publications express the breadth of his interests in biopolitics, ecology, environmental control, and many other subjects.

359

ARTHUR A. CAMPBELL is Deputy Director of the Center for Population Research, National Institute of Child Health and Human Development, National Institutes of Health. Since 1950, when he finished his graduate work at Columbia, Mr. Campbell has conducted research in the fields of fertility, family planning, and population problems in general. He has published more than twenty-five books and articles covering many aspects of these subjects. His memberships include American Statistical Association, American Public Health Association, International Union for the Scientific Study of Population, and he is presently on the Board of Directors of the Population Association of America.

DOUGLASS CATER is currently Senior Advisor to the Academy for Educational Development. He was educated at Harvard College and Harvard School of Public Administration. After wartime service with the OSS, he held editorships on the *Reporter Magazine* with intermittent leaves-of-absence to serve as consultant within the government. In 1964 he became a Special Assistant to President Johnson. He has authored and co-authored several books on Washington and Government.

ANSLEY J. COALE has served on the faculty of Princeton University since 1947. Since 1959 he has been Professor of Economics and Director of the Office of Population Research. He was educated at Princeton, receiving his Ph.D. in economics. He has specialized in the mathematical and statistical aspects of demography, and the economic implications of population growth. Professor Coale has served on many national boards and has written many books and papers. Included among these are co-authored books on *Population Growth and Economic Development, New Estimates of Fertility and Population in the U.S.,* and *Regional Model Life Tables and Stable Population.*

ROBERT C. COOK is a consultant in population and genetics currently associated with the National Parks and Conservation Association, and other organizations. He was the Director and President of the Population Reference Bureau from 1952 to 1968, and Editor of the *Journal of Heredity* from 1922 to 1960. His long experience in writing and editing in these related fields of genetics and demography have afforded him a unique overview of the population problem.

JERRY W. COMBS is Chief of the Behavioral Sciences Branch of the Center for Population Research in the National Institute of Child Health and Human Development. Receiving his Ph.D. at Columbia University in Sociology, he has taught in several universities and served in several Federal agencies. He is a fellow in several learned societies and author of many books and papers. Dr. Combs is responsible for the creation of a program seeking the broad determinants of population change. He brings to this position years of training in many aspects of demography.

PHILIP A. CORFMAN has been Director of the Center for Population Research of the National Institute of Child Health and Human Development since the Center was founded in August 1968. He received his medical degree from Harvard in 1954 and his subsequent specialty training in obstetrics and gynecology at Harvard-affiliated hospitals. He spent four years in clinical practice in upstate New York and two years in full time medical research at Columbia University prior to coming to NIH in 1964.

JOHN C. CUTLER has, since 1967, been Director of the Population Division and Professor of International Health, Graduate School of Public Health, University of Pittsburgh. During 1968-69, he was Acting Dean of the GSPH and acting head of the Department of Public Health Practice. He organized the Family Planning Council of Allegheny County, and is a member of the Medical Advisory Committee to Pittsburgh Planned Parenthood Center. He has an M.D. from Western Reserve and an M.P.H. from Johns Hopkins. From 1943 until his retirement from the Public Health Service in 1967, he worked in venereal disease, research control, and in public health administration within the Public Health Service, the World Health Organization, and the Pan American Health Organization. He was Assistant Surgeon General in the PHS in 1958-59, and Deputy Director, Pan American Sanitary Bureau, Regional Office for the Americas of WHO, 1960-67. Dr. Cutler is Chairman of the International Committee of the Association for Voluntary Sterilization, and a member of the Advisory Committee on Population to the Secretary General of the Organization of American States.

FRANK FRASER DARLING is Vice President of the Conservation Foundation and Vice President of the International Union for the Conservation of Nature and Natural Resources. Educated at the University of Edinburgh, he holds Doctor of Science, Ph.D., and LL.D. degrees. During his early years Sir Frank Fraser Darling did research in animal genetics, particularly on farm animals. His constant interest in wild animals led him into ecology and conservation in areas as far afield as Scotland, Africa, and Alaska. He was for years Senior Lecturer in Ecology and Conservation at the University of Edinburgh. As an author he has to his credit a long list of books and articles concerned with nature and nature's proper balance. He was knighted in 1970.

SANFORD S. ELBERG is Dean of the Graduate Division of the University of California at Berkeley. Within the broad fields of medicine and biology, he is an epidemiologist and has done work in immunology and bacteriology. He has been internationally recognized for his work on brucellosis. A member or fellow in many learned societies, including The American Academy of Microbiology, The Biochemical Society of Great Britain and the AAAS, Dr. Elberg has contributed to the field of science as a researcher, teacher, consultant, and administrator throughout an impressive career.

RONALD FREEDMAN has held various positions at the University of Michigan since 1947 in the fields of sociology and population studies. He is at present Director of the Population Studies Center and Professor of Sociology. He serves as a consultant to the National Institutes of Health, U.S. Bureau of the Census, Population Council, Ford Foundation, and Taiwan Population Studies Center. He was a member of the Committee on Population, National Academy of Science. His publications include *Principles of Sociology; Population, the Vital Revolution* (1964); *The Sociology of Human Fertility*, and *Family Planning in Taiwan*. He has been President of the Population Association of America and Vice-President of the International Union for the Scientific Study of Population.

MOYE W. FREYMANN is presently Professor of Public Health and Population Planning and Director of the Carolina Population Center. He has an M.D. from Johns Hopkins and a D.P.H. from Harvard. He has worked extensively on population problems both in the United States and abroad, particularly in India and Iran. Dr. Freymann is a fellow in both the Public Health and Sociological Associations and a member of other professional societies.

OSCAR HARKAVY has been Program Officer in Charge of the Population Office of the Ford Foundation since 1963, having been associated with that organization since 1953. He has been a consultant for the Department of Health, Education, and Welfare, an author of scientific papers on population and economics, and he is a member of several learned societies including the American Economic Association, the American Finance Association and the Population Association of America. He is a fellow of The AAAS. Dr. Harkavy received his Ph.D. in Economics from Syracuse.

WILLIS W. HARMAN currently is Director, Educational Policy Research Center, Stanford Research Institute. Most recently he served as a principal consultant to the National Goals Research Staff at the White House. He has been a professor in the School of Engineering at Stanford University, with which he has been affiliated since 1952. He is also a professor in the new area of engineering-economic systems planning. Dr. Harman has written texts in electrical engineering and has published scientific papers on a variety of subjects. His publications since 1952 reflect his increasing involvement with problems of policy formulation and the economic systems. He has conducted a regular seminar on human potentiality since 1956 and finds himself increasingly concerned about the human condition.

LILLIAN H. HARVEY is the Dean of the School of Nursing, Tuskegee Institute, Alabama. She has served on the staff of that institution, first as Director, School of Nursing, and Director of Nursing Service, John A. Andrew Memorial Hospital, 1944-47. She was appointed Dean, School of Nursing in 1948, at which time, Tuskegee Institute established the first baccalaureate program in nursing in Alabama. She holds membership in the American Nurses Association and National League for Nursing. She has served on the Nursing Advisory Board for the American National Red Cross; Kellogg Foundation; Board of Directors, National League for Nursing; American Journal of Nursing Company; member, Education Committee, President's Commission on the Status of Women and currently she serves as a member of the Comprehensive Health Planning Committee, State of Alabama.

PAUL S. HENSHAW has had a varied career which expresses his many interests. Currently he is visiting Professor, Department of Government, University of Arizona. A biophysicist with a Ph.D. in zoology from the University of Wisconsin, he served for many years with the U.S. Atomic Energy Commission. He was a principal biologist with the Manhattan Project in 1944-45. He has been deeply involved in U.S. and international public health and in the early 1950s served as Director of Research in the Planned Parenthood Federation of America. He is author of books and papers in the fields of population, biology, and radiation. His memberships include AAAS, Radiation Research Society, and the Population Association of America.

REUBEN L. HILL is Professor of Sociology and Research Professor in the Family Study Center at the University of Minnesota. He holds a Ph.D. from the University of Minnesota. He holds a Ph.D. from the University of Wisconsin. He is the author of many scientific books and papers and has been a consultant on population and social problems to various Federal agencies. In 1963 he received the Ernest W. Burgess award for distinguished family research. He is fellow or member of several learned societies, and President, 1970-74, of The International Sociological Association.

NORMAN A. HILMAR is Chief, Program Liaison Branch of the Center for Population Research, National Institute of Child Health and Human Development. He has a Ph.D. in sociology from Cornell University. As a commissioned officer in the Public Health Service, Dr. Hilmar has worked in program planning and evaluation in the Office of the Surgeon General and in the Bureau of Disease Prevention and Environmental Control. He has taught sociology at various universities, authored several scientific papers and holds memberships which include the AAAS, the Population Association of America, and Planned Parenthood-World Population.

CHARLES J. HITCH became President of the nine-campus University of California in January, 1968. His educational experience includes highest honors at the University of Arizona and a Rhodes Scholarship. He was the first American Rhodes Scholar to become an Oxford don and served as a Fellow of Queen's College, Oxford, for thirteen years. President Hitch has been chairman of the Research Council of the Rand Corporation and in the early 1960's was Assistant Secretary of Defense (Comptroller). He is largely responsible for the introduction of the techniques of program budgeting and systems analysis into Defense and other Federal departments. He joined the University of California in 1965.

HUDSON HOAGLAND is President Emeritus of The Worcester Foundation for Experimental Biology. With a Ph.D. from Harvard in psychology, he is holder of many honorary doctorates. He has been a teacher, an administrator, and a consultant to government, industry, and academia throughout his colorful career. His affiliations are numerous as are his interests and writings. His wide interests include work in oceanography, neurophysiology, endocrinology and psychopharmacology. He is past president of The American Academy of Science and is a member of the Board of Directors of AAAS.

SYLVAN J. KAPLAN was Head, Population Research Centers Programs, Center for Population Research at the time this book was written. He holds a Ph.D. in psychology from Stanford University. Currently, he is Chief, Division of Plans and Objectives, National Park Service. He has served also in Government on The National Goals Research Staff of the White House, the Defense Atomic Support Agency, and the Peace Corps. He has served on faculties as a teacher, department head, and dean. He has authored scientific papers in psychology, radiation biology, poverty and other social issues, and military history. His memberships include the American Psychological Association, the Radiation Research Society, and the Population Association of America.

JOSEPH F. KAUFFMAN is President of Rhode Island College. He formerly was Professor of Counseling and Behavioral Studies and Dean of Student Affairs at the University of Wisconsin; he was Dean of Students at Brandeis University before going to Wisconsin. Dr. Kauffman holds a doctorate in counseling and guidance from Boston University. Apart from two years as Director of Training for the Peace Corps, most of Dr. Kauffman's work has related to youth guidance, development, and counseling. His memberships include American College Personnel Association, American Sociology Association, Personnel and Guidance Association. His publications include *Education,* Potomac, 1966; co-author of *College and the Student,* American Council on Education, 1966; *Student Personnel Services in Higher Education Part I* summer 1964 and *Part II* fall of 1964, Educational Record.

FORREST E. LINDER is Professor of Biostatistics, School of Public Health, University of North Carolina at Chapel Hill. He holds a Ph.D. in psychology and mathematics from the University of Iowa. His lengthy career in the U. S. Public Health Service as a statistician and demographer has benefited countless organizations, private, national, and international. He has acted as consultant on vital statistics and demography to the U. S. Public Health Service, the United Nations, the national governments of Uruguay and India, The Ford Foundation, the World Health Organization and many others. He has written many scientific papers including "The Increased Scope of Demographic Investigations Through the Use of Sampling Surveys" (U. N. World Population Conference 9/25) and "Health of the American People" (Scientific America 6/66).

WILLIAM K. LINVILL has been Professor of Engineering at Stanford University since 1960 and chairman of the Department of Engineering-Economic Systems at Stanford since 1967. He holds a Sc.D. degree from M.I.T. He is an expert on multivariable systems analysis and coordinated systems planning. He is a member of several professional societies, including the Institute of Electrical and Electronics Engineering and the Instrument Society. Prior to joining the Stanford faculty, he was a member of the senior staff of the Rand Corporation.

WILLIAM T. LIU is Professor of Sociology and Anthropology at the University of Notre Dame. He holds a doctorate from Florida State University and did his postdoctoral work at the University of Chicago. His particular sociological emphasis has been in the family processes, values, and religion in the changing world. His geographic area of interests include Taiwan, Hong Kong, Singapore, and the Philippines. He has membership in AAAS, American Sociological Association, National Council of Family Relations, etc. His principal works include: *Chinese Society Under Communism* (John Wiley, 1967); *Family and Fertility* (Notre Dame Press, 1967), *Catholics: USA, Perspectives for Change*, which he edited. He is currently working on a monograph dealing with family and fertility in the Philippines. He contributes in many social science journals.

JAMES L. LIVERMAN is Associate Director for Biomedical and Environmental Sciences at the Oak Ridge National Laboratory. He is a biochemist with special interest in plant physiology. He has worked for the Atomic Energy Commission and several universities. He has done work in radiation and cell physiology. He holds a Ph.D. in plant physiology biorganic chemistry from the California Institute of Technology. His memberships include AAAS, the Society of Plant Physiology, Chemical Society, and the Radiation Research Society.

CHARLES W. LLOYD is Director of the Training Program of the Physiology of Reproduction and Clinical Research Unit and Senior Scientist at the Worcester Foundation for Experimental Biology, having been with the Foundation since 1962. He has a wide background in endocrinology with work done at several hospitals and universities. His memberships include AAAS, The Society for Clinical Investigation, the Endocrine Society, the Physiology Society, the Society for Experimental Biology, the College of

Physicians, the Federation for Clinical Research, and the New York Academy of Science.

ROBERT K. MCCORMICK has worked in Europe, Africa, and the Pacific as a correspondent for the National Broadcasting Company. Currently, he serves NBC as a Congressional correspondent. Before that, he was head of the Washington Bureau of *Collier's Magazine,* when he devoted much of his time to attempting to popularize scientific subjects, such as the therapeutic effects of urea, and the development of hundred-octane gasoline. Before going to *Collier's,* he worked on the *Washington Daily News,* where Ernie Pyle was one of his editors. His interest in population goes back to the early thirties.

HERMAN P. MILLER has served as Chief of the Population Division at the Bureau of the Census since 1966 and Professor of Economics at Temple University since 1967. He has a Ph.D. in economics from American University. He is a statistics expert and has several books to his credit, including *Rich Man, Poor Man* (1964), and *Poverty American Style* (1966). Dr. Miller is affiliated with the American Statistical Association, the American Economic Association, Conference on Income and Wealth—National Bureau of Economic Research, Population Association of America, and the International Conference on Income and Wealth.

ARNOLD S. NASH is a Professor at the University of North Carolina and is presently serving as a Research Consultant on the Humanities to the National Goals Research Staff, The White House. He was educated at the University of Liverpool; Ripon Hall, Oxford; and the London School of Economics. He has been in North America since 1939 and is now Professor of the History and Sociology and Religion and a member of the staff of the Carolina Population Center where he is chairman of an interdisciplinary graduate seminar on the humanities and social sciences in their approaches to the population question. He served as a consultant on the ethical and social aspects of dialysis and kidney transplantation to the Committee of the U. S. Bureau of the Budget on renal disease. He has lectured extensively in Europe and Asia on the role of the university in society. He is the author of *The University and the Modern World* and has edited and contributed to various symposia and articles in America, Britain, Germany, and France.

D. WARNER NORTH is a member of the Decision Analysis Group at Stanford Research Institute. He holds a Ph.D. in operations research from Stanford University as well as graduate degrees in physics and mathematics. He has applied decision analysis to a variety of problems facing industry and government, including weather modification and the planning of a national electrical power system. His memberships include the Institute of Management Sciences, the Operations Research Society of America, and the IEEE System Science and Cybernetics Group.

JAMES PEPPER is a student at the Georgetown University Law Center. He was graduated in 1969 with a B.A. in history from St. Vincent College, where he was active in student government, publications, and other activities.

PAGE S. PROCTER is Senior Vice President of J. Walter Thompson advertising agency where he is creative supervisor for some twenty clients. He has a Ph.D. in English from Yale University, where he taught before going into the business world in 1955.

ROGER REVELLE is Richard Saltonstal Professor of Population Policy and Director of the Center for Population Studies at Harvard University. He is also Deputy Foreign Secretary of the National Academy of Sciences, and Vice-President of the American Academy of Sciences. Professor Revelle was formerly University Dean of Research for the nine campuses of the University of California. From 1961 to 1963 he was science adviser to the Secretary of the Interior. Revelle College of the University of California, San Diego, is named for him.

SHELDON J. SEGAL is Vice-President and Medical Director of the Biomedical Division of the Population Council. He holds a Ph.D. in zoology and biochemistry from the University of Iowa. He has done research and published in the fields of endocrinology and embryology and acted as consultant to numerous organizations, including the Ford Foundation, Planned Parenthood, and the National Institute of Child Health and Human Development. He is a member of the Obstetrics and Gynecology Advisory Committee of the Food and Drug Administration, the Medical Committee of Planned Parenthood Federation of America, AAAS, Population Association, Fertility Society, Endocrine Society, Association of Anatomy, Society of Zoology, Eugenics Society, British Society for the Study of Fertility, Indian Society for the Scientific Study of Reproduction, and the International Institute of Embryology.

GEORGE J. STOLNITZ is Professor of Economics and Director of the International Development Research Center, Indiana University. He has his Ph.D. in economics and demography from Princeton. He has been a consultant to, or member of advisory committees for, Ford Foundation, National Academy of Sciences, Social Science Research Council, U. S. Bureau of the Census, Agency for International Development, National Institute for Child Health and Human Development, Population Reference Bureau, and the Department of Health, Education, and Welfare, as well as to various state government bodies and business firms. His memberships include the American Economics Association, American Statistical Association, Econometrics Society, International Union for the Scientific Study of Population, and the Population Association of America. He has published in the areas of demography, economic development, and statistical methods.

J. Mayone Stycos is Director of the International Population Program at Cornell University, where he has been on the faculty since 1957. He received his Ph.D. in sociology from Columbia University. As a long-time authority of fertility and family planning, he has acted as consultant to many organizations, including the Population Council, Population Reference Bureau, NICHD, Planned Parenthood, and the Organization of American States. His memberships include the Sociology Association and the Population Association. His latest publications include *Ideology, Faith, and Family Planning in Latin America: Studies in Public and Private Opinion on Fertility Control* (1971) forthcoming; *Children of the Barriada* (1970); *Human Fertility in Latin America* (1968); and co-authorship (Taplinger) of *Population Dilemma in Latin America* (1966).

Conrad Taeuber is Associate Director of the Bureau of the Census. Since the Federal Emergency Relief Act of 1934, he has had a special expertise in agricultural and rural sociological problems. Dr. Taeuber holds a Ph.D. from the University of Minnesota. His memberships include Fellow of the American Statistics Association, AAAS, American Sociology Association, Population Association of America (former president), Inter-American Statistical Institute (President), the Rural Sociological Society, International Statistical Institute, and Sociological Research Association. He has contributed to numerous social science journals and has authored *Rural Migration in the United States* (with C. E. Lively) 1939, *The Changing Population of the United States* (with Irene Taeuber) 1958.

George Tarjan is Professor of Psychiatry in the Schools of Medicine and Public Health and Program Director of Mental Retardation in the Neuropsychiatric Institute. Department of Mental Hygiene, at the University of California at Los Angeles. He has served on the faculty at UCLA since 1953. He was educated in Hungary, receiving his M.D. degree from the Peter Pasmany University. He is a member of the President's Committee on Mental Retardation; the American Psychiatric Association, where he was Vice-President 1967-68 and has been Secretary since 1969; and the American Association on Mental Deficiency.

Calvin W. Taylor joined the faculty of the University of Utah in 1946 and today is Professor in the Department of Psychology. He has a Ph.D. in psychology from the University of Chicago. Author of many learned papers and several books, he is best known for his specialty in occupation and personnel analysis, in the field of creativity and multiple talents, and in architectural psychology.

Alvin Weinberg is Director of the Oak Ridge National Laboratory in Oak Ridge, Tennessee. A nuclear physicist (Ph.D. from the University of Chicago) who received the Atoms for Peace award in 1960, he was also a member of the U. S. scientific team that visited nuclear installations in

Russia in 1959, the Science Advisory Board of the U. S. Air Force, the President's Science Advisory Committee, and was the recipient of the Lawrence Memorial award of the U. S. Atomic Energy Committee. His memberships include the National Academy of Science, the American Physical Society, the American Nuclear Society (president 1959-60), and the American Academy of Arts and Sciences.

IRAM J. WEINSTEIN is manager of the Systems Evaluation Department at the Stanford Research Institute and lecturer at the Stanford University Institute of Engineering Economic Systems and the University of California Extension. He holds the Ph.D. in electrical engineering from Stanford. Dr. Weinstein has worked on industrial projects for the Raytheon Company, has been a consultant to the Institute of Defense Analysis, and has been a member of the Newport summer study on ballistic missile defense. His major interest has been a system analysis. His memberships include the Operation Research Society of America, and the Science Research Society of America.

LEORA WOOD WELLS is a free-lance writer who specializes in publications and reports of conferences and research in the health, welfare, and behavioral science fields. Her clients include many Federal agencies, universities, and foundations. A member of Phi Beta Kappa, Mrs. Wells is a graduate of the University of Illinois and did graduate work at Stanford University. Formerly a writer in the United States Children's Bureau and a child welfare case worker in public and private agencies, Mrs. Wells also teaches adult writing courses.

ANTHONY WIENER is Chairman of the Research Council of the Hudson Institute, a nonprofit public policy research institute. He is co-author with Herman Kahn of *The Year 2000: A Framework for Speculation,* and author of many reports and articles on a wide range of political and social issues. He has served as Chairman of the White House Urban Affairs Research Committee, as Research Consultant to the President's National Goals Research Staff, and in numerous other advisory positions. His experience includes teaching political science at M.I.T., research at the M.I.T. Center for International Studies, research at the U. S. Joint Commission on Mental Illness and Health, the U. S. Educational Policy Research Center, the Society for the Investigation of Human Ecology. Dr. Wiener has an A.B. from Harvard College and a J.D. from Harvard Law School.

SAMUEL M. WISHIK is Director of the Division of Program Development and Evaluation at the International Institute for the Study of Human Reproduction at Columbia University. He received his M.D. degree from Columbia University and his M.P.H. degree from Johns Hopkins University. His professional practice includes service at Kings County Hospital in Brooklyn, New York; Babies Hospital, Rumson, New Jersey; Willard Parker

Hospital in New York; Queensboro Hospital of Communicable Diseases, Jamaica, Long Island; and Children's Hospital, Pittsburgh, Pennsylvania. As an academician he has served as Professor of Maternal and Child Health, as Associate Dean of Academic Affairs, and also as Director of the Population Unit at the Graduate School of Public Health, University of Pittsburgh. At present he is also Professor of Public Health Practice, School of Public Health and Administrative Medicine, Columbia University. His memberships include American Pediatrics Society, American Public Health Association, and the American Academy of Pediatrics.

RICHARD W. YOUNG is Senior Vice President, Research and Development for the Polaroid Corporation. He received his A.B. and M.A. degrees from Dartmouth College and his Ph.D. from Columbia University where he was a Cramer Traveling Fellow and a Cyanamid Fellow. Prior to joining the Polaroid Corporation in 1962, he was with the American Cyanamid Company as a Research Chemist, Chemotherapy Division 1950-56, as a Group Leader of Pesticide Chemicals, Agricultural Division 1956-58, as Director of Chemical Research 1958-60, and as Central Research Division Director 1960-62. He has been a member of the visiting committee of physical science at Case Western Reserve since 1965 and is Chairman of the Scientific Advisory Committee of the Massachusetts Eye and Ear Hospital, Boston, Massachusetts. His other memberships include AAAS, American Chemical Society, British Chemical Society, the Royal Photography Society, and the Society of Photographic Scientists and Engineers.

NAME INDEX

SUBJECT INDEX

A

Abortions
  Europe, family planning, 48
  government's role, 53-54
  Japan, 24
    family planning, 48
  law, liberalization needed?, 300
  limitation in population control, 337
  media's coverage of subject, 331
  necessary measure, 62
  role in fertility reduction, 51
Academic disciplines, role in technological transition, 176
Academic world, technology exploitation, 167-168
  see also Colleges, and Universities
Action
  guidance, knowledge needed, 255
  policy relationship, 334-342
  relation to "science," 198
Action-oriented research, university's role, 217-218
Action programs, university's limitations, 251
"Acts of God," *see* Natural disasters
"Acts of Man," effects on population figures, 20-21
Advertising industry, role in social problems' solution, 235
Advertising techniques, ideas for population centers, 295
AEC laboratories, 226, 227
  environmental studies, 348
  programs, 228
  teaching activities, 212
  see also Atomic Energy Commission
Africa
  cholera epidemic, 23
  family planning, 253
  news penetration, 332
  population studies, 148

studies on at U. of Michigan, 136
Age distribution
  analysis, 153
  changes forecast, 81-84
  in stationary population, 85
Age group relationship
  economic and social implications, 38
  fertility rate's role, 37-39
Age level, effect on political power, 39
Agency for International Development, 65
  assistance by U. of Michigan, 137
  funding of population centers, 286, 287
  international directory sought, 327
  population problems information center possibility, 328
  publications on population data, 325
  see also AID
Aging population, in zero growth population, 313
Agricultural Experiment Station, U. of California, 212-213
Agriculture
  green revolution, food problem solution, 97
  plan for future good, 96
  pollution factor, 64
  role in population increase, 14, 15-16
AID, *see also* Agency for International Development
Air Pollution Technical Information Center (APTIC), 328
America
  applied research approach, 211
  family restriction, attitude toward, 57-58
  family size, education relationship, 151
  population problems, specific focus urged, 304-305